W9-CQO-788

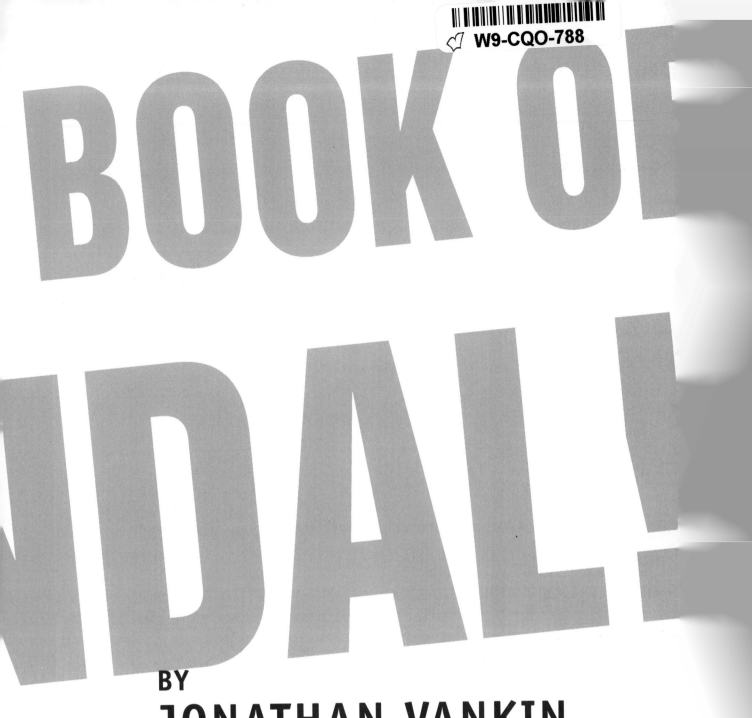

BOOK OF
NDAL!

BY
JONATHAN VANKIN

AND 54 OF
THE WORLD'S
TOP COMIC ARTISTS!

PARADOX PRESS
NEW YORK

DC COMICS

JENETTE KAHN
PRESIDENT & EDITOR-IN-CHIEF

PAUL LEVITZ
EXECUTIVE VICE PRESIDENT & PUBLISHER

ANDREW HELFER
GROUP EDITOR

JIM HIGGINS
ASSISTANT EDITOR

AMIE BROCKWAY
ART DIRECTOR

RICHARD BRUNING
VP-CREATIVE DIRECTOR

PATRICK CALDON
VP-FINANCE & OPERATIONS

DOROTHY CROUCH
VP-LICENSED PUBLISHING

TERRI CUNNINGHAM
VP-MANAGING EDITOR

JOEL EHRLICH
SENIOR VP-ADVERTISING & PROMOTIONS

LILLIAN LASERSON
VP & GENERAL COUNSEL

BOB ROZAKIS
EXECUTIVE DIRECTOR-PRODUCTION

THE BIG BOOK OF SCANDAL! Published by Paradox Press. Cover and compilation copyright © 1997 Paradox Press. All Rights Reserved. Factoid, Paradox Press and related logo are trademarks of DC Comics. Paradox Press is an imprint of DC Comics, 1700 Broadway, New York, NY 10019. A division of Warner Bros. - A Time Warner Entertainment Company.

Printed in Canada. First Printing.

See page 191 for individual copyright holders.

Front and back cover designed by Steve Vance.

Front cover illustration by John Cebollero.

Front cover photograph by Marc Witz.

Title page illustration by Stephen DeStefano.

Publication design by Brian Pearce.

Principal Letterer: Bob Lappan.

Additional Lettering: Agnes Pinaha

DEDICATED
with love, to Deb,
who's always in search
of a good scandal.

TABLE OF CONTENT

I'VE BEEN IN THIS BUSINESS A LONG TIME, THE NEWS BUSINESS, BUT I DON'T COVER BUDGETS, FOREIGN POLICY OR TAX REFORM. MY BEATS? SEX, MONEY, FAME, DRUGS, DECEPTION, MURDER. YOU KNOW-- THE GOOD STUFF. IN A WORD...

SCANDAL!!!

Introduction

I KNOW WHAT YOU'RE THINKING. I'M A SLEAZEBAG. A PARASITE. MAYBE I AM. BUT FACE IT, WITHOUT ME, YOU'D PROBABLY NEVER READ A PAPER. YOU LOVE THIS STUFF.

HEY HANDSOME! WANNA PARTY?

AND WHY NOT? WHAT'S A SCANDAL, ANYWAY? IT'S WHEN SOME BIG SHOT TURNS OUT TO BE HUMAN AFTER ALL. THAT'S ALL. BIG SHOTS ARE LIKE ANYBODY. THEY GET GREEDY, THEY GET HORNY. THEY GET JUST PLAIN STUPID.

WHEN THEY GET CAUGHT, THAT'S A SCANDAL.

YOU LOVE TO SEE PEOPLE BREAK TABOOS. THERE'S NOTHING MORE FASCINATING THAN THE FORBIDDEN.

FLASH!!

BUT SOCIETY HAS TO HOLD TABOO-BREAKERS IN DISGRACE. THAT'S HOW WE ENFORCE THE RULES OF ACCEPTABLE BEHAVIOR.

IN OTHER WORDS, I'M SOCIETY'S COP. CURSE ME ALL YOU WANT. I'M JUST DOING YOUR DIRTY WORK.

DAMMIT, WHERE'S THAT STORY?

DON'T GET YER PANTIES IN A BUNCH, CHIEF! IT'S COMIN'!

THERE'S SOMETHING ELSE. EVER HEAR THE WORD SCHADENFREUDE? IT MEANS TAKING PLEASURE IN THE MISFORTUNE OF OTHERS.

THE WORD'S GERMAN-- BUT WE ALL KNOW THE FEELING. IT'S JUST SOMETHING WE'RE NOT VERY PROUD OF. BUT, HEY, I'M HERE TO TELL YOU-- IT'S OK!

GUILTY

guilty

Gui

Gui

WELL, ENOUGH OF THIS IDLE CHITCHAT. LET'S GET TO THE GOOD STUFF. YOU'RE ABOUT TO TAKE A JOURNEY THROUGH A **WORLD** OF SHAMEFUL, OUTRAGEOUS AND DISGRACEFUL BEHAVIOR. YOU LUCKY DEVIL.

YOU'LL SEE RICH AND FAMOUS PEOPLE LAID LOW BY LUST, GREED, VICE -- A WHOLE **MENAGERIE** OF CHARACTER FLAWS.

BUT THERE'S ONE FLAW THAT CROPS UP MORE THAN ANY OF THE OTHERS -- IN ALMOST EVERY STORY! **PRIDE!** AS IT SAYS IN **HERE**, "PRIDE GOETH BEFORE DESTRUCTION AND A HAUGHTY STEP BEFORE A FALL."

THE BIBLE? SURE, I READ IT. **FULL** OF SCANDALS! KNOW WHAT ELSE I READ? GREEK TRAGEDIES. **EVERY ONE** WAS A SCANDAL -- A KING OR QUEEN KAYOED BY PRIDE. THE GREEKS CALLED IT **HUBRIS**.

LOOK AT OL' OEDIPUS. HE WHACKED HIS DAD AND BEDDED HIS MOM. THEN HE FELT SO BAD HE COULDN'T BEAR TO LOOK AT HER. IF THAT'S NOT A SCANDAL, I DON'T KNOW WHAT IS.

YAAAAH!

ALL I'M SAYING IS THAT SCANDAL IS AS OLD AS CIVILIZATION ITSELF. PROBABLY EVEN OLDER. OUR PRIMAL URGES NEVER LEFT US. SCANDALS ARE AN IMPORTANT PART OF **HISTORY!**

BRAIN!

Y'KNOW, I'VE COMPARED SCANDALS TO TRAGEDY. BUT ACTUALLY, THERE ARE FEW THINGS **FUNNIER** THAN WATCHING SELF-IMPORTANT IDIOTS MAKE JERKS OF THEMSELVES.

MUST BE OVER 18 TO RENT THESE TAPES.

SLUTS IN LOVE

JUGS OVER BROADWAY

XXX

SAY, AREN'T YOU...?

EGAD!

THE BOOK YOU'RE HOLDING IS A **COMIC**, AFTER ALL. WHAT BETTER FORMAT FOR A SURVEY OF THE HUMAN COMEDY? THERE'S NOTHING LIKE A LITTLE **SATIRE** WITH YOUR SLEAZE.

I SAID, WHERE'S MY **STORY**?!

JUST HANG ON, CHIEF!

BAT MAN

NON-STOP SEXXX LIVE! ALL NUDE!

GIRLS GIRLS GIRLS

SO, TURN THE PAGES AND ENJOY THE VOYEURISTIC VOYAGE TO THE DEPTHS OF SCANDAL.

BUT REMEMBER... WE'RE ALL GUILTY OF **SOMETHING**.

CHAPTER ONE

TAWDRY TINSELTOWN

Hollywood: a town where debauchery is a recognized lifestyle choice. What better spot, then, to commence our chronicle of appalling behavior in exalted places? The movie business wasn't always as sleazy as it appears to our jaded eyes today. Prior to 1922, Americans had little reason to believe that their motion picture heroes were anything but the milk-sipping pillars of wholesome goodness their studio publicists pretended them to be. Then along waddled a rotund comic called "Fatty." Suddenly Hollywood morphed into, as preeminent scandalophile Kenneth Anger forever dubbed it, "Babylon."

Hollywood scandals come in a variety of flavors. Yet whether we're talking about the rakish exploits of Errol Flynn, the sordid death of Thelma Todd, or the financial profligacy of an entire studio in the cinematic disaster that was *Cleopatra,* movieland possesses a weird, dreamlike quality that makes the stars feel like—stars: distant, unreachable, existing in some inscrutable space far above our own. Unfortunately for the stars, they do live on Earth. And they live in a society that insists on gawking voyeuristically at their private conduct while relentlessly passing judgment upon it. So let's indulge in a bit of that right now, shall we...?

"FATTY" ARBUCKLE:
NO TEARS FOR THE FAT MAN

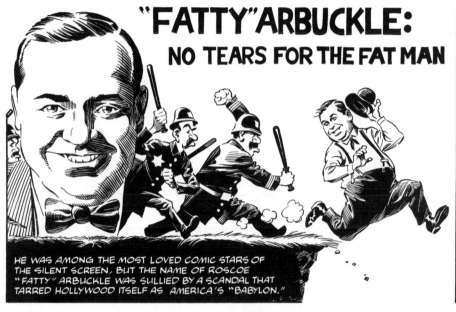

HE WAS AMONG THE MOST LOVED COMIC STARS OF THE SILENT SCREEN, BUT THE NAME OF ROSCOE "FATTY" ARBUCKLE WAS SULLIED BY A SCANDAL THAT TARRED HOLLYWOOD ITSELF AS AMERICA'S "BABYLON."

WHILE ARBUCKLE PROSPERED, ON THE LOW END OF THE HOLLYWOOD SPECTRUM, YOUNG VIRGINIA RAPPE-- WHO KNEW (SO TO SPEAK) ARBUCKLE AND MANY OTHER STARS-- STRUGGLED TO MAKE IT.

MACK SENNETT'S KEYSTONE STUDIO HIRED HER, BUT IN THE PROCESS OF CURRYING FAVOR WITH HER COLLEAGUES SHE SPREAD VENEREAL DISEASE ALL OVER THE LOT.

GET RID OF HER! THEN FUMIGATE THIS WHOLE PLACE!

THE PATH TO SUCCESS WASN'T EASY ON WOMEN IN HOLLYWOOD. VIRGINIA REPORTEDLY UNDERWENT NUMEROUS ABORTIONS.

ALSO NO PICNIC IN THOSE DAYS.

SEPT. 3, 1922. ROSCOE WRAPPED AN ARDUOUS SHOOT: THREE SIMULTANEOUS FEATURES. HE DROVE TO SAN FRANCISCO FOR A WEEKEND OF R AND R...

...HOLLYWOOD STYLE.

ROSCOE TOOK THREE SUITES IN THE PLUSH ST. FRANCIS HOTEL, SETTLING IN FOR A LONG WEEKEND. HOOCH FLOWED LIKE IT WASN'T EVEN ILLEGAL.

TWO DAYS INTO THE MARATHON PARTY, TO ROSCOE'S SURPRISE...

MY GOD! VIRGINIA! LONG TIME, NO SEE!

VIRGINIA WAS ACCOMPANIED BY MAUDE DELMONT, A SHADY CHARACTER WITH A KNOWN HISTORY OF EXTORTION AND BLACKMAIL. WHO INVITED THEM TO THE PARTY IS UNCERTAIN.

VIRGINIA TOOK THE MOVIE STAR ASIDE...

ROSCOE, I NEED DOUGH FOR ANOTHER ABORTION! HELP ME, PLEASE!

I'D LIKE TO, VIRGINIA. BUT ABORTION? I DON'T KNOW...

MEANWHILE, MAUDE DELMONT SLAMMED BACK 10 WHISKEYS.

A SEASONED VETERAN, NO DOUBT!

A FEW MINUTES LATER, AND FOR NO DISCERNABLE REASON, VIRGINIA WIGGED OUT...

I CAN'T BREATHE! GET THESE RAGS OFFA ME!

JEEZ, VIRGINIA-- CALM DOWN!

THE REST OF THE WELL-SOUSED REVELERS TOOK LITTLE NOTICE AS THE HALF-NAKED VIRGINIA STAGGERED OFF INTO THE BATHROOM.

ARBUCKLE ATTEMPTED TO FOLLOW HER, BUT SOMETHING WAS JAMMED AGAINST THE BATHROOM DOOR. PUSHING AGAINST IT, HE DISCOVERED...

VIRGINIA? MY GOD-- WHAT'S WRONG!?

HE LAID HER ON THE BED OF HIS ADJOINING BEDROOM.

THEY WERE ALONE BEHIND THE LOCKED BEDROOM DOOR FOR 10 TO 15 MINUTES BEFORE ROSCOE EMERGED.

VIRGINIA'S SICK. I GAVE HER SOME WATER.

ROSCOE AND THE LIQUORED-UP DELMONT CLASHED OVER HOW TO AID THE FRANTIC YOUNG ACTRESS.

GET OUTTA HERE AND MINDJER OWN BIZHNISH! (HIC!)

YOU SHUT UP, OR I'LL THROW YOU OUT THE WINDOW!

FOUR DAYS LATER, VIRGINIA DIED AT WAKEFIELD SANITARIUM, A MATERNITY HOSPITAL. THE CAUSE OF DEATH: A RUPTURED BLADDER CAUSED BY, THE CORONER SAID, "AN EXTERNAL FORCE."

ONCE SHE RECOVERED FROM HER BINGE, DELMONT CAME UP WITH AN IDEA. SHE TELEGRAPHED SOME ASSOCIATES IN L.A.

WESTERN UNION TELEGRAM

LOSANGELES CALIF 1921

WE HAVE ROSCOE ARBUCKLE IN A HOLE HERE STOP CHANCE TO MAKE SOME MONEY OUT OF HIM STOP

MAUDE DELMONT

SHE TOLD THE POLICE AND THE PRESS:

ARBUCKLE BRUTALLY RAPED VIRGINIA, CRUSHING HER WITH HIS GREAT GIRTH!

ROSCOE WAS CHARGED WITH MURDER.

DELMONT KEPT CHANGING HER STORY, BUT THE DA PRESSED THE CASE. THE CHARGE WAS DROPPED TO MAN-SLAUGHTER.

I DIDN'T *EXACTLY* SEE THEM GO INTO THE BEDROOM. DID I MENTION I HAD AN AFFAIR WITH ARBUCKLE?

RUMORS RAN WILD, FUELED BY THE PRESS. THE BELIEF THAT ROSCOE RAPED VIRGINIA WITH A SODA BOTTLE HAS BECOME A HOLLYWOOD LEGEND.

THE SCANDAL HAD REPERCUSSIONS. ONCE SACROSANCT, MOVIE STARS FOUND THEMSELVES UNDER PUBLIC ATTACK.

HOLLYWOOD IS A FLESHPOT TEEMING WITH DEGENERATES LIKE ARBUCKLE, CHAPLIN AND PICKFORD!

THE FIRST TRIAL ENDED IN A HUNG JURY, THANKS MAINLY TO ONE WOMAN WHO LATER ADMITTED...

I ALWAYS PLANNED TO VOTE GUILTY NO MATTER WHAT THE EVIDENCE SAID.

AFTER A SECOND HUNG JURY, THE THIRD TIME WAS A CHARM.

ACQUITTAL IS NOT ENOUGH FOR ROSCOE ARBUCKLE. WE FEEL A GREAT INJUSTICE HAS BEEN DONE HIM...

...THERE WAS NOT THE SLIGHTEST PROOF TO CONNECT HIM WITH A CRIME.

BUT ROSCOE'S EXONERATION WASN'T GOOD ENOUGH FOR HOLLYWOOD CENSOR WILL HAYS, APPOINTED BY THE STUDIOS AS SCANDAL DAMAGE CONTROL.

ARBUCKLE IS BANNED FROM THE MOTION PICTURE BUSINESS AND HIS UNRE-LEASED MOVIES MAY NOT BE SHOWN.

THOUGH THE BAN WAS EVENTUALLY LIFTED, ROSCOE NEVER CLIMBED BACK FROM OBSCURITY. ON JUNE 28, 1933, HIS ACHING HEART GAVE OUT, ENDING THE FUNNY MAN'S SAD STORY.

As the late teens turned into the Roarin' 20's, Americans were beginning a sexual awakening. No one helped to wake them up better than RUDOLPH VALENTINO...

THE GREAT LOVER

But he spent his career dodging nasty rumors about his own sexuality.

He spoke little English, but he was damned handsome... that got him to Hollywood. In 1919, he married actress Jean Acker.

They never consummated the marriage. As it happened, she was a lesbian.

In 1921, Valentino starred as "THE SHEIK" — a movie that made him a sensation. His very glance had the power to knock women out, LITERALLY.

They threw themselves at him hysterically. Sometimes they'd disrobe right in front of him.

RUDY! Ohh, RUDY!!

Yaaaah!!

In 1922, he married actress Natacha Rambova. He had neglected to divorce Jean Acker first. That landed him in a bigamy rap.

Oh YEAH— she was a lesbian too.

But his biggest problem was his image. Women loved him, but men found him effeminate.

Royal Velvet SKIN CREME FOR MEN

He didn't help himself by doing advertisements for face cream... "It leaves your skin so smooth."

...Or by dressing so flamboyantly. Editorialists railed against him.

DO WOMEN LIKE THE SORT OF "MAN" WHO PATS PINK POWDER ON HIS FACE IN A PUBLIC WASHROOM?!

Their attacks stung him deeply.

Even as he lay dying of peritonitis, in extraordinary pain, the innuendoes were on his mind. He asked his doctors...

AND NOW, DO I ACT LIKE A PINK POWDER PUFF?

The secrets of his sexuality, if there were any, never did emerge. He died prematurely, at 31 — sending women all over the world into grief-stricken histrionics.

AND RUMOR HAD IT, SOME MEN, TOO.

TEN YEARS LATER, THE NOW-REMARRIED ETHEL MAY TANNER HAPPENED TO TAKE HER DAUGHTER TO THE MOVIES. SHE MADE A STARTLING DISCOVERY.

THAT'S YOUR FATHER!

AS "TAYLOR," HE'D SUDDENLY BECOME A CELEBRITY. HE MOVED TO DIRECTING AND ROSE SWIFTLY TO PRESIDENT OF THE SCREEN DIRECTORS GUILD.

TAYLOR

HE ALSO GAINED A REP AS QUITE THE LADIES' MAN.

RUMOR HAD IT THAT POLICE FOUND GRAPHIC PHOTOS OF TAYLOR WITH SEVERAL FAMOUS ACTRESSES.

HOO, BROTHER!

THE INTIMATE LOVE LETTERS FROM "VIRGINAL" TEEN STAR MARY MILES MINTER, HOWEVER, WERE MORE THAN A RUMOR.

YES, I LOVED BILLY--

--LIKE A FATHER!

THE STAR'S DOMINEERING MOTHER, CHARLOTTE SHELBY, HAD A FORTUNE RIDING ON MARY'S PURE-AS-SNOW IMAGE. SHE'D ALREADY PULLED A GUN ON ONE OF MARY'S DIRECTOR/LOVERS TO PROTECT IT.

NEIGHBOR FAITH MACLEAN SAW A "FUNNY-LOOKING" MAN WALKING CALMLY FROM TAYLOR'S HOUSE THE NIGHT OF THE MURDER. D.A.'S INVESTIGATOR ED C. KING BELIEVED IT WAS THE WIDELY DESPISED SHELBY IN DRAG.

MANY IN HOLLYWOOD SOCIAL CIRCLES SHARED THAT SUSPICION.

OR WAS IT THE MYSTERIOUS EDWARD SANDS, TAYLOR'S FORMER VALET? HE BURGLARIZED TAYLOR'S HOME TWO MONTHS BEFORE THE MURDER...

...TAKING JEWELRY AND TAYLOR'S ENTIRE STASH OF DISTINCTIVE, GOLD-TIPPED CIGARETTES.

SANDS TORMENTED TAYLOR. HE PAWNED SOME OF THE BURGLED GOODS, USING THE NAME "WILLIAM DEANE TANNER!" THEN HE SENT TAYLOR THE RECEIPT.

I WANT ED SANDS ARRESTED FOR GRAND LARCENY!

SANDS WAS SIGHTED IN L.A. THE DAY OF THE MURDER AND SUPPOSEDLY HEARD TO SAY:

I'M HERE TO GET BILL TAYLOR!

SANDS COULD HAVE BEEN THE MAN SPOTTED LURKING OUTSIDE TAYLOR'S HOUSE TWO HOURS AFTER THE SHOOTING.

THE LURKER LEFT BEHIND TWO CIGARETTE BUTTS -- WITH GOLD TIPS. AFTER TAYLOR'S DEATH, SANDS VANISHED FOR GOOD.

TAYLOR HAD A "LONG-LOST" BROTHER, DENIS. RUMORS CIRCULATED THAT DENIS WAS SANDS, BUT CONTEMPORARY RESEARCHERS HAVE SINCE DISCOUNTED THE TALE.

WHAT ABOUT MABEL NORMAND? SHE VISITED TAYLOR THAT FATEFUL EVENING.

THE KILLER SNUCK IN AS TAYLOR WALKED HIS "BLESSED BABY" OUT...

...AND PLUGGED TAYLOR MOMENTS AFTER NORMAND DEPARTED.

BLAM

NORMAND HAD A SERIOUS HANKERING FOR WHITE POWDER. HER HABIT TOPPED OUT AT $2,000 PER MONTH, A STAGGERING SUM FOR 1922. BUT THAT TOTAL PROBABLY ALSO INCLUDED BLACKMAIL PAYOFFS.

TAYLOR ONCE THRASHED NORMAND'S DOPE DEALER, WHO DELIVERED THE "STUFF" TO HER HOME.

TAKE *THAT*, SIR!

CRACK

HE THEN GRABBED THE DOPE AND MABEL'S CASH.

AND I'LL TAKE *THAT!*

HE RATTED OUT NORMAND'S SUPPLIERS TO THE FEDS.

YOU DON'T UNDERSTAND! SHE'S NOT JUST A STAR, SHE'S THE WOMAN I LOVE!

FIVE DAYS BEFORE HIS DEATH, TAYLOR SPOKE OF HIS ANTI-DRUG CRUSADE TO A NON-HOLLYWOOD FRIEND, WHO LATER HELD A PRESS CONFERENCE.

BILL TAYLOR THREATENED TO MAKE AN EXAMPLE OF THE DRUG PEDDLERS IN HOLLYWOOD, BUT THEY GOT TO HIM FIRST.

NO L.A. PAPERS RAN THE STORY.

STILL HOOKED ON PARTYING, NORMAND WAS AT A 1923 NEW YEAR'S EVE BASH WHEN HER CHAFFEUR SHOT THE HOST WITH MABEL'S GUN.

BLAM

THE SCANDALS AND DRUGS RUINED HER. MABEL DIED IN 1930 OF CONSUMPTION. SHE ASKED A FRIEND:

DO YOU THINK THEY'LL EVER FIND OUT WHO KILLED BILL TAYLOR?

MARY MILES MINTER, ALSO DESTROYED BY THE TAYLOR SCANDAL, RETREATED INTO OBSCURITY AND OBESITY. SHE LATER CLAIMED:

BILL AND I LOVED EACH OTHER AND WERE SECRETLY ENGAGED.

FAMED DIRECTOR KING VIDOR LOCATED MINTER IN 1967. SHE SEEMED MENTALLY SHAKY, BUT HE ASKED HER ABOUT THE TAYLOR CASE. MINTER ADMITTED NOTHING, BUT AT ONE POINT BURST INTO TEARS.

MY MOTHER KILLED EVERYTHING I EVER LOVED!

SHE DIED IN 1984, THE LAST SURVIVOR OF THE TAYLOR MYSTERY.

ALL-AMERICAN JUNKIE

AFTER THE ARBUCKLE AND TAYLOR SCANDALS SHOOK HOLLYWOOD, STUDIOS COMPILED A "DOOM BOOK," LISTING 117 FILMLAND NAMES WHOSE PRIVATE LIVES MADE THEM, SHALL WE SAY, "DANGEROUS." WHEN PARAMOUNT MOGUL ADOLPH ZUKOR SAW IT...

NO! NOT OUR *BIGGEST ATTRACTION!* NOT--*WALLACE REID!!*

IMPECCABLY HANDSOME AND CHARMING, REID WAS HOLLYWOOD'S MR. PERFECT-- THE ICON OF THE YOUNG AMERICAN MAN.

HIS PICTURES, SUCH AS *DOUBLE SPEED* AND *THE DANCING FOOL*, BROUGHT $2 MILLION PER YEAR INTO PARAMOUNT'S COFFERS.

HE EVEN HAD THE PERFECT ROMANCE WITH HIS LEADING LADY, DOROTHY DAVENPORT. THEY WERE UTTERLY DEVOTED TO EACH OTHER. ALL OF HOLLYWOOD LOVED THE COUPLE.

BUT SOON, RUMORS SPREAD THROUGH HOLLYWOOD. A POPULAR TABLOID HINTED OF A PROMINENT MALE STAR HOOKED ON DRUGS, BUT THE PUBLIC REMAINED IN THE DARK.

WHEN HE COLLAPSED ON THE SET OF A MOVIE IN 1922, THE STUDIO CALLED IT "OVERWORK".

CUT! CUT!

THEN THEY QUIETLY CHECKED HIM INTO A SANITARIUM.

DOROTHY FELT SHE COULD KEEP WALLY'S SECRET NO LONGER.

WALLY SUFFERS FROM A TERRIBLE ADDICTION-- MORPHINE!

NO! NOT-- *WALLACE REID!!*

WALLY FOUGHT HARD, BUT HIS WITHDRAWAL BROUGHT ON PNEUMONIA.

TELL THEM, MAMA! -*KOFF*- WE'RE GOING TO MAKE IT!

HE DIED ON JANUARY 18, 1923 AT AGE 31.

DOROTHY DAVENPORT CARRIED ON. HER NEXT MOVIE WAS A DRUG-SCARE POTBOILER TITLED *HUMAN WRECKAGE*.

FROM THAT FILM ON, SHE BILLED HERSELF AS "MRS. WALLACE REID."

FACTOID BOOKS

CHARLIE CHAPLIN

...CREATED ONE OF THE MOST BELOVED CHARACTERS IN MOVIE HISTORY: THE LITTLE TRAMP. CHAPLIN WAS AMERICA'S FIRST CINEMATIC GENIUS...

...YET EVEN HE COULDN'T AVOID THE SPECTRE OF SCANDAL...

CHAPLIN'S PROBLEM WAS HIS WEAKNESS FOR WOMEN --ESPECIALLY YOUNG ONES. HIS TROUBLES BEGAN WITH 16-YEAR-OLD MILDRED HARRIS.

CHAR-LIEEE! I'M PREG-NAAANT!

EVER THE GENTLEMAN, CHAPLIN MARRIED HER. SHE LAUNCHED HER OWN FILM CAREER, WITH HELP FROM MOGUL LOUIS B. MAYER.

FROM NOW ON, YOU'RE MILDRED CHAPLIN! AND WE'RE CHAPLIN-MAYER PRODUCTIONS!

CHAPLIN NEVER HELD HIS YOUNG BRIDE IN MUCH REGARD.

HOW'S LIFE WITH MILDRED?

SHE'S PLEASANT ENOUGH TO LOOK AT, BUT A MENTAL LIGHTWEIGHT!

HER PROPOSED NAME-CHANGE PLOY SPARKED A HUGE FIGHT.

YOU'RE A MEDIOCRE ACTRESS TRYING TO TRADE ON MY GOOD NAME!

YEAH, WELL GUESS WHAT? I'M NOT REALLY PREGNANT!

CHAPLIN AVOIDED HER. SHE WAS REDUCED TO TRYING TO CATCH HIS ATTENTION AS HE LEFT THE STUDIO.

CHARLIE! OH, CHARLIE!

JUST IGNORE HER. PRETEND WE DON'T HEAR.

BUT MILDRED WAS PREGNANT AFTER ALL.

WE'LL CALL HIM CHARLES CHAPLIN JR.!

WE CERTAINLY SHALL NOT!

THE BABY, BORN WITH A SEVERE INTESTINAL DEFECT, DIED TWO DAYS LATER.

INEVITABLY, MILDRED FILED FOR DIVORCE, CLAIMING "MENTAL CRUELTY." SHE BAD-MOUTHED CHAPLIN TO THE PRESS.

BEFORE I CAME ALONG HE DIDN'T HAVE A DECENT PAIR OF SOCKS!

MAYER, MILDRED'S "MANAGER," DEMANDED A LARGE SETTLEMENT, WHICH LED TO AN ANGRY CONFRONTATION WITH CHAPLIN AT THE ALEXANDRIA HOTEL.

SOCK!

NOT A GREAT MOVE BY CHARLIE.

CHAPLIN SETTLED THE DIVORCE IN 1920 FOR $100,000. MILDRED'S BRIEF POST-CHAPLIN CAREER PEAKED WITH THE 1936 THREE STOOGES SHORT MOVIE MANIACS.

ALCOHOLISM GOT THE BETTER OF HER. SHE DIED IN 1944.

FOUR YEARS AFTER THE DIVORCE-- AT THE AGE OF 35-- CHAPLIN SLIPPED AGAIN, TAKING UP WITH 15-YEAR-OLD ACTRESS LITA McMURRAY.

MRS. McMURRAY! I SAY, WHAT A PLEASANT SURPRISE! (Heh heh)

HE WAS ALSO, IT SEEMED, MYSTIFIED BY THE MECHANICS OF CONCEPTION.

MY DAUGHTER IS PREGNANT!

BUT... BUT HOW?

DOES THE PHRASE "STATUTORY RAPE" MEAN ANYTHIN' TO YA?

THE McMURRAYS --LITA'S MOTHER AND ATTORNEY UNCLE ED-- PUSHED FOR MARRIAGE TO SECURE A CHUNK OF CHAPLIN'S FORTUNE. THEY SNUCK OFF TO MEXICO.

DO YOU, SEÑOR CHAPLEEN, TAKE...?

YER DARN RIGHT HE DOES! NOW GET ON WITH IT!

THE PRESS GOT THE STORY AND MILKED IT DRY...

LITTLE TRAMP ROBS CRADLE

I THINK IT'S TIME YOU WENT INTO EARLY RETIREMENT, MY DEAR.

LITA GOT HER MAN, BUT LOST HER PART IN CHAPLIN'S CLASSIC, THE GOLD RUSH.

LITA AND CHAPLIN HAD TWO SONS IN JUST OVER A YEAR OF MARRIAGE, BUT IT WAS A DOOMED UNION. SHE LEFT IN 1926.

CHAPLIN WAS RELIEVED...

...UNTIL LITA FILED A LURID, 52-PAGE DIVORCE COMPLAINT IN JANUARY OF 1927.

COURT

COURTHOUSE ATTENDANCE FOR THE COMPLAINT WAS BIGGER THAN FOR A CHARLIE CHAPLIN MOVIE.

REPRESENTED BY UNCLE ED, LITA ACCUSED CHAPLIN OF ALL SORTS OF SORDID DEEDS.

HE FORCED HER TO SUBMIT TO HIS DEGENERATE PERVERSIONS!

THE "PERVERSION" AS DEFINED IN SECTION 288a OF THE PENAL CODE: ORAL SEX.

CALIFORNIA PENAL CODE

CHAPLIN, YOU DOG!

IT WAS STILL A CRIME IN THOSE DAYS.

TO CHAPLIN'S FURTHER HUMILIATION, MIMEOGRAPHS OF LITA'S DIVORCE COMPLAINT SOLD THOUSANDS ON STREETCORNERS.

CHAPLIN SEX PERVERSIONS! READ 'EM ALL RIGHT HERE!

A COURT ORDERED CHAPLIN TO PAY $3,000 PER MONTH. HIS COUNTEROFFER OF JUST $25 PER WEEK EARNED HIM NATIONWIDE SCORN.

CHAPLIN WOULD LET HIS OWN CHILDREN GO WITHOUT MILK!

SHAME ON YOU, CHARLIE CHAPLIN!

FINALLY, LITA PLAYED HER TRUMP CARD. SHE WENT TO CHAPLIN'S SECRET LOVER, MARION DAVIES.

TELL CHARLIE TO SETTLE UP OR I'LL TELL THE WORLD ABOUT YOU TWO!

THAT DID IT. CHAPLIN SETTLED FOR A RECORD-BREAKING $650,000.

PLEASURE DOIN' BUSINESS WITH YA, CHARLIE OL' PAL!

LITA'S LEGACY LINGERED. THE ONCE-LOVABLE "LITTLE TRAMP" WAS NOW SEEN AS A SEX-DEVIANT --A THREAT TO SOCIETY ITSELF.

COME ON, HONEY! THAT'S A BAD MAN!

CHAPLIN WAS AT IT AGAIN, WHEN, IN 1941, AFTER ANOTHER FAILED MARRIAGE, HE PURSUED A YOUNG ACTRESS NAMED JOAN BARRY.

I CAN TELL YOU'RE TALENTED! YOU'RE SO FRESH AND ALIVE!

AFTER CHAPLIN SIGNED HER TO A STUDIO CONTRACT, SHE SLEPT WITH HIM.

THIS ISN'T BECAUSE YOU'RE MY BOSS, CHARLIE. I'M DOING THIS FOR LOVE!

UH HUH.

CHAPLIN SOON TIRED OF JOAN AND TRIED TO END THE RELATIONSHIP --BUT JOAN WASN'T HAVING ANY OF IT...

I'M GOING TO KILL MYSELF AND TAKE YOU WITH ME!

I HAVE A BETTER IDEA, JOAN! COME TO BED!

AND SO THEY DID.

I'VE NEVER DONE IT WITH A LOADED GUN POINTED AT MY HEAD BEFORE!

BUT JOAN WASN'T PLACATED. THE NEXT NIGHT -- CHRISTMAS EVE --SHE PLASTERED CHAPLIN'S HOUSE WITH MUDBALLS.

SSPLATT!

YOU KNOW YOU LOVE ME, CHARLIE!

WHILE ALL THIS WAS GOING ON, CHAPLIN MET THE WOMAN WHO, AT LAST, PROVED TO BE THE TRUE LOVE OF HIS LIFE.

OONA O'NEILL, THE 17-YEAR-OLD DAUGHTER OF CELEBRATED PLAYWRIGHT EUGENE O'NEILL.

CHAPLIN ALSO BECAME INTERESTED IN LEFT-WING POLITICS. HIS HITLER SPOOF, **THE GREAT DICTATOR**, SEEMED TO SOME TO EMBODY A COMMUNIST PARTY LINE.

ALL-POWERFUL GOSSIP COLUMNIST HEDDA HOPPER WAS A STAUNCH RIGHT-WINGER AND HATED CHAPLIN. SHE WAS DELIGHTED WHEN JOAN BARRY BURST INTO HER OFFICE AND DECLARED...

I'M PREGNANT WITH CHARLIE CHAPLIN'S BABY!

HOPPER VILIFIED CHAPLIN. FEDERAL PROSECUTORS SAW THEIR BIG CHANCE.

IT'S TIME TO PUT THAT *PINKO* BEHIND BARS!

LOS ANGELES POST
CHAPLIN SIRES LOVE CHILD

THEY CHARGED HIM WITH VIOLATION OF THE MANN ACT BY TRANSPORTING JOAN, A MINOR, ACROSS STATE LINES FOR IMMORAL PURPOSES, BECAUSE HE ONCE BOUGHT HER A TRAIN TICKET TO NEW YORK.

JOAN TRIED BLACKMAIL.

FOR 65 GRAND I WON'T PRESS CHARGES!

SORRY, JOAN. I'LL SEE YOU IN COURT.

HIS PUBLIC IMAGE CRASHED. ALONG WITH EVERYTHING ELSE, THE PRESS CRITICIZED CHAPLIN, BRITISH BY BIRTH, FOR "FAILING" TO TAKE U.S. CITIZENSHIP.

I DIDN'T KNOW ANYONE CONSIDERED ME AN ENGLISHMAN.

HE SEEMED TO CATCH A BREAK WHEN BLOOD TESTS RULED HIM OUT AS THE FATHER OF JOAN'S BABY.

THAT'S A RELIEF!

UNBELIEVABLY, A JURY RULED THAT HE HAD TO PAY CHILD SUPPORT ANYWAY.

SOMEONE'S GOT TO PAY. MIGHT AS WELL BE HIM.

HE WAS ACQUITTED --NARROWLY-- ON THE MANN ACT CHARGE.

SOMEHOW, DESPITE ALL THE TURMOIL, CHAPLIN WENT ON TO COMPLETE ONE OF HIS FINEST FILMS, MONSIEUR VERDOUX.

CLAP CLAP CLAP

CHAPLIN WAS SO UNPOPULAR BY THEN THAT THE FILM, TODAY CONSIDERED A CLASSIC, FLOPPED.

THE FINAL BLOW CAME IN 1952, WHEN HE WAS SAILING BACK FROM A PROMOTIONAL TOUR OF LONDON.

QUEEN ELIZ

TERRIBLE NEWS, MR. CHAPLIN! YOU'VE BEEN BANNED FROM THE UNITED STATES AS A COMMUNIST SYMPATHIZER!

THE GREAT AMERICAN MOVIEMAKER WAS EXILED FROM AMERICA.

I DO NOT WANT TO CREATE ANY REVOLUTION. ALL I WANT TO DO IS CREATE A FEW MORE FILMS. IT MIGHT AMUSE PEOPLE. I HOPE SO.

FINALLY, 20 YEARS LATER, HE RETURNED --BRIEFLY. HE ACCEPTED A SPECIAL ACADEMY AWARD . THEN HE RETURNED TO SWITZERLAND.

FIVE YEARS LATER, CHARLIE CHAPLIN DIED PEACEFULLY IN HIS SLEEP. HE WAS 88.

FACTOID 100% TRUE BOOKS

IN THE EARLY DAYS OF TALKIES, THELMA TODD WAS HOLLYWOOD'S BEST-LOVED FUNNY GIRL. CUTE, SEXY AND FULL OF LAUGHS, THEY CALLED HER...

...the Ice cream blonde

HOW, THEN, DID THIS BRIGHT YOUNG STAR END UP DEAD IN HER GARAGE, ASPHYXIATED BY FUMES FROM HER OWN PACKARD CONVERTIBLE?

THEY FOUND HER MONDAY MORNING, DECEMBER 16, 1935. SHE WAS 30 YEARS OLD. AT FIRST, HER DEATH SEEMED LIKE A SUICIDE.

BUT SUICIDE DIDN'T EXPLAIN THE BLOOD ALL OVER HER FACE AND CLOTHES.

AN' IF THE DAME'S TRYIN' TO DO HERSELF IN, WHY'S SHE LEAVE THE TOP DOWN?

THE ICE CREAM BLONDE HAD SURELY BEEN MURDERED. BUT BY WHOM? HER LOVER ROLAND WEST-- ACCLAIMED DIRECTOR OF SUCH THRILLERS AS THE BAT WHISPERS-- CAME UNDER SUSPICION.

YOU'RE NOT SLEEPIN' HERE TONIGHT, TODDY!

LEMME IN, YOU #$@%&!!

BAM BAM BAM

WEST ADMITTED THAT WHEN THELMA RETURNED FROM A PARTY SATURDAY NIGHT, HE'D LOCKED HER OUT AND THEY'D HAD A TERRIBLE FIGHT.

HIS MOTIVE? THELMA MAY HAVE GIVEN IT AWAY EARLIER THAT EVENING.

I'M HAVING A WILD FLING WITH A RICH BUSINESSMAN FROM SAN FRANCISCO. ROLLY HAS NO IDEA!

ONE POPULAR HOLLYWOOD RUMOR HELD THAT WEST SET UP AN ALIBI, PAYING SOME WOMAN TO POSE AS THELMA AND MAKE A SCENE OUTSIDE HIS DOOR WHILE, INSIDE, HE PUMMELLED HIS LOVER INTO UNCONSCIOUSNESS BEFORE BRINGING HER DOWN TO THE GARAGE.

IT'S THE PERFECT MURDER... JUST LIKE IN MY 1929 CLASSIC, ALIBI!

BAM BAM BAM

THERE WAS NEVER A SHRED OF EVIDENCE, BUT IN HOLLYWOOD, RUMOR OF SCANDAL WAS ENOUGH. WEST NEVER WORKED AGAIN.

YOU'RE *POISON,* WEST! GET OUTTA HERE!

HE DIED IN OBSCURITY 17 YEARS LATER.

THERE WAS A MORE LIKELY — AND MORE SINISTER — SCENARIO. THELMA GOT MIXED UP WITH CHARLES "LUCKY" LUCIANO, THE CRIMINAL GENIUS WHO *CREATED* THE MODERN MAFIA.

I'LL MAKE HER AN OFFER SHE CAN'T REFUSE.

IN THOSE DAYS, L.A. WAS STILL OPEN TERRITORY FOR THE MOB. NEW YORK'S LUCIANO BATTLED CHICAGO'S CAPONE GANG FOR CONTROL.

THAT DAME TODD'LL HELP ME GET A PIECE O' THIS ACTION.

SPECIFICALLY, LUCIANO WANTED A PIECE OF THELMA'S SIDEWALK CAFE RESTAURANT.

TO THE MOBSTER, THELMA'S JOINT WITH ITS HOLLYWOOD CLIENTELE WAS THE PERFECT SPOT FOR AN UNDERWORLD CASINO.

KNOWING THELMA'S WEAKNESS FOR A GOOD TIME, LUCIANO WOOED HER -- WITH DRUGS.

THESE'LL CURE YOUR ILLS, SUGAR!

BUT THELMA DESPISED THE MOBSTER. WHEN HE TRIED TO MUSCLE IN ON HER RESTAURANT, SHE DEFIED HIM.

FORGET IT, CHARLIE! YOU'RE FINISHED IN LOS ANGELES! I'M TURNING *STATE'S EVIDENCE!*

THUS, THELMA SIGNED HER OWN DEATH WARRANT.

THE BROAD KNOWS TOO MUCH. TAKE CARE OF HER.

THE TODD INVESTIGATION WAS BOTCHED. OR WAS A COVER-UP ORCHESTRATED BY LUCIANO? THE BEST A GRAND JURY COULD DECIDE WAS...

THELMA TODD DIED OF CARBON MONOXIDE POISONING.

TODD WAS MAKING "*THE BOHEMIAN GIRL*" WHEN SHE DIED, BUT MOST OF HER SCENES WERE CUT OUT WHEN THE FILM WAS RELEASED. IN HER BRIEF APPEARANCE, THE ICE CREAM BLONDE WEARS A BROWN WIG.

HER DEATH REMAINS UNSOLVED.

MaryAstor's Little Blue Book

CENSORED

Diary

MARY ASTOR WAS ONE OF HOLLYWOOD'S MOST POPULAR FEMALE LEADS. WITH HER PRIM GOOD LOOKS AND NEATLY BOBBED HAIRDO, SHE PLAYED SOPHISTICATED LADIES. SHE WAS HARDLY CUT OUT FOR SEXPOT ROLES.

EXCEPT IN REAL LIFE.

ONE DAY IN 1935 HER HUSBAND, DR. FRANKLIN THORPE, WAS RUMMAGING THROUGH HER DRESSER DRAWER.

THOSE CUFFLINKS HAVE TO BE IN HERE SOMEW... SAY, WHAT'S THIS?

CURIOUS, HE FLIPPED THROUGH THE PAGES OF THE BLUE-BOUND DIARY.

"RAMPANT IN AN INSTANT... STAYING POWER... MADE LOVE ALL NIGHT LONG...?" WHAT THE... *MARY!*

Diary

MARY'S DIARY DETAILED HER AFFAIR WITH NEW YORK PLAYWRIGHT AND MAN-ABOUT-TOWN GEORGE S. KAUFMAN--BY APPEARANCES AN UNLIKELY LOTHARIO.

THE DIARY TOLD A DIFFERENT STORY-- LEAVING LITTLE TO THE IMAGINATION.

THORPE WAS SHATTERED.

MARY! ÷SOB!÷ PLEASE STOP SEEING HIM! I *NEED* YOU!!!

FINE, FINE! JUST STOP YOUR SOBBING.

SHE WOULDN'T END THE AFFAIR. THE ONLY REASON MARY WAS AT ALL CONCILIATORY: KAUFMAN WAS IN L.A. THAT VERY WEEKEND.

I DIDN'T WANT TO BE ALL UPSET WHEN I SAW *YOU*, GEORGE, SWEETIE!

THORPE TOOK HIS REVENGE BY BEDDING A BEVY OF SHOWGIRLS.

AND THEN I'M GOING TO DIVORCE THAT *TRAMP* AND GET CUSTODY OF OUR DAUGHTER!

THEIR MARRIAGE WAS FINISHED ANYWAY. BUT MARY HAD A MOTHER'S INSTINCT.

I'LL NEVER GIVE *YOU* UP, LITTLE MARILYN! I'LL FIGHT THEM!

BUT WOULD THE RAUNCHY DIARY PROVE THAT SHE WAS AN *UNFIT MOTHER?*

SHE WON A VICTORY AS THE TRIAL OPENED.

IRRELEVANT AS EVIDENCE! BUT, UH, *INTERESTING* NONETHELESS.

BUT THORPE WAS PLAYING FOR KEEPS. HE-- OR SOMEONE-- LEAKED EXPLICIT DIARY EXCERPTS TO THE PRESS.

I THINK YOU'LL ENJOY THESE.

OKAY-- YOU SEEM LIKE A *RELIABLE* SOURCE!

THE EXCERPTS CONTAINED MORE THAN ENOUGH STEAMY PROSE TO KEEP THE READING PUBLIC ENTERTAINED, INCLUDING THIS MEMORABLE PASSAGE:

AH, DESERT NIGHT-- WITH GEORGE'S BODY PLUNGING INTO MINE, NAKED UNDER THE STARS!

OF COURSE, NEWSPAPERS COULDN'T PRINT THE STEAMIER STUFF. BUT READERS EN- JOYED THE GAME OF FILL-IN-THE-BLANKS.

"...HE *BLANKED* THE LIVING DAYLIGHTS OUT OF ME!"

WAIT! WAIT! DON'T TELL ME...

THE DAILY BLAB
ASTOR KAUFMAN IN RED HOT LOVE NEST!

IN THE DIARY ASTOR LAUDED KAUFMAN'S SEXUAL ENDURANCE. BUT THE PLAYWRIGHT NEVER COMMENTED ON THE CASE EXCEPT ONCE TO SAY...

I'LL TELL YOU THIS-- I DID *NOT* KEEP A DIARY!

STAGE DOOR

WITHOUT THE DIARY IN THE COURTROOM, MARY WON HER CASE. THE JUDGE LET HER KEEP HER DAUGHTER. BUT NOT THE DIARY.

A FITTING FATE FOR THIS WANTON *PORNOGRAPHY!*

PERHAPS IT WAS A SIGN OF CHANGING TIMES, BUT THE SENSATIONAL SCANDAL EVENTUALLY SUBSIDED WITH NO EFFECT ON MARY'S CAREER. SHE HAD MANY MEMORABLE ROLES TO COME, INCLUDING A CLASSIC IN *THE MALTESE FALCON.*

SORRY, SHWEETHAHT. YOU'RE TAKIN' THE *FALL!*

SHE PASSED AWAY IN 1987 AT AGE 81.

25

HIS WHOLE LIFE WAS A SCANDAL THAT HAD HOLLYWOOD-HATING MORALISTS OUTRAGED. BUT IN THE 30s AND 40s, ANY YOUNG MAN IN AMERICA WOULD GIVE HIS RIGHT ARM TO BE...

IN LIKE FLYNN

IN 1935, RAFFISH AND HANDSOME 25-YEAR-OLD AUSSIE ERROL FLYNN ARRIVED IN HOLLYWOOD WITH AN IMPRESSIVE, IF MOSTLY FALSE, RESUME OF ACCOMPLISHMENTS.

IT ALL BEGAN WHEN I BOXED IN THE 1928 OLYMPICS...

THAT SUMMER, HE GOT HIS BIG BREAK. DIRECTOR MICHAEL CURTIZ PICKED THE UNKNOWN FLYNN TO STAR IN *CAPTAIN BLOOD*, A DECISION CURTIZ SOON REGRETTED.

STOP ACTING LIKE A @!$#% HAM, YOU%#&!@!!

IF HIS OVERACTING WASN'T ANNOYING ENOUGH, FLYNN'S HABIT OF SHOWING UP DRUNK DIDN'T EXACTLY ENDEAR HIM EITHER.

HEY (HIC!)! WHICH END DO YOU HOLD THIS THING? (HIC!)

CUT! CUT! @&#$!

ERROL FLYNN IN THE ADVENTURES OF ROBIN HOOD

NONETHELESS, *CAPTAIN BLOOD* WAS A BLOCKBUSTER THAT LAUNCHED THE CAREER OF THE DASHING FLYNN VIRTUALLY OVERNIGHT.

ALL THE BETTER FOR HIS RAKISH LIFESTYLE.

I BELIEVE THERE'S A ROLE FOR YOU IN MY NEW PICTURE, MY DEAR. SHALL WE DISCUSS IT-- UPSTAIRS?

OH, THANK YOU MR. FLYNN. THIS COULD BE MY *BIG BREAK*!

THE FIRST HINT OF PROBLEMS CAME WHEN FLYNN TRIED TO JOIN THE WAR EFFORT.

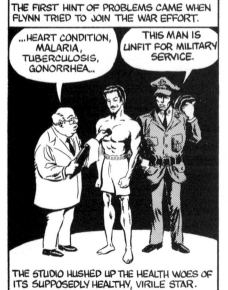

...HEART CONDITION, MALARIA, TUBERCULOSIS, GONORRHEA...

THIS MAN IS UNFIT FOR MILITARY SERVICE.

THE STUDIO HUSHED UP THE HEALTH WOES OF ITS SUPPOSEDLY HEALTHY, VIRILE STAR.

THE RESULT: FLYNN CAME OFF AS HEALTHY, VIRILE--AND YELLOW.

WHY DONTCHA FIGHT FOR REAL, YA PRETTY-BOY HOLLYWOOD SISSY!

BUT HIS REAL TROUBLE BEGAN IN 1942 WHEN HIS WOMANIZING WAYS CAME BACK TO HAUNT HIM...

MR. FLYNN, YOU'RE UNDER ARREST FOR STATUTORY RAPE.

STATU-WHAT?

...OR SO IT SEEMED.

HIS ACCUSER, 17-YEAR-OLD BETTY HANSEN, HAD A DUBIOUS PAST AND MADE A LESS THAN COMPELLING WITNESS.

WELL, HE RIPPED MY CLOTHES OFF, BUT I DIDN'T HAVE NO OBJECTIONS.

FLYNN WAS NOT INDICTED.

THE D.A. TRIED FLYNN ANYWAY, ADDING AN ANCIENT COMPLAINT BY VIVACIOUS (BUT UNDERAGED) "DANCER" PEGGY SATTERLEE WHO, ABSURDLY, APPEARED IN COURT WEARING PIGTAILS.

HE RAVISHED ME ABOARD HIS YACHT AS I GAZED AT THE MOON.

FLYNN WAS HUMILIATED. HANSEN'S CLAIM THAT HE KEPT HIS SOCKS ON DURING SEX BECAME A NATIONAL JOKE.

JUST A MOMENT, DARLING. MY TOESIES ARE CHILLY.

IRONICALLY, GIVEN FLYNN'S MANY SINS, HE WAS TRIED FOR THE ONES HE APPARENTLY DIDN'T COMMIT. AFTER FLYNN WAS EASILY ACQUITTED BY THE JURY, THE JUDGE INFORMED THEM:

I KNOW I'VE ENJOYED THIS CASE AND I THINK YOU HAVE, TOO.

THE TRIAL'S CONCLUSION MARKED THE START OF FLYNN'S STEEP DECLINE. HE BECAME A PARODY OF HIS OWN PHILANDERING PERSONA, OPENLY CHEATING ON HIS SECOND WIFE.

MASHED POTATOES TONIGHT, ERROL?

WITH GRAVY, PLEASE, MY DEAR!

HE ADDED A NASTY DRUG HABIT TO HIS DRUNKENNESS, DEMANDING THAT HIS WIFE SHOOT HIM UP.

IF YOU WON'T DO IT, I'LL DO IT MYSELF!

IN 1959, AT AGE 50, FLYNN DIED, HIS BODY EXHAUSTED AND HIS SOUL WEARY FROM A LIFE OF DISSIPATION.

I WANTED PEOPLE TO TAKE ME SERIOUSLY, BUT I NEVER GAVE THEM A REASON TO.

EVEN LONG AFTER HIS DEATH, SCANDAL FOLLOWED FLYNN. A 1979 BOOK ALLEGED THAT HE WAS A NAZI SPY.

THE CHARGE SEEMED UNLIKELY. BUT THEN AGAIN, FLYNN NEVER EXPECTED TO BE REMEMBERED WELL.

IN APRIL 1958, AS SHE WAS FILMING *THE LADY TAKES A FLYER*, A STRANGER CALLING HIMSELF JOHN STEELE CALLED ON HER.

OH, MY--! DO YOU HAVE A MONEY TREE?

JUST THE LEAVES, BABY!

LANA FELL FOR "STEELE", BUT SOON LEARNED A FRIGHTENING SECRET ABOUT HER NEW PARAMOUR.

THE MAN YOU'RE SEEING IS REALLY A GANGSTER NAMED JOHNNY STOMPANATO!

LANA CONFRONTED JOHNNY.

YOU LIED TO ME! I THINK WE'D BETTER NOT SEE EACH OTHER ANYMORE!

DARLIN', JUST TRY AND GET AWAY FROM ME!

IT TURNED OUT JOHNNY WAS BODY-GUARD TO L.A. CRIME LORD MICKEY COHEN.

SOME THOUGHT COHEN BANKROLLED JOHNNY'S COURTSHIP OF LANA, HOPING JOHNNY WOULD MARRY HER--AND HER MONEY!

NOTHING, NOT JOHNNY'S THREATS OR HIS SHADY PAST, DISSUADED LANA. SHE WAS NUTS FOR HER GANGSTER BEAU.

STILL, IMAGE ALWAYS CAME FIRST FOR THE GREAT MOVIE STAR. SHE KNEW THAT THIS ROMANCE MUST STAY IN THE CLOSET.

SAY, WHATCHA GOT IN THERE, LANA?

OH, UH, NOTHING!! NOTHING AT ALL!

JOHNNY INGRATIATED HIMSELF WITH LANA'S TROUBLED BUT BELOVED DAUGHTER, CHERYL CRANE.

THERE YA GO, KID! AIN'T SHE A BEAUT?

LANA FLEW OFF TO LONDON TO FILM A MOVIE CALLED *ANOTHER TIME, ANOTHER PLACE*. BY HERSELF.

FAREWELL, MY LOVE-- FOR NOW!

CATCH YA LATER, TOOTS!

BUT JOHNNY HAD OTHER IDEAS.

GIMME A TICKET TO LONDON-- AND MAKE IT SNAPPY!

LANA'S COSTAR WAS A YOUNG SCOTTISH BODYBUILDER-TURNED-ACTOR NAMED SEAN CONNERY. HE HAD A REPUTATION AS SOMETHING OF A LADIES' MAN, AND JOHNNY DIDN'T LIKE THAT ONE BIT. WHEN THE MOBSTER SHOWED UP, UNEXPECTED, ON THE LONDON SET...

STAY AWAY FROM THE KID, YA PUNK! OR I'LL LET YA HAVE IT!

CONNERY'S RESPONSE--?

POW

FRUSTRATED, JOHNNY TOOK IT OUT ON LANA.

YOU'LL NEVER GET RID OF ME! AND IF YA TRY, I'LL CUT THAT PRETTY FACE!

LANA, TERRIFIED, CONTINUED THE RELATIONSHIP, EVEN PAYING FOR THEIR VACATION IN ACAPULCO.

BUT SHE STILL KEPT THE AFFAIR SECRET. WHEN SHE WAS NOMINATED FOR AN OSCAR IN 1958, IT WAS CHERYL WHO ACCOMPANIED HER, NOT JOHNNY.

POP!

POP!

ON APRIL 4, 1958 CHERYL, AGE 14, WAS HOME FROM SCHOOL. BUT THAT DIDN'T STOP JOHNNY FROM STARTING A TERRIBLE FIGHT.

DON'T ARGUE IN FRONT OF THE CHILD!

I'LL SHUT UP WHEN YOU COUGH UP SOME MORE CASH!!

CHERYL LISTENED AS THE QUARREL TURNED MORE VIOLENT.

I WANT YOU OUT, JOHNNY! WE'RE FINISHED!

YOU TRAMP! I'LL CUT YER FACE UP AND IF I CAN'T DO IT, I'LL HIRE SOMEONE!!

SHE RAN DOWNSTAIRS TO THE KITCHEN.

DON'T WORRY, MOTHER! I'LL PROTECT YOU!

CHERYL RUSHED BACK TO THE BEDROOM AND--

OH MY GOD!! CHERYL!!!

CLUTCH!

THERE WAS NO WAY TO KEEP THE AFFAIR A SECRET ANYMORE.

HE'S DEAD, ALL RIGHT. THE KID GOT HIM A GOOD ONE!

IT WAS THE BIGGEST HOLLYWOOD SCANDAL SINCE FATTY ARBUCKLE. THE PRESS EXCORIATED LANA AS A "WANTON" WOMAN AND AN UNFIT MOTHER.

GELES TIMES

CHERYL IS NOT THE JUVENILE DELINQUENT HERE. LANA IS!

ANNOYED BY THE KILLING... AND BY HAVING TO FOOT THE BILL FOR THE FUNERAL... MICKEY COHEN HANDED LANA'S LOVE LETTERS TO THE L.A. HERALD-EXAMINER.

HAVE A FIELD DAY!

THE EMBARRASSING LETTERS MADE LANA LOOK MORE LIKE A PATHETIC SCHOOLGIRL THAN A WANTON SEX FIEND.

OH, DARLING! WHEN NEAR ME YOU MAKE DREAMS COME TO LIFE WITH THE REALNESS OF YOU!

AT THE CORONER'S INQUEST, LANA GAVE WHAT THE CYNICAL PRESS CALLED THE PERFORMANCE OF HER LIFE, NEARLY FAINTING.

IT WORKED. THE KILLING WAS RULED "JUSTIFIABLE." CHERYL WAS FREED.

LANA'S NEXT FILM, IMITATION OF LIFE, WAS HER BIGGEST HIT EVER. BUT FROM THEN ON, HER GLAMOUR WAS TAINTED BY RIDICULE.

CHERYL GREW UP TO WORK IN HER FATHER'S RESTAURANT BUSINESS. LANA FINISHED HER CAREER ON THE DINNER THEATER CIRCUIT AND DIED IN 1995.

HOLLYWOOD

FACTOID BOOKS

THE LOVES OF INGRID BERGMAN

SHE WAS THE SILVER SCREEN'S TOP FEMALE STAR OF THE 1940s-- THE SWEDISH-BORN HEIR TO ANOTHER ETHEREAL SCANDINAVIAN BEAUTY, GARBO.

HERE'S LOOKING AT YOU, KID.

SHE WAS ALREADY A STAR IN SCANDINAVIA WHEN HOLLYWOOD BIGSHOT DAVID O. SELZNICK SAW HER 1936 FILM, INTERMEZZO.

I WANT A DEAL TO REMAKE THAT PICTURE -- WITH THE GIRL!

SHE WAS RELUCTANT TO LEAVE HER HUSBAND, A MEDICAL STUDENT, AND THEIR DAUGHTER.

IF I SUCCEED, COME JOIN ME IN A YEAR.

IT WASN'T THE LAST TIME SHE WOULD LEAVE THEM.

SUCCEED SHE DID. WHILE THE NEW INTERMEZZO WAS A BOX OFFICE LETDOWN, CRITICS WENT WILD FOR INGRID. SHE WAS POISED FOR STARDOM.

RARE BEAUTY, FRESHNESS, VITALITY, AND ABILITY!

INCANDESCENT! ANOTHER GREAT LADY OF THE SCREEN!

THE MOST GIFTED AND ATTRACTIVE STUDIO RECRUIT IN MANY MOONS!

BUT SELZNICK COULDN'T FIND A WORTHY FOLLOW-UP FOR HIS NEW STAR. INSTEAD, HE SIMPLY MOVED HER INTO A PLUSH MANHATTAN APARTMENT.

I'M GOING MAD FROM LACK OF WORK.

THE WAIT APPEARED OVER WHEN ERNEST HEMINGWAY HIMSELF ANOINTED INGRID TO STAR IN THE FILM OF HIS BEST-SELLER ABOUT THE SPANISH CIVIL WAR.

YOU'RE MY MARIA!

BUT PARAMOUNT ORIGINALLY CAST SOMEONE ELSE, SO INGRID, DESPERATE, JUMPED AT AN OFFER FROM WARNER BROS. TO STAR IN A WARTIME ROMANCE CALLED CASABLANCA.

PLAY IT, SAM. PLAY "AS TIME GOES BY."

LITTLE KNOWN IN THE U.S., ROBERTO ROSSELLINI HELPED DEFINE THE BURGEONING "NEOREALIST" STYLE OF ITALIAN CINEMA.

HOLLYWOOD IS A FACTORY CHURNING OUT SAUSAGES! HERE IN ITALY I HAVE *FREEDOM!*

MORE IMPORTANT, HOWEVER, HE WAS A NOTORIOUS PLAYBOY. JOWLY AND BALDING, HE SEEMED LIKE NO DON JUAN, BUT FOR SOME REASON, WOMEN COULDN'T KEEP THEIR HANDS OFF HIM.

PERHAPS IT WAS HIS REMARKABLE TALENT FOR MANIPULATING WOMEN'S EMOTIONS. HE MADE INGRID FEEL LIKE A QUEEN.

LADIES AND GENTLEMEN-- MY NEW STAR!

INEVITABLY INGRID AND HER NEW DIRECTOR BEGAN A TORRID ROMANCE. BOTH, OF COURSE, WERE MARRIED.

THE AFFAIR BLOSSOMED AS THEY FILMED THEIR FIRST MOVIE TOGETHER, *STROMBOLI,* ON THE VOLCANIC ITALIAN ISLAND OF THE SAME NAME. THE PICTURE WAS FINANCED BY RKO WHICH STILL SAW INGRID AS A MAJOR BOX OFFICE DRAW.

ROSSELLINI WAS NOT ONLY CHARMING, HE WAS CONTROLLING. HE KNEW ALL THE EMOTIONAL PLOYS.

IF YOU EVER WORK FOR ANOTHER DIRECTOR, I WILL DRIVE MY FERRARI OFF A CLIFF!

NEWS OF THE AFFAIR LEAKED. IMMEDIATELY REPORTERS INVADED THE TINY ISLAND.

GET HER! YOU'LL NEVER ESCAPE, BERGMAN!

IT WAS A FULL-BLOWN SCANDAL, AND INGRID'S "PURE" IMAGE WAS BLOWN.

THE WHOLE THING DEPRESSED INGRID. IT ALL SEEMED OUT OF HER CONTROL.

INGRID, PLEASE--! YOU'LL LOSE YOUR HUSBAND *AND* YOUR CHILD!

I KNOW.

BACK IN BEVERLY HILLS, PETTER-- WHO LOATHED PUBLICITY-- WAS REPELLED BY THE SCANDAL. HE REALIZED HE WAS LOSING HIS WIFE FOR GOOD.

INGRID, IT'S TIME YOU GREW UP!

THE SCANDAL COULDN'T HAVE COME AT A WORSE TIME FOR HOLLYWOOD. THE TINSELTOWN EMPIRE WAS UNDER SIEGE.

ARE YOU NOW OR HAVE YOU EVER BEEN-- A COMMUNIST?!

UNDER POLITICAL PRESSURE, THE LAST THING HOLLYWOOD NEEDED WAS A MORAL SCANDAL.

THEY'RE SAYING YOUR FILMS COULD BE BANNED!

YOUR CAREER COULD BE RUINED!

THEN WHAT WILL THEY SAY WHEN THEY FIND OUT I'M PREGNANT?!

THE PREGNANCY WAS A CLOSELY GUARDED SECRET, AT LEAST UNTIL INGRID'S PUBLICIST CONFIDED IN THE HEAD OF RKO, HOWARD HUGHES.

YOU UNDERSTAND, MR. HUGHES, IF THIS GETS OUT, IT COULD KILL THE PICTURE!

OF COURSE. YOU CAN COUNT ON ME.

THE NEXT DAY...

THAT TRAMP!

IN 1950 AMERICA, A MARRIED WOMAN HAVING A BABY BY A MARRIED MAN WHO WASN'T HER HUSBAND...

LOS ANGELES
HERALD EXAMINER
INGRID BERGMAN BABY DUE IN THREE MONTHS AT ROME

FIRE AND FLOOD

...WELL, IT WASN'T TOO COOL.

THE ANTI-INGRID OUTCRY REACHED THE U.S. SENATE.

BERGMAN IS A FREE-LOVE CULTIST, A POWERFUL FORCE FOR EVIL!

INGRID AND HER NOW-PUBLIC LOVER HOLED UP FOR A MONTH. WHEN THEY WENT OUT...

POP

STOP IT, YOU DEVIL!

IN FEBRUARY, 1950 INGRID GAVE BIRTH TO ROBERTO ROSSELLINI'S SON. THEY NAMED HIM--

ROBERTINO!

ROSSELLINI WAS A PROUD ITALIAN PAPA. HE COULDN'T WAIT TO SHOW OFF HIS NEW BOY TO THE WORLD.

UNFORTUNATELY, THE WORLD WASN'T QUITE READY.

EVIL! EVIL! EVIL!

A CHILD OF SIN!

WHEN *STROMBOLI* WAS RELEASED, THERE WERE CALLS TO BAN IT. BUT WORSE HAPPENED. NOBODY BOUGHT A TICKET.

STROMBOLI! INGRID BERGMAN

ROBERTO ROSSELLINI

BOX OFFIC

STROMBOLI WAS THE FIRST OF SIX STRAIGHT BERGMAN/ROSSELLINI DISASTERS.

IN 1952 INGRID AND ROBERTO -- NOW MARRIED -- HAD TWINS.

YESS!

BY NOW INGRID WAS A PARIAH IN THE U.S. SHE WAS, IN EFFECT, EXILED.

INGRID WANTED PIA TO COME TO ITALY. SHE SUED TO MAKE IT HAPPEN. THAT DIDN'T TURN OUT TOO WELL EITHER.

I DON'T LOVE MY MOTHER, YOUR HONOR. SHE DOESN'T SEEM TO CARE ABOUT ME.

NOR WERE THINGS EXACTLY BLISSFUL IN THE ROSSELLINI HOUSEHOLD.

THWACK

YAAAAA!

ROSSELLINI WAS SUBJECT TO FREQUENT BLACK MOODS.

WITH HER CAREER AND *LIFE* IN TATTERS, BY 1956 INGRID GREW IMMUNE TO ROSSELLINI'S EMOTIONAL ACROBATICS.

I HAVE AN OFFER FROM 20TH CENTURY-FOX -- AND I'M TAKING IT!

NO! INGRID! I SHALL KILL MYSELF!

FREED FROM ROSSELLINI, INGRID WAS BACK TO HER BEST. HER NEXT FILM, ANASTASIA, WON HER A SECOND ACADEMY AWARD.

AS IF THEY'D ALWAYS WANTED TO, AMERICANS FORGAVE HER COMPLETELY.

IN 1977 ROSSELLINI DIED OF A HEART ATTACK.

THE FAMOUS FILMMAKER'S ESTATE: $200 IN THE BANK... AND A MILLION IN DEBTS.

INGRID WON A THIRD OSCAR IN 1975. IN HER FINAL ROLE SHE PLAYED ISRAELI PRIME MINISTER GOLDA MEIR IN A TV MOVIE... AND WON AN EMMY.

SHE DIED IN 1982 ON HER 67TH BIRTHDAY.

ONCE, THERE WAS A POOR SOUTHERN BOY WHO GREW UP TO BECOME AN AMERICAN LEGEND. HIS NAME WAS ELVIS AND TO MOST, HE WAS "THE KING." BUT TO HIS MANY HANGERS-ON AND SYCOPHANTS, HE WAS SIMPLY...

E!

IN THE 1950s, WHEN AMERICAN TEENS WERE TREATING ELVIS LIKE A GOD, AMERICAN GROWNUPS CONDEMNED HIS "LEWD" PELVIC GYRATIONS. HIS PERFORMANCES WERE WIDELY BANNED.

♪ YOU AIN'T NOTHIN' BUT A HOUND DOG ♪

SHWING SHWING

BUT THE PHENOMENON COULDN'T BE STOPPED. ON A 1956 ED SULLIVAN SHOW, ELVIS — SHOWN ONLY FROM ABOVE THE WAIST — SCORED A STAGGERING 82 PERCENT SHARE, UNBELIEVABLE BY TODAY'S STANDARDS.

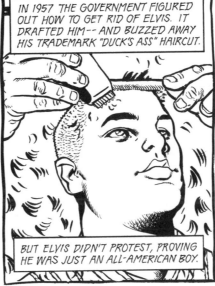

IN 1957 THE GOVERNMENT FIGURED OUT HOW TO GET RID OF ELVIS. IT DRAFTED HIM-- AND BUZZED AWAY HIS TRADEMARK "DUCK'S ASS" HAIRCUT.

BUT ELVIS DIDN'T PROTEST, PROVING HE WAS JUST AN ALL-AMERICAN BOY.

WHILE STATIONED IN GERMANY, HE DISCOVERED AN ALL-AMERICAN PASTIME: DRUGS. HE TOOK DEXEDRINE TO STAY UP FOR ALL-NIGHT MANEUVERS.

UH, ELVIS...

GONE, DADDY, GONE!

AFTER HIS DISCHARGE, ELVIS RETREATED INTO HIS LAVISH MEMPHIS PLAYHOUSE, GRACELAND, AND MADE GRADE-B MOVIES FOR MOST OF THE '60s.

HE SURROUNDED HIMSELF WITH SUBSERVIENT FOLLOWERS WHO CALLED THEMSELVES "THE MEMPHIS MAFIA." THEY SAW TO HIS EVERY NEED, INCLUDING HIS NEW DRUG HABIT.

HERE Y' GO, E!

THANGYAVERREMUCH!

IN ADDITION TO HIS NEWFOUND FONDNESS FOR PRESCRIPTION DRUGS, ELVIS ALSO FOUND A GIRLFRIEND IN GERMANY. HE MET PRISCILLA WHEN SHE WAS JUST 14.

THEY WED IN 1967, EIGHT YEARS LATER.

BUT THEIR RELATIONSHIP WAS FAR FROM TYPICAL. BEFORE THEY WERE MARRIED, FRIENDS SAID, HE DIRECTED PRISCILLA IN SEVERAL SEXUAL VIDEOS FOR HIS PERSONAL ENJOYMENT.

ONE MORE TIME, HONEY — WITH *FEELIN'*!

ODD FOOTNOTE: HE DIDN'T LIKE HIS WOMEN NUDE; A WHITE BRA AND PANTIES REALLY TURNED HIM ON.

THEY SAID THAT THE KING WAS ALSO PARTIAL TO VOYEURISM. HE PUT TWO-WAY MIRRORS IN GRACELAND GUEST BEDROOMS, THEN SAT BACK TO WATCH THE ACTION.

♪ I GOT A HUNK, A HUNK O' BURNIN' LOVE! ♪

IN 1966, ELVIS TOOK ON MEMPHIS DOCTOR GEORGE "DR. NICK" NICHOPOULOS AS HIS PERSONAL PHYSICIAN, TO KEEP HIM SATIATED WITH PRESCRIPTION PILLS.

THANKS, DOC, THESE'LL MAKE ME FEEL A WHOLE LOT BETTER.

IN 1968, AFTER A SEVEN-YEAR HIATUS FROM LIVE PERFORMANCES, ELVIS RETURNED IN A "COMEBACK" TV SPECIAL. HE WAS BETTER THAN EVER.

HE FOLLOWED THE SPECIAL WITH A STRING OF HIT SINGLES AND A TRIUMPHANT, IF GRUELING, RUN OF TWICE-A-NIGHT SHOWS IN LAS VEGAS.

THANGYAVERREMUCH!

ONE NIGHT HE VISITED THE WHITE HOUSE AND OFFERED HIS SERVICES TO PRESIDENT NIXON TO HELP FIGHT THE "WAR ON DRUGS." RATHER IRONIC, ALL THINGS CONSIDERED.

PERHAPS IT WAS A SIGN. HIS RESURGENT FAME ONLY MADE HIS ALREADY ERRATIC BEHAVIOR A LOT MORE BIZARRE.

KA-BLAM

DAMN SOAP OPERAS!

IN 1973, PRISCILLA DIVORCED HIM.

AS IF THE DRUGS WEREN'T ENOUGH, THE KING STARTED TO EAT LIKE ONE, HIDING HIMSELF UNDER LAYERS OF FAT.

MORE FUDGSICLES!

HIS GIRTH AND THE DRUGS ATE AWAY AT HIS PRECARIOUS HEALTH. EVERY PERFORMANCE BECAME AN ORDEAL.

I CAN'T HELP -- KOFF -- FALLING IN LOVE -- WHEEZ -- WITH Y-Y-Y...

IN 1977 THREE OF ELVIS' EX-BODYGUARDS PUBLISHED A TELL-ALL BOOK DETAILING THE KING'S DEBAUCHERY AND DRUG ADDICTION. ELVIS FANS WERE OUTRAGED. THEY TRIED TO SABOTAGE SALES.

GOD SAVE THE KING!!

A FEW MONTHS LATER, ON AUGUST 16, 1977, THE KING WAS DEAD-- IN THE BATHROOM.

THERE WERE 12 DIFFERENT DRUGS IN HIS SYSTEM. HE WAS 42.

ELVIS WORSHIPPERS EVERYWHERE WERE ABSOLUTELY CRUSHED. MANY LOOKED FOR SOMEONE TO BLAME.

-- WAAAAA! -- ELLLLL-VIIIISSSS! -- WAAAH!!!

DR. NICK TOOK THE FALL. HE'D PRESCRIBED 11,000 DOSES OF VARIOUS DRUGS FOR ELVIS IN THE 15 MONTHS BEFORE THE KING'S DEATH.

I WAS ONLY TRYING TO HELP.

HE WAS TRIED-- BUT ACQUITTED.

OTHER FANS DEALT WITH THE DEATH OF ELVIS BY DENYING IT. IN THE TWO DECADES SINCE ELVIS DIED, HE'S BEEN SEEN ALMOST EVERYWHERE, THE DISGRACES OF HIS FINAL YEARS SUBSUMED BY THE DESIRE TO SEE HIM LIVE ON.

ELVIS LIVES!

FINAL FOOTNOTE: DR. NICK LOST HIS LICENSE IN 1995 FOR OVERPRESCRIBING DRUGS.

ON THE EARLY 1960s, 20TH CENTURY FOX LAUNCHED A MONUMENTAL EPIC, PLANNED AS THE GREATEST MOTION PICTURE EVER MADE. BEFORE IT WAS OVER, CLEOPATRA, THE STIRRING SAGA OF THE TRAGICALLY AMOROUS EGYPTIAN QUEEN, WOULD GO DOWN IN HISTORY AS:

THE SCANDAL THAT SANK A STUDIO

— AND IT MADE FOR A PRETTY CRAPPY MOVIE, TOO!

IN 1958, FOX BEGAN FILMING A LOW-BUDGET REMAKE OF THE EPIC CLEOPATRA. THE PROJECTED COST WAS $210,000 — LESS THAN THAT OF THE SILENT ORIGINAL, MADE IN 1917.

WHEN MGM PULLED OUT ALL THE STOPS FOR ITS OWN COSTUME EPIC, BEN-HUR, FOX CHIEF SPYROS SKOURAS PREVIEWED THE SPECTACLE AND SCRAPPED HIS LOW-BUDGET FLICK.

FOX WAS ALREADY IN DEEP FINANCIAL TROUBLE. IT HUNG ALL ITS HOPES ON THE SUCCESS OF THE RELAUNCHED, BIG-BUDGET CLEOPATRA.

AND THE SUCCESS OF THE MOVIE HUNG ON HOLLYWOOD'S GREATEST STAR AND QUEEN DIVA: ELIZABETH TAYLOR.

KNOWING SHE WAS CALLING THE SHOTS, TAYLOR MADE SOME HEFTY DEMANDS. AN UNPRECEDENTED MILLION-DOLLAR SALARY, FOR OPENERS...

...AND $3000 A WEEK EXPENSES, AND $1500 A WEEK FOR MY HUSBAND, AND A FIRST CLASS HOTEL SUITE, AND 10% OF THE GROSS, AND...

SETS WORTH MILLIONS WENT UP AT LONDON'S PINEWOOD STUDIOS. BY SEPT. 28, 1960, FILMING WAS READY TO BEGIN.

THERE WAS ONE SMALL PROBLEM: THAT VERY MORNING, LIZ WOKE UP WITH A HEAD COLD.

AH-CHOO!

HER COLD TURNED INTO A FIVE-WEEK ABSENCE, AS THE CRIPPLED PRODUCTION RAN UP HUGE BILLS. THE PRESS PLACED BLAME SQUARELY ON LIZ.

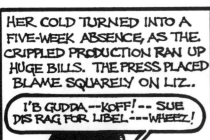

I'B GUDDA --KOFF!-- SUE DIS RAG FOR LIBEL ---WHEEZ!

HER ABSENCE WAS COSTLY, BUT THE PROBLEMS RAN FAR DEEPER. FOR ONE THING, THE SCRIPT-- WHAT SCRIPT THERE WAS -- WAS CONTINUALLY BEING RE-WRITTEN.

FOX HAD ALREADY SPENT $8 MILLION FOR 10 MINUTES OF TAYLOR-LESS FOOTAGE. SKOURAS HIRED VETERAN DIRECTOR JOSEPH MANKIEWICZ TO SAVE THE PICTURE -- AND THE FINANCIALLY HEMORRHAGING STUDIO!

GET FOOTAGE WITH LIZ! ONLY SHE CAN SAVE THIS COMPANY!

SOON LIZ, ACCOMPANIED BY SINGER EDDIE FISHER, HER COMPLIANT FIFTH HUSBAND, WAS OUT OF THE HOSPITAL AND BACK IN HER HOTEL SUITE.

EDDIE! GET ME SOME **#$% COFFEE!

BUT LIZ HAD LITTLE TO DO, WHILE MANKIEWICZ HAD THE SETS REBUILT AND RE-WROTE THE SCRIPT IN A SPEED-INDUCED FRENZY.

THEN, WITHOUT WARNING, LIZ BECAME SICK AGAIN, THIS TIME WITH PNEUMONIA. SHE FOUGHT FOR HER LIFE.

THE WHOLE LONDON PRODUCTION WAS SCRAPPED.

LIZ CLAIMED TO HAVE ACTUALLY DIED AND COME BACK, A MIRACULOUS TALE THAT HELPED REBUILD HER INCREASINGLY SULLIED PUBLIC IMAGE.

IT WAS LIKE I HAD JUST COME OUT OF MY OWN WOMB!

GROSS ME OUT!

ONCE HEALTHY AGAIN, LIZ AGREED TO START THE FILM OVER -- ON HER TERMS.

ANOTHER MILLION BUCKS! AND FILM IT SOMEWHERE SUNNY THIS TIME!

ANYTHING YOU SAY, LIZ! ONLY YOU CAN SAVE THIS COMPANY!

THE MASSIVE PRODUCTION MOVED TO ROME.

THE FILM'S LLOYDS OF LONDON INSURERS PUSHED TO REPLACE TAYLOR WITH MARILYN MONROE, BUT MET WITH STUDIO RESISTANCE.

GET THIS STRAIGHT! LIZ TAYLOR IS CLEOPATRA!

BUT THE STUDIO AGREED TO OTHER CAST CHANGES AND MADE THE FATEFUL DECISION TO HIRE WELSH ACTOR RICHARD BURTON FOR THE PIVOTAL ROLE OF MARC ANTONY.

BURTON WAS A WORLD-CLASS DRINKER — AND HOLLYWOOD CASANOVA.

SHOOTING BEGAN IN SEPTEMBER, 1961, AGAIN WITHOUT A SHOOTING SCRIPT.

LINE, PLEASE!

DAMMIT, LIZ, I'M WRITING AS FAST AS I CAN!

RAVAGED BY LABOR WOES, CORRUPTION AND THEFT, THE PRODUCTION CONTINUED TO BLEED MONEY. FOX SHARE-HOLDERS WERE OUTRAGED.

CLEOPATRA'S RUINING US, SKOURAS, AND IT'S GONNA BE YOUR ASS!

GENTLEMEN, RELAX! WE HAVE A GREAT ASSET: ELIZABETH TAYLOR!

SKOURAS WAS DEPOSED IN 1962 BY THE WALL STREET MONEYMEN.

MEANWHILE, THE STAR DIDN'T EXACTLY HELP THE CAUSE WITH HER PRODIGIOUS INTAKE OF PRESCRIPTION DRUGS.

DO ME AGAIN, DR. FEELGOOD!

GROOVY!

SHE ALSO CONSUMED PRODIGIOUS AMOUNTS OF STUDIO MONEY, LIVING LIKE A QUEEN IN A 14-ROOM ROMAN VILLA.

CLEOPATRA'S GOT NUTHIN' ON LIZ TAYLOR! HA HA HA HA!

IN JANUARY, 1962, TAYLOR AND BURTON PLAYED THEIR FIRST SCENES TOGETHER. IT WAS CLEAR TO ALL ON THE SET THAT THEY WEREN'T ENTIRELY ACTING.

BRRR

ZZAP

EVERYONE WAS WAITING FOR THE LEGENDARY LADYKILLER TO MAKE HIS MOVE. BUT AT FIRST, BURTON DISMISSED THE GLAMOUR GIRL.

NAAAH! HER CHEST IS OVER-DEVELOPED AND HER LEGS ARE TOO SHORT.

BUT IT WASN'T LONG BEFORE HE FULFILLED THE EXPECTATIONS OF HIS ADMIRERS, ANNOUNCING ONE MORNING . . .

GENTLEMEN, I FINALLY SHTUPPED ELIZABETH TAYLOR IN THE BACK SEAT OF MY CADILLAC!

WELL DONE!

BRAVO!

VERY NICE INDEED!

LE SCANDALE, AS BURTON CAME TO CALL THE AFFAIR, WAS READY TO BLOW WORLDWIDE. MANKIEWICZ AND FOX BOSSES TRIED TO RATIONALIZE WHAT THEY COULDN'T CONTROL.

BURTON IS A GOOD INFLUENCE ON LIZ AS AN ACTOR, RIGHT?

THE PUBLICITY WILL HELP AT THE BOX OFFICE! GEE— HEH-HEH —THIS IS GREAT!

THE LAST TO KNOW WAS LIZ'S HUSBAND, EDDIE FISHER . . . .

BAD NEWS, OLD BOY. I'M AFRAID I'M SHTUPPING YOUR WIFE.

. . . AND BURTON'S LONG-SUFFERING WIFE SYBIL, WHO'D ALREADY ENDURED DOZENS OF BRAZEN AFFAIRS, ALWAYS KNOWING HE'D RETURN TO HER.

THIS TIME WAS DIFFERENT.

GUILT-RIDDEN, BURTON WAS TORN BETWEEN HIS ANGELIC WIFE AND HIS NEW FOUND SEX KITTEN.

LADIES, PLEASE! I'M ONLY ONE MAN, ALBEIT ONE WITH A GROSSLY OUTSIZED LIBIDO!

WHEN SYBIL FINALLY THREATENED TO LEAVE, BURTON GAVE IN AND DUMPED LIZ, WHO PROMPTLY GUZZLED AN OVERDOSE OF PILLS.

IT'S BEEN FUN, LUV, BUT MY WIFE COMES FIRST.

THIS'LL TEACH YOU!

HER SUICIDE ATTEMPT WAS ANOTHER FINANCIAL AND P.R. DISASTER FOR FOX, WHICH FRANTICALLY TRIED TO COVER UP THE TRUTH.

LIZ TAYLOR IS IN THE HOSPITAL WITH, UH . . . FOOD POISONING! YEAH, THAT'S THE TICKET!

THIS TIME, BURTON DUMPED HIS WIFE OF 12 YEARS AND CAME CRAWLING BACK TO LIZ.

MY DARLING, I'M SO SORRY!

HEY, IT WORKED!

THE AFFAIR CONTINUED. PUBLICATION OF A PAPARRAZZI'S PHOTO OF LIZ AND DICK LOUNGING ABOARD A LUXURY YACHT CONFIRMED THE WORLD'S SUSPICIONS.

LOVE CRUISE
LIZ & DICK
SENSAT...

LIZ, WHOSE STORMY MARITAL HISTORY HAD ALREADY TARNISHED HER REPUTATION, WAS VILIFIED IN THE WORLD'S PRESS — NOT WITHOUT SOME JUSTIFICATION — AS A WANTON HOMEWRECKER. EVEN THE VATICAN CONDEMNED HER.

ELIZABETH TAYLOR IS A WOMAN OF LOOSE MORALS!!

THEIR RELATIONSHIP WAS STORMY. USUALLY DRUNK, THEY BATTLED MIGHTILY. ACCORDING TO FOX PRESIDENT SKOURAS, ONE SUCH QUARREL LEFT LIZ UNABLE TO WORK FOR MORE THAN THREE WEEKS.

HIT ME WID YER BEST SHOT, LOVER BOY!

HER ABSENCE WAS COSTLY— BOTH IN TERMS OF DOLLARS AND PUBLIC RELATIONS.

LIZ HAD, UH... ER... A CAR ACCIDENT! JUST A LITTLE FENDER BENDER! THAT'S THE TICKET!

EVEN WHEN SHE WORKED, LIZ AND DICK WOULD OFTEN SHOW UP DRUNK FROM LONG, WINE-SODDEN ITALIAN LUNCHES.

♪ SHOW ME THE WAY TO GO HOME! I'M TIRED AND I WANNA GO TO BED... ♪

THE FOX BRASS FINALLY GOT FED UP. THEY ATTEMPTED TO INVOKE THE "MORALS CLAUSE" IN LIZ'S CONTRACT.

DEAR MISS TAYLOR, PLEASE DESIST IN YOUR AFFAIR WITH MR. BURTON OR 20TH CENTURY FOX WILL BE FORCED TO SUE.

LIZ WAS HAVING NONE OF THAT!

IF THEY SEND THAT *#$@% LETTER, I WALK! AND IF I WALK, I TAKE THE WHOLE %#*@ STUDIO DOWN WITH ME!

IN JUNE, 1962, FOX DISPATCHED THREE TOP EXECUTIVES TO ROME! THEIR MISSION: FIRE ELIZABETH TAYLOR AND SHUT DOWN THE PRODUCTION. TAYLOR BATTLED THEM WITH HER CHARM.

HEY, BOYS! WELCOME TO ROME!

THEY ALSO BROUGHT BAD NEWS ABOUT THE MOVIE'S FINANCES.

THOUSANDS OF DOLLARS ARE UNACCOUNTED FOR. NUMEROUS QUESTIONABLE EXPENSES HAVE BEEN CHARGED TO THE PRODUCTION.

SOMEHOW, HOWEVER, THEY LEFT AGREEING TO CONTINUE BOTH FINANCING THE FILM AND EMPLOYING TAYLOR.

SEE YA LATER, LIZ!

KEEP UP THE GOOD WORK!

THE FILM FINALLY WRAPPED; THEN MANKIEWICZ HAD A BRILLIANT IDEA...

WE'LL RELEASE THE MOVIE IN TWO INSTALLMENTS — A FULL SEVEN HOURS!

THAT'LL BE THE DAY, JOE!

CRITICS HATED THE FINAL, FOUR-HOUR FILM, SINGLING OUT ELIZABETH'S PERFORMANCE FOR SPECIAL EXCORIATION.

OVERWEIGHT, OVERPAID AND UNDER-TALENTED.

SHE FALLS FLAT— DISASTROUSLY SO.

MONOTONY IN A SLIT SKIRT.

Z

THE CLEOPATRA FIASCO COST FOX A RECORD $42 MILLION, AND EARNED BACK JUST HALF OF THAT.

THE STUDIO WAS PUSHED TO THE EDGE OF BANKRUPTCY, FORCED TO SELL ITS ENTIRE BACK LOT, LEVERAGING ALL OF ITS ASSETS, INCLUDING ITS CLASSIC FILM LIBRARY. SHARE PRICES DROPPED BY HALF.

20TH CENTURY FOX

LIZ AND DICK MARRIED IN MONTREAL IN 1964. FOR YEARS THEY WERE THE WORLD'S MOST FAMOUS COUPLE, RIVALED ONLY BY ARISTOTLE AND JACKIE ONASSIS.

I DRINK (HIC!)— I MEAN, I DO...

THE CLEOPATRA DEBACLE BEHIND THEM, THEY HAD ONLY EACH OTHER TO RUIN. THEY DIVORCED ACRIMONIOUSLY IN 1974, REMARRIED THE NEXT YEAR, THEN DIVORCED AGAIN IN 1976. BURTON DIED SUDDENLY IN 1984, JUST AS HE WAS FINALLY TRYING TO BEAT HIS ALCOHOLISM.

FACTOID 100% TRUE BOOKS

PRODUCER ROBERT EVANS REACHED THE HEIGHTS OF HOLLYWOOD SUCCESS IN THE 1970s, BUT IN THE EARLY 80s HE WAS FINDING OUT THAT IN HOLLYWOOD, BUSINESS CAN BE *MURDER.*

MURDER, MAYHEM AND THE COTTON CLUB

EVANS ROSE TO PRODUCTION CHIEF OF PARAMOUNT WITHOUT PRODUCING A MOVIE. HE UNLEASHED A STRING OF HITS, INCLUDING ROSEMARY'S BABY AND THE ODD COUPLE.

HEY, THIS IS EASY!

THE GODFATHER, DIRECTED BY YOUNG FRANCIS COPPOLA, WAS A MASTERPIECE AND THE BIGGEST MONEYMAKER EVER.

ALL BECAUSE *I* RE-EDITED COPPOLA'S TERRIBLE FIRST CUT.

BUT AS A STUDIO EXEC, HE GOT NO SCREEN CREDIT.

HE STRUCK OUT ON HIS OWN. HIS FIRST INDEPENDENT PRODUCTION WAS ANOTHER INSTANT CLASSIC.

FORGET IT, JAKE, IT'S *CHINATOWN.*

HEY, PRODUCING MOVIES IS EASY!

BUT A STRING OF FLOPS—AND A COCAINE CONVICTION—LEFT EVANS REELING. THEN HE HAD AN IDEA.

WHAT I NEED TO DO IS PRODUCE *AND* DIRECT.

ALL HE NEEDED WAS A PROJECT.

HE FOUND IT IN AN UNLIKELY SOURCE -- A PICTURE BOOK ABOUT A LEGENDARY JAZZ-AGE HARLEM NIGHTCLUB.

GANGSTERS, MUSIC, WOMEN! THIS ONE HAS IT ALL!

EVANS HAD HIS SETTING. NOW ALL HE NEEDED WAS A STORY... A MERE DETAIL.

WHEN HE PITCHED THE IDEA TO STUDIOS, HE HIT A MAJOR OBSTACLE.

YOU'RE BEAUTIFUL, BOB, BUT WHO WANTS TO SEE A MOVIE ABOUT BLACK PEOPLE?

DID I TELL YOU YOU'RE BEAUTIFUL?

HE CONNECTED WITH SHADOWY ARMS MERCHANT ADNAN KHASHOGGI. THE MULTI-BILLIONAIRE PUT UP $2 MILLION IN START-UP MONEY.

FEEL FREE TO GAMBLE AT MY PRIVATE CASINO, MR. EVANS.

WHAT THE HECK! I'LL ROLL THE DICE!

EVANS HIRED *GODFATHER* AUTHOR MARIO PUZO TO WRITE THE SCRIPT. SOON *EVERYONE* WAS INTERESTED. EXCEPT KHASHOGGI.

THIS SCRIPT STINKS!

YOU JUST WANT CONTROL OF THIS MOVIE! WELL, IT'S MINE! SO GOOD RIDDANCE!

EVANS PITCHED THE IDEA FRANTICALLY TO POTENTIAL INVESTORS.

GANGSTERS, ANYONE? MUSIC? HOW ABOUT SOME NAKED...

COTTON CLUB

HE SECURED $8 MILLION FROM OVERSEAS DISTRIBUTORS, JUST ENOUGH TO MOVE AHEAD.

EVANS VISITED COPPOLA, WITH WHOM HE'D BATTLED MIGHTILY ON *GODFATHER*, TO ASK HIS OPINION OF THE SCRIPT.

UNWORKABLE!

MILLIONS IN DEBT HIMSELF, COPPOLA AGREED TO WRITE A WHOLE NEW SCRIPT FOR $500,000.

EVANS MET *LANEY JACOBS*, INTRODUCED TO HIM AS A RICH WIDOW. HE DIDN'T KNOW HER REAL STORY. HE JUST NEEDED MONEY.

I HAVE A FRIEND WITH CONTACTS IN HIGH PLACES.

THE FRIEND WAS ROY RADIN, PROMOTER OF GRADE-Z ROADSHOWS STARRING SUCH ACTS AS "THE HARMONICA RASCALS" AND "PIERRE DUPONT AND HIS WONDER DOG SPARKY."

A SINISTER CHARACTER, RADIN WAS ACCUSED BY *WELCOME BACK KOTTER* ACTRESS MELANIE HALLOR OF BEATING AND RAPING HER-- AND VIDEOTAPING IT.

AUTHOR MAURY TERRY THOUGHT THAT RADIN WAS IN A DRUGS-AND- -PORNOGRAPHY RING WITH TIES TO A SATANIC CULT.

IN ANY CASE, RADIN HAD A FAUSTIAN PROPOSITION FOR EVANS.

MY FRIENDS IN THE PUERTO RICAN GOVERNMENT WILL FRONT US $35 MILLION. *TEMPTING,* ISN'T IT?

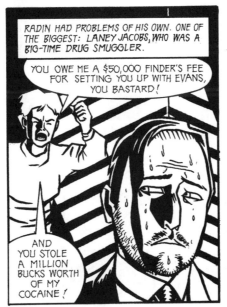

RADIN HAD PROBLEMS OF HIS OWN. ONE OF THE BIGGEST: LANEY JACOBS, WHO WAS A BIG-TIME DRUG SMUGGLER.

YOU OWE ME A $50,000 FINDER'S FEE FOR SETTING YOU UP WITH EVANS, YOU BASTARD!

AND YOU STOLE A MILLION BUCKS WORTH OF MY COCAINE!

ONE NIGHT, JACOBS PICKED UP RADIN IN A LIMO TO GO TO DINNER AT A FASHIONABLE L.A. RESTAURANT.

COME ON, ROY. LET'S GO FOR A RIDE.

MIDWAY THROUGH THE RIDE, JACOBS GOT OUT AND TWO OF HER "FRIENDS," BILL MENTZER AND ALEX MARTI GOT IN.

THEY TOOK RADIN TO A DESERTED FIELD OUTSIDE OF L.A., AND...

BLAM

BLAM

WHEN EVANS HEARD THAT RADIN WAS MISSING, HE FREAKED OUT.

THATA WAY

THEY *KILLED* HIM! I'M SURE OF IT! AND *I'M* NEXT!

HE DISAPPEARED FOR A WHILE.

HE LIVED, BUT HE HAD OTHER PROBLEMS. WITH FINANCING IN PLACE FROM A LAS VEGAS CASINO OWNER, *COTTON CLUB* PRODUCTION STARTED--WITH COPPOLA DIRECTING.

I'M IN CHARGE HERE, EVANS. SOMEBODY'S GOTTA MAKE THE DECISIONS!

COULD YOU AT LEAST WRITE A SCRIPT BEFORE YOU START SHOOTING?

THAT WASN'T COPPOLA'S METHOD. HE BROUGHT IN PULITZER PRIZEWINNING NOVELIST WILLIAM KENNEDY TO CRANK OUT DAILY REWRITES.

WOW! DEADLINES! JUST LIKE THE OLD DAYS ON THE NEWSPAPERS!

MIDNIGHT OIL

WHEN COPPOLA WON AN ARGUMENT OVER HIS CASTING OF FRED GWYNNE, EVANS KNEW HE'D LOST "HIS" MOVIE.

BUT FRANCIS-- HE'S *HERMAN MUNSTER!*

THE FILM'S STAR, RICHARD GERE, GOT SO FED UP WITH THE FIASCO, HE WALKED OUT.

RICHARD, CAN WE TALK ABOUT THIS?

BAD KARMA, MAN!

GERE RETURNED. THEN IT WAS COPPOLA WHO TOOK OFF, FLYING TO LONDON FOR THREE DAYS.

FRANCIS, CAN WE TALK ABOUT THIS?

I'M CATCHING A CONCORDE!

YOU COULDN'T REALLY BLAME COPPOLA. HE'D BEEN FILMING FOR SIX WEEKS AND STILL HADN'T BEEN PAID.

I PROMISED TO BE TOLERANT AND HELPFUL, BUT THIS IS TOO MUCH.

ONCE PAID, COPPOLA RETURNED -- AND WAS GREETED BY UNFLATTERING PRESS REPORTS GENERATED BY EVANS.

COPPOLA'S BLOWN THIS MOVIE'S BUDGET UP TO $40 MILLION.

COPPOLA DIDN'T TAKE THE ATTACKS LIGHTLY.

YOU'VE DOUBLE-CROSSED ME FOR THE LAST TIME, EVANS!

BUT COPPOLA STILL CONTROLLED THE MOVIE.

IN THE END, THE COST TOPPED $47 MILLION. IT DIDN'T FLOP AT THE BOX OFFICE, BUT IT WAS FAR FROM THE SMASH IT NEEDED TO BE TO BREAK EVEN.

THIS FILM DIED AS A RESULT OF SLOW POISONING.

EVANS NEXT TRIED TO RECREATE HIS GREATEST SUCCESS, PRODUCING A SEQUEL TO CHINATOWN.

FORGET IT, BOB, IT'S THE TWO JAKES.

IT WAS A FAR CRY FROM THE ORIGINAL.

THE COTTON CLUB CONTINUED TO HAUNT EVANS. IN 1988, ROY RADIN'S KILLERS WERE ARRESTED.

YOU HAD A DEAL WITH RADIN, EVANS! YOU'RE A SUSPECT!

WHAT?!?

EVANS WAS CALLED TO TESTIFY, BUT ON THE ADVICE OF HIS LAWYER, ALL HE SAID WAS...

I REFUSE TO ANSWER ON THE GROUNDS THAT MY ANSWERS MAY INCRIMINATE ME.

NO EVIDENCE CONNECTS EVANS TO RADIN'S DEATH, WHICH HAD MORE TO DO WITH DRUGS THAN MOVIES. BUT THE COTTON CLUB REMAINS THE ONLY MOVIE TO HAVE A MURDER NAMED AFTER IT.

THAT MOVIE DROVE ME CRAZY!!

FACTOID BOOKS

DON SIMPSON PRODUCED SOME OF THE BIGGEST HITS OF THE 1980's-- HE DEFINED THE MOVIES OF THAT DECADE AND REDEFINED HOLLYWOOD. BUT LIKE THE RACE CAR DRIVERS IN HIS MOVIE, *DAYS OF THUNDER*, HE LIVED ON THE

FAST TRACK

IN THE END, HE DIED THERE.

AS A YOUTH, THE WILDLY INCLINED SIMPSON COULDN'T WAIT TO ESCAPE HIS STRICT BAPTIST UPBRINGING IN ISOLATED ANCHORAGE, ALASKA.

BANISH YOUR IMPURE THOUGHTS OR GOD WILL STRIKE YOU DOWN!

ONLY IF HE CAN CATCH ME! I AM OUTTA HERE!

HE FLED TO THE ONE PLACE THAT WOULD NOT ONLY ALLOW HIM TO INDULGE HIS APPETITES, BUT WOULD STAND UP AND APPLAUD THEM.

GIMME ANOTHER ONE! OH, GOD! YES!!

FORGET GOD, HONEY! WE'RE IN HOLLYWOOD!

SPANK! SPANK!

IN *THE 70's* SIMPSON, ALONG WITH MICHAEL EISNER AND JEFFREY KATZENBERG WAS IN A GROUP OF FAST-RISING EXECUTIVES WHO, IN THE NEXT DECADE WOULD COME TO DOMINATE THE BUSINESS.

BUT HIS UNQUENCHABLE THIRST FOR DOPE, BOOZE AND HOOKERS BROUGHT HIM CRASHING DOWN. BY THE END OF THE DECADE HE WAS OUT OF A JOB.

OFFICE FOR RENT

RING, YOU #@$*!! RING!!

HE WENT INDEPENDENT, TEAMING WITH THE MORE STAID JERRY BRUCKHEIMER, WHOSE STABILITY HELPED ANCHOR THE MORE MANIC SIMPSON. THEY PRODUCED *FLASHDANCE* FOR $10 MILLION. IT EARNED $175 MILLION. SIMPSON BEGAN TO SEE HIMSELF AS NOT MERELY A DEAL MAKER, BUT AN ARTIST.

IT'S THE AUTEUR THEORY OF PRODUCING.

FLASHDANCE

WHAT A FEELING.

HE CELEBRATED HIS SUCCESS WITH MORE DRUGS-- AND BY BECOMING ONE OF HOLLYWOOD'S BIGGEST JERKS.

WHERE'S MY ASSISTANT?!

THESE PANTS ARE PRESSED, DAMMIT! I TOLD HIM: FLUFF AND FOLD! FLUFF AND %$#&@ FOLD!!!

SIMPSON AND BRUCKHEIMER TURNED OUT A STREAK OF BLOCKBUSTERS, INCLUDING *TOP GUN* AND *BEVERLY HILLS COP*. STAR VEHICLES, SHORT ON STORY BUT FILLED WITH ACTION-PACKED MOMENTS, THEIR MOVIES WERE PERFECT FOR THE ALL-FLASH, NO-SUBSTANCE REAGAN DECADE.

BUT FAME AND WEALTH COULDN'T VANQUISH SIMPSON'S INNER DEMONS. HE BATTLED HIS WEIGHT AND HAD PLASTIC SURGERY.

I DUNNO, DOC. MAKE ME LOOK LIKE TOM CRUISE OR SOMETHING.

SCHPURTZZ!

THEIR BLOATED, 1990 STOCK CAR RACING EPIC *DAYS OF THUNDER* WAS FAR FROM A SMASH.

THIS MOVIE SUCKS!

SIMPSON RETREATED INTO HIS BEL AIR HOME, RARELY COMING OUT.

HE HIT A LOW WHEN DR. STEPHEN AMMERMAN WAS FOUND DEAD OF AN OD IN SIMPSON'S GUEST HOUSE IN OCTOBER, 1995.

FRIENDS HELD SIMPSON, WITH HIS UNRE-STRAINED DRUG HABITS, RESPONSIBLE.

ON JANUARY 19, 1996, SIMPSON HIMSELF WAS FOUND DEAD IN HIS BATHROOM.

THE L.A.P.D. CONCLUDED:

THIS MAN DIED OF NATURAL CAUSES.

IN OTHER WORDS, THIS BEING HOLLY-WOOD, NATURALLY HE DIED OF A DRUG OVERDOSE.

THE TWO DEATHS SPARKED AN INVESTIGA-TION-- AND A LAWSUIT FROM DR. AMMER-MAN'S FAMILY.

YOUR HONOR, SIMPSON AND OTHERS CAUSED AMMERMAN'S DEATH WITH ILLEGAL DRUGS, THEN CONSPIRED TO COVER UP THE CIRCUMSTANCES.

SHORTLY BEFORE HIS DEATH, SIMPSON TOLD AN INTERVIEWER...

I'VE ALWAYS BEEN ABLE TO KIND OF TEETER ON THE PRECIPICE.

BUT WHEN THE FAME SLIPPED AWAY, HE FELL WITH IT.

FACTOID 100% TRUE BOOKS

TO ALL OUTWARD APPEARANCES, SHE WAS A NICE JEWISH GIRL, DAUGHTER OF A PROMINENT PHYSICIAN. BUT IN HER SECRET IDENTITY, SHE STRUCK FEAR IN THE HEARTS OF THE MOVIE INDUSTRY'S MOST POWERFUL MEN. SHE WAS...

HEIDI FLEISS, HOLLYWOOD MADAM

IN L.A., YOU SEE THEM ALL OVER TOWN. THEY TURN UP AS "DATES" FOR VISITING ARAB BUSINESSMEN...

...AS "GOOD FRIENDS" TO POWERFUL MOVIE PRODUCERS...

...BUT MOST IMPORTANT, AT THE HOMES AND HOTELS OF WEALTHY, GLAMOROUS MEN, PROVIDING EVENINGS OF ECSTASY—STARTING AT $1,500 PER NIGHT.

ANYTHING YOU WANT, BABY-- ANYTHING! (CALIFORNIA RESIDENTS ADD 7.5% SALES TAX.)

THEY ARE-- HOLLYWOOD CALL GIRLS.

IN THE EARLY 1990s, ALL OF THE BEST GIRLS WERE HEIDI'S GIRLS. AT AGE 27, SHE WAS TINSELTOWN'S MOST POWERFUL MADAM, RUNNING HER OPERATION FROM HER MILLION-DOLLAR BEVERLY HILLS MANSION.

SHE LIVED THE PART. SHE HUNG OUT IN TONY SPOTS LIKE JACK NICHOLSON'S MONKEY BAR.

HEY! I NEVER USED HER SERVICES!

BUT HE WAS A GODDAM GREAT LOVER!

SHE RAN HER OWN CLUB, "ON THE ROX," WHICH DREW SUCH CLIENTELE AS ROCK STAR BILLY IDOL, ABOUT WHOM HEIDI ONCE SAID...

HE WANTS GIRLS TO SHOVE EVERYTHING IN SIGHT UP HIS BUTT!

THEY ALSO SEIZED HEIDI'S NOTORIOUS "BLACK BOOKS" FILLED WITH NAMES OF THE RICH AND FAMOUS (AND MARRIED!)-- ALL IN CODE, OF COURSE.

K to P / S to M

A to D / KINKY

STILL, THEIR VERY EXISTENCE SENT HOLLYWOOD INTO A PANIC-- AND A FRENZY OF GOSSIP.

I'M GLAD MY HUSBAND ISN'T IN THERE! AND I'M ONLY SURE OF THAT BECAUSE I'M SINGLE!

THE PRESIDENT OF COLUMBIA PICTURES HAD HIS LAWYER DENY EVERYTHING.

MR. NATHANSON HAS NEVER DONE BUSINESS WITH THE ALLEGED MS. FLEISS.

NATHANSON WAS REACTING TO RUMORS; HE HADN'T ACTUALLY BEEN ACCUSED OF ANYTHING.

FACING DRUG AND PANDERING CHARGES, HEIDI WAS ARROGANT AS EVER. WAS SHE GOING TO PLAY HER ACE-IN-THE-HOLE AND NAME NAMES?

SHE KEPT HER MOUTH SHUT-- AND WAS CONVICTED.

BUT SOMEONE WIRETAPPED HEIDI'S PHONE AND RECORDED SEVERAL TOP MOVIE STARS AND PRODUCERS, AS WELL AS MILLIONAIRE BUSINESSMEN, CALLING HER.

WOW!

HEIDI EVEN BOUGHT A COPY OF THE TAPE.

HEIDI'S EX-GIRLS MADE AN INDUSTRY OF THEIR ANONYMOUS REVELATIONS. FOR INSTANCE, THERE WAS THE HOLLYWOOD BIGSHOT WHO HIRED GIRLS JUST TO WATCH HIM SMOKE CRACK.

BEAM ME UP, SCOTTY!

HEIDI THEN FACED TAX EVASION CHARGES. IN THAT TRIAL, CHARLIE SHEEN WAS FORCED TO TESTIFY THAT HE'D SPENT A STAGGERING $50,000 ON "HEIDI GIRLS".

I GUESS IT REALLY ADDS UP, DOESN'T IT? HEH-HEH.

HEIDI'S FATHER, PEDIATRICIAN-TO-THE-STARS PAUL FLEISS, WENT DOWN ON MONEY-LAUNDERING CHARGES.

AS ALWAYS, HOLLYWOOD SURVIVED. BUT HEIDI TOOK THE FALL. WHEN SHE WAS FINALLY SENTENCED TO 37 MONTHS ON TAX CHARGES IN JANUARY, 1997, SHE WAS A DIFFERENT PERSON.

I MADE TERRIBLE CHOICES! -SOB!- I CAN'T SAY HOW SORRY I AM!!

FACTOID BOOKS

Woody and Mia

WOODY ALLEN AND MIA FARROW GREW UP IN DIFFERENT WORLDS. WOODY (BORN ALLAN KONIGSBERG) WAS A LOWER MIDDLE CLASS BROOKLYN JEWISH KID. MIA CAME FROM HOLLYWOOD WITH A MOVIE STAR MOTHER AND A DIRECTOR FOR A DAD.

THEY BOTH WENT INTO SHOW BIZ. THE TEENAGE WOODY CRANKED OUT THOUSANDS OF GAGS FOR COMEDIANS AND NEWSPAPER COLUMNISTS.

"I JUST MADE A FORTUNE -- I WAS DOWNTOWN AUCTIONING OFF MY *PARKING SPACE*."

THE TEENAGE MIA MARRIED FRANK SINATRA.

DOO-BEE DOO-BEE DOOO.

WOODY MADE HIS MARK IN HOLLYWOOD AS WRITER, DIRECTOR, AND STAR OF SUCH ZANY COMEDIES AS TAKE THE MONEY AND RUN AND BANANAS.

IN THE '70s HE STARTED MAKING "SERIOUS" FILMS AND BUILT A REPUTATION AS AMERICA'S TOP ART-FILM DIRECTOR.

MIA, A DEVOUT CATHOLIC, WON RAVES IN THE MACABRE HORROR FLICK ROSEMARY'S BABY IN WHICH SHE GIVES BIRTH TO THE ANTICHRIST.

WAHHHH!

MIA HAD BEEN A FLOWERCHILD AND GOT INTO TRANSCENDENTAL MEDITATION.

WOODY WAS THE STEREOTYPE OF THE RECLUSIVE NEW YORK INTELLECTUAL.

OMM OMM OMM OMM

YET SOMEHOW WOODY AND MIA BEGAN A ROMANCE. THEY BECAME NEW YORK'S MOST CELEBRATED COUPLE.

THEIR MANY DIFFERENCES ONLY MADE THEM MORE INTERESTING.

I LOVE THE CITY.

I'D RATHER BE IN CONNECTICUT.

I LOVE LATE DINNERS AT FANCY RESTAURANTS.

QUIET DINNERS AT HOME ARE DIVINE!

I LIKE GOING TO KNICKS GAMES.

SPORTS ARE SO STUPID!

THEY DIDN'T EVEN LIVE TOGETHER, KEEPING APARTMENTS ON OPPOSITE SIDES OF CENTRAL PARK.

WE HAVE OUR OWN LIVES. IT'S FUN BUT NOT SMOTHERING.

THERE WAS ANOTHER HUGE DIFFERENCE. MIA LOVED KIDS — SO MUCH THAT SHE ADOPTED CHILDREN ALMOST COMPULSIVELY. WOODY HAD NO INTEREST IN HER CHILDREN.

SHE'S ADDICTED TO BABIES!

SO IMAGINE HER SURPRISE IN JANUARY, 1992 WHEN IN WOODY'S APARTMENT SHE DISCOVERED --

I'M SEEING THE FACE OF EVIL!!

-- NUDE — AND EXPLICIT — POLAROIDS OF HER COLLEGE-AGE KOREAN DAUGHTER, SOON-YI, WHOM MIA HAD ADOPTED WITH HER SECOND HUSBAND, COMPOSER ANDRE PREVIN.

LAY BACK AND GIMME YOUR MOST EROTIC POSES! LET YOURSELF GO!

THAT WAS HOW MIA DISCOVERED THAT WOODY WAS HAVING AN AFFAIR WITH HER DAUGHTER.

WHEN MIA CONFRONTED HER NOW-FORMER LOVER, SHE COULDN'T BELIEVE WOODY'S RESPONSE.

HAVING AN AFFAIR WITH ME IS GOOD FOR SOON-YI, IT GAVE HER A LITTLE CONFIDENCE.

REPORTEDLY, MIA'S REACTION TO SOON-YI WASN'T EXACTLY EXEMPLARY EITHER.

HOW COULD YOU?!!

THWAK

MIA HAD ALSO BEEN LONG CONCERNED ABOUT WOODY'S "INAPPROPRIATE" ATTENTION TO THEIR ADOPTED DAUGHTER, DYLAN.

MIA MAINTAINED HE WAS "OBSESSED" WITH HER, DOING THINGS LIKE GETTING INTO BED AND CUDDLING THE SEVEN-YEAR-OLD WHILE WEARING JUST HIS UNDERWEAR.

SO OVERWHELMED WAS THE CHILD BY WOODY'S ATTENTION THAT SHE WOULD SOMETIMES LOCK HERSELF IN THE *BATHROOM* DURING HIS VISITS.

DYLAN, HONEY, IT'S OKAY--DADDY'S LEAVING SOON.

NOK NOK

FOR EIGHT MONTHS THEY'D KEPT THEIR PRIVATE WAR PRIVATE. THEN IN AUGUST, WHEN THEY WERE CLOSE TO A COMPREHENSIVE LEGAL SETTLEMENT, MIA MADE A STUNNING ACCUSATION.

WOODY *MOLESTED* DYLAN! SHE SAID SO ON *VIDEOTAPE!*

WOODY WAS NORMALLY PRIVATE TO THE POINT OF PARANOIA. NOW HE SUDDENLY CALLED A PRESS CONFERENCE.

THESE CHARGES ARE TOTALLY FALSE AND OUTRAGEOUS! I'M SUING FOR *CUSTODY* OF MY CHILDREN!

THE PRESS TREATED THE SCANDAL AS REAL NEWS. IN THE SUMMER OF 1992 THE WOODY/MIA SPLIT PUSHED THE REPUBLICAN CONVENTION OFF THE COVERS OF NATIONAL MAGAZINES.

MIA RECEIVED SUPPORT FROM HER FRIENDS. FOR EXAMPLE, EX-HUSBAND SINATRA WHO, MIA SAID, MADE AN INTERESTING OFFER.

YA WANT THAT I SHOULD BREAK HIS LEGS?

BUT EVEN WOODY'S MANY SUPPORTERS NOTED ODD SIMILARITIES BETWEEN HIS LIFE AND ART.

IN THE FILM MANHATTAN, WOODY HAS AN AFFAIR WITH THE TEENAGE MARIEL HEMINGWAY.

BLAH BLAH BLAH

A JUDGE DENIED WOODY'S CUSTODY BID, LAMBASTING WOODY FOR--

-- SELF-ABSORPTION, LACK OF JUDGMENT, DEFICIENCIES AS A PARENT...

WOODY, HE NOTED, DIDN'T EVEN KNOW THE NAMES OF HIS OWN CHILDREN'S TEACHERS, DOCTOR, OR PETS.

CONNECTICUT STATE AUTHORITIES SAID THEY BELIEVED WOODY HAD INDEED MOLESTED DYLAN. BUT ODDLY, THEY DECIDED NOT TO PROSECUTE.

WE WANT TO SPARE THE CHILDREN FURTHER *SUFFERING.*

DISPLAYING EITHER GREAT STRENGTH OR UTTER OBLIVIOUSNESS, WOODY CONTINUED WORKING AS IF NOTHING HAD HAPPENED.

HIS NEXT FILM, HUSBANDS AND WIVES--ABOUT MARITAL INFIDELITY AND BETRAYAL--OPENED IN 800 THEATERS NATIONWIDE.

DIRECTOR

THE 1950s WERE A KIND OF GOLDEN ERA FOR BAD BOYS. THEY STARTED WITH JAMES DEAN, THE *REBEL WITHOUT A CAUSE* HIMSELF.

DEAN PERFORMED THE ULTIMATE ACT OF BAD-BOYISM.

HE GOT KILLED.

DEAN'S DEATH WAS THE BEST THING THAT EVER HAPPENED TO HIM COMMERCIALLY. *REBEL*, RELEASED POSTHUMOUSLY, WAS A BLOCKBUSTER.

DEAN'S RIVAL BAD BOY WAS MONTGOMERY CLIFT. HE WAS SO SCREWED UP ON BOOZE AND PILLS THAT SOMETIMES HE'D BE SEEN SLEEPWALKING NAKED THROUGH THE STREETS OF L.A.

BUT THE QUINTESSENTIAL BAD BOYS AND KINGS OF COOL CALLED THEMSELVES THE RAT PACK: DEAN MARTIN, FRANK SINATRA, SAMMY DAVIS JR., PETER LAWFORD AND JOEY BISHOP.

HEY, BABE...

DOLL...

DIG THOSE CRAZY CATS!

GARÇON! ANOTHER MARTINI!

MAZEL!

CHIEF RAT FRANK SINATRA THOUGHT HE WAS A LAW UNTO HIMSELF. HE REVELED IN DOING WHATEVER THE HELL HE WANTED.

THIS HOTEL FURNITURE'S FOR SQUARES! TOSS IT OUT THE WINDOW!

YOU GOT IT, FRANK!

BRITISH BAD BOYS PETER O'TOOLE AND PETER FINCH ONCE SHOWED UP TOASTED AT THE *WRONG* FUNERAL.

PARDON ME, MADAM, BUT WHO ARE YOU?

THE WIDOW! AND YOU'RE *PISSED!*

IN 1977, *CHINATOWN* DIRECTOR ROMAN POLANSKI WAS CHARGED WITH DRUGGING AND RAPING A 13-YEAR-OLD GIRL.

NO, I JUST WANT TO TAKE YOUR PICTURE!

REALLY!

HE AVOIDED JAIL BY FLEEING THE COUNTRY.

THE 1980s SAW A NEW BREED OF YOUNG ACTORS TAKE UP THE BAD BOY MANTLE.

DISLL LOIN YA TA TAKE MY PITCHA!

SEAN PENN MARRIED MADONNA AND STARTED PUNCHING OUT PHOTOGRAPHERS.

THE ASSAULT CHARGE ON THE PHOTOGRAPHER AND A DRUNK DRIVING RAP SPELLED TWO MONTHS IN JAIL FOR PENN.

AT LEAST THIS BAD BOY KNEW WHERE HE STOOD.

I THINK I'M MORE FAMOUS AS MADONNA'S HUSBAND AND AS SOMEONE WHO HITS PHOTOGRAPHERS THAN AS AN ACTOR.

BUT MADONNA SOON DIVORCED HIM.

THEN THERE WAS ROB LOWE.

LIKE MOST ACTORS, WHAT I REALLY WANT TO DO IS DIRECT.

FOR HIS FIRST DIRECTORIAL EFFORT, HE PICKED UP TWO YOUNG WOMEN IN AN ATLANTA BAR AND VIDEOTAPED THEM HAVING SEX WITH HIM, AND EACH OTHER. ONE OF THE GIRLS WAS JUST 16, TWO YEARS BELOW LEGAL AGE.

LIGHTS, CAMERA — ACTION! IF YOU KNOW WHAT I MEAN.

CRIMINAL CHARGES WERE DROPPED, BUT HIS CAREER — ONCE SEEMINGLY BOUND FOR GREATNESS — NEVER FULLY RECOVERED.

IN 1994, BRITISH STAR HUGH GRANT GOT CAUGHT WITH A HOOKER ON L.A.'s SLEAZY SUNSET STRIP.

I'VE GOT JUST 60 QUID, er... DOLLARS!

HONEY, THAT'S ALL IT TAKES!

GRANT WON FORGIVENESS BY BRAVELY APPEARING ON THE TONIGHT SHOW AND OTHER TALK SHOWS, TO SHEEPISHLY APOLOGIZE.

WHAT WERE YOU THINKING?

AND LET'S NOT FORGET THE DARK SIDE OF ALL THIS BAD BOYISH FUN — AS SUCH MISBEHAVING STARS AS JOHN BELUSHI AND RIVER PHOENIX FOUND OUT.

THEY AIN'T MISBEHAVIN' ANYMORE — THOSE BAD BOYS ARE DEAD.

CHAPTER TWO

SOCIETY SLEAZE

The world teems with people who, whether due to birth, money or some particular talent, have reached the unshakable conclusion that they are much more marvelous than everybody else. But even a king must answer to his subjects. In modern times, public scandals serve as the corrective for egos out of control. If England's Charles and Diana had been ordinary folks, their tormented marriage would have remained an anonymous debacle. O.J. Simpson would have been just an everyday *alleged* wife-killer if he hadn't fashioned himself as a public icon. If Michael Jackson wasn't one of the most famous people on the planet, he'd—well, he'd *still* be weird.

The point is, there are perils to social climbing. The higher you reach beyond the great unwashed masses, the more you find yourself enslaved to their oh-so-common code of correct conduct. Once you slip, you fall hard.

THE TURN OF THE CENTURY WAS NEW YORK'S "GILDED AGE." NO FIGURE EMBODIED ITS OPULENCE, VIGOR AND ABANDON LIKE STANFORD WHITE, ARCHITECT OF THE CITY'S MOST FAMOUS BUILDINGS AND ARBITER OF TASTE FOR THE SOCIAL ELITE. FITTING, THEN, THAT HIS DEATH WAS, IN ITS TIME, THE

MURDER OF THE CENTURY

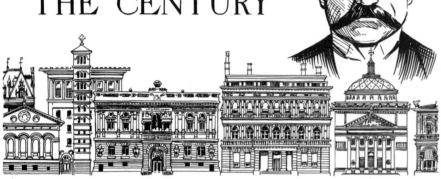

AT THE TOP OF NEW YORK'S "RULING SET," WHITE PURSUED WORK AND PLEASURE WITH EQUAL ARDOR.

IN 1900, A BEAUTIFUL, 16-YEAR-OLD MODEL NAMED FLORENCE EVELYN NESBIT ARRIVED IN NEW YORK, ESCORTED BY HER WIDOWED MOTHER. SHE CREATED AN INSTANT SENSATION.

SHE WON A ROLE IN THE POPULAR MUSICAL *FLORODORA*. WHITE HAD BEEN COLLECTING HER MAGAZINE CLIPPINGS FOR MONTHS WHEN HE FINALLY SAW HER IN PERSON.

THAT YOUTHFUL FLOWER ON THE END! I MUST PLUCK HER!

HE INVITED HER TO HIS SUMPTUOUS HOUSE ON 24TH ST. WHERE SHE TASTED CHAMPAGNE FOR THE FIRST TIME.

WOOO! IT TICKLES MY NOSE!

BUT JUST ONE GLASS, MY DEAR. YOU ARE SO YOUNG.

IN WHITE'S BEDROOM HUNG A RED VELVET SWING. PERFECT FOR A CLEAR VIEW UP A YOUNG LADY'S SKIRT.

WHEEE! OH, MR. WHITE! IT'S SUCH FUN!

YOU LOOK ESPECIALLY LOVELY FROM THIS ANGLE, MY CHILD.

WHILE WHITE, MARRIED AND 50, OPENLY KEPT EVELYN AS HIS MISTRESS, MOTHER NESBIT WELCOMED HIM. ESPECIALLY WHEN HE WILLINGLY COVERED THE BILLS.

MR. WHITE, YOU ARE THE PERFECT GENTLEMAN. EVELYN IS INDEED BLESSED.

MEANWHILE, ANOTHER MULTIMILLIONAIRE BECAME OBSESSED WITH EVELYN.

BUT EVELYN WAS NOT THAW'S ONLY OBSESSION.

THE NE'ER-DO-WELL SCION OF A PITTSBURGH MINING FAMILY, THAW'S HATRED OF WHITE BEGAN WITH AN INCIDENT IN 1902.

THE GIRLS HAD INDEED ACCEPTED THAW'S INVITATION--THEN WENT TO A SOIREE WITH WHITE INSTEAD.

IT WAS PAYBACK FOR THAW'S EARLIER SNUB OF ONE OF THE GIRLS.

THE TABLOIDS GOT AHOLD OF THE STORY. THAW, NEVER STABLE IN THE FIRST PLACE, WENT NUTS.

REPULSED BY THAW'S WEIRDNESS, EVELYN STUCK WITH THE MORE RESPECTABLE WHITE. HER MOTHER TRUSTED WHITE COMPLETELY.

FOR SOME REASON, THE CHAMPAGNE DIDN'T AGREE WITH EVELYN THAT NIGHT.

WHEN SHE WOKE UP THE NEXT MORNING, SHE KNEW WHAT HAD HAPPENED.

STILL, SHE CONTINUED THE AFFAIR.

WHEN EVELYN FELL ILL IN 1903, THAW, UNDAUNTED, SHOWERED HER WITH AFFECTION.

WHEN HE OFFERED TO PAY FOR A EUROPEAN TOUR, EVELYN AND HER WARY MOTHER ACCEPTED.

EVELYN WAS STILL IRKED AT WHITE FOR THWARTING HER ROMANCE WITH JOHN BARRYMORE (BEFORE BARRYMORE BECAME A FAMOUS ACTOR AND DRUNK).

IN EUROPE, THAW POPPED THE QUESTION. BUT HE GAVE THE RELUCTANT EVELYN AN EASY OUT.

NATURALLY, MY LOVE, I CAN MARRY YOU ONLY IF YOU ARE STILL PURE.

DOES THE TIME THAT STANFORD WHITE RAPED ME COUNT?

NEEDLESS TO SAY, THAW DIDN'T TAKE *THAT* NEWS VERY WELL.

THAW HAD ANOTHER ECCENTRICITY EVELYN SOON LEARNED ABOUT. HE GOT HIS ROCKS OFF BY WHIPPING PEOPLE. ONE NIGHT HE APPEARED IN HER BEDROOM, BUCK NAKED.

HARRY, IS THAT Y... OH MY GOD, HARRY!!

YOU KNOW YOU LOVE IT, SWEETHEART!

CRACK!!

IT TOOK HER WEEKS TO RECOVER.

AUDACIOUSLY, THAW BEGGED FOR FORGIVENESS.

DARLING, I DON'T KNOW WHAT CAME OVER ME. I'M SO ASHAMED!

NOT ASHAMED ENOUGH, APPARENTLY. HE REPEATED THE BEATING TWICE.

BACK IN NEW YORK, SHE FOUND WHITE HAD *COOLED* TO HER. HIS RESPONSE TO HER HORROR STORY ABOUT THAW WAS LESS THAN FERVENT.

I'LL CONTACT MY LAWYER FOR YOU. NOW I MUST RETURN TO MY WORK.

ON APRIL 5, 1905, MOST LIKELY OUT OF SPITE, EVELYN MARRIED HARRY K. THAW.

BUT HIS APPARENT VICTORY IN ROMANCE FAILED TO COOL THAW'S OBSESSION WITH WHITE.

ON JUNE 25, 1906, WHITE AND THE THAWS CROSSED PATHS AT THE OPENING OF A NEW MUSICAL.

SO AS I WAS SAYING...

WHITE -- THAT BLACKGUARD!

THAW FINALLY SAW THE CHANCE TO ACT ON HIS LONG-BURNING GRUDGE.

BLAM! BLAM! BLAM!

THE GREAT ARCHITECT DIED INSTANTLY OF A BULLET THROUGH THE EYE.

CALMLY, THAW CONCOCTED A MOTIVE DESIGNED TO WIN PUBLIC SYMPATHY.

I WAS MERELY AVENGING THE HONOR OF MY WIFE. THAT BEAST WHITE RAVISHED HER.

HE PLED TEMPORARY INSANITY.

EVELYN TESTIFIED ABOUT THE RAPE.

AND WHEN I WOKE UP, MY OWN BLOOD COLORED THE SHEETS, AND STANNY LAY BESIDE ME IN ALL HIS NAKED GLORY.

THE PUBLIC WAS, AS THAW HOPED, OUTRAGED.

READ ALL ABOUT IT! HERO THAW GAVE MONSTER WHITE WHAT HE DESERVED!

EVELYN'S GRAPHIC TESTIMONY BECAME A SCANDAL OF ITS OWN, WITH CALLS TO BAN ITS PUBLICATION.

HOLY TOLEDO!

OH MY!

THAW TRIAL SHOCKER

THE SCANDAL BLACKENED NOT ONLY WHITE'S MEMORY, BUT THE WHOLE UPPER CLASS.

THE RICH ARE NOTHING BUT A BUNCH OF MORAL DEGENERATES AND PERVERTS! THIS *PROVES* IT!

THAW'S FAMILY HIRED THE NATION'S FINEST DEFENSE LAWYER, DELPHIN DELMAS, WHO CAME UP WITH AN INSANITY DEFENSE HE CHRISTENED "DEMENTIA AMERICANA."

THAT SPECIES OF INSANITY THAT INSPIRES EVERY AMERICAN TO BELIEVE HIS HOME AND THE PURITY OF HIS WIFE IS SACRED.

FIVE JURORS BOUGHT IT, BUT SEVEN DIDN'T. THAW WOULD GET A SECOND TRIAL.

MAYBE HE'S CRAZY, MAYBE HE ISN'T. WHO KNOWS?

A NEW SET OF LAWYERS FARED BETTER. THAW WAS ACQUITTED BY REASON OF INSANITY.

AND YOU KNOW WHAT THAT MEANS. OFF TO THE BUGHOUSE WHERE YOU BELONG!

DESPITE HER LURID TESTIMONY ABOUT THE RAPE, EVELYN CLAIMED GREAT ADMIRATION FOR WHITE.

EXCEPT FOR THAT ONE THING, STANNY WAS THE NICEST MAN I'VE EVER KNOWN.

THAW DIVORCED EVELYN AND ESCAPED FROM THE ASYLUM IN 1915. HIS LAWYERS MANEUVERED TO KEEP HIM OUT, BUT THEY WERE POWERLESS WHEN HE WAS ARRESTED IN 1917 FOR WHIPPING A 19-YEAR-OLD BOY.

THWACK

YEEE-OOOW!!

HE WAS FREED IN 1924. UNTIL HIS DEATH IN 1947, HE FOUGHT OFF LAWSUITS FROM SHOWGIRLS WHO CLAIMED HE'D WHIPPED THEM.

EVELYN LOST HER BEAUTY TO HEROIN ADDICTION. SHE OPENED A STRING OF NIGHTCLUBS THAT ALL FAILED.

SHE USED TO BE SOMEBODY. I'M NOT SURE WHO.

HER MOMENT OF GLORY CAME IN 1955 WHEN HOLLYWOOD FILMED HER LIFE STORY. **THE GIRL IN THE RED VELVET SWING** STARRED JOAN COLLINS AS EVELYN.

SHE DIED IN 1966 AT AGE 81. BUT NOT BEFORE GIVING ONE, FINAL INTERVIEW.

STANNY WAS LUCKY. HE DIED. I LIVED.

the PRINCESS & THE ICE QUEEN

IN 1994 ANGELIC NANCY KERRIGAN REIGNED ATOP THE WORLD OF U.S. AMATEUR FIGURE SKATING. HER ONLY CHALLENGER: SKATING'S SMOKING, SWEARING, POOL-SHOOTING BAD GIRL, TONYA HARDING.

A MEETING IN LATE DEC., 1993: JEFF GILLOOLY, HARDING'S EX-HUSBAND, PLOTS AGAINST KERRIGAN.

WE GOTTA TAKE HER OUT!

OR WE COULD JUST WHACK HER IN THE KNEE.

JAN. 6. THE U.S. NATIONAL CHAMPIONSHIPS. KERRIGAN WAS COMING OFF THE ICE AFTER PRACTICE WHEN--

THWACK

--YAAAAA! WHY ME?! WHY ME?!

WITH KERRIGAN OUT OF THE WAY, HARDING SKATED TO HER FIRST NATIONAL CROWN AND QUALIFIED FOR THE OLYMPICS.

HARD-GAL HARDING HAD A KNACK FOR SAYING THE WRONG THING.

TONYA, WHAT ARE YOUR THOUGHTS ON WINNING?

ALL I'M THINKING ABOUT ARE DOLLAR SIGNS.

AND HER BODYGUARD COULDN'T KEEP HIS MOUTH SHUT.

GILLOOLY ORDERED THE ATTACK. I GOT HIM ON TAPE.

THE EX-HUSBAND DECIDED HE WASN'T GOING DOWN ALONE.

YEAH, I'M GUILTY-- BUT TONYA KNEW ABOUT IT FROM DAY ONE!

FIGHTING THE CHARGE, TONYA FULFILLED HER LIFELONG DREAM OF SKATING IN THE OLYMPICS, BUT HER SKATE LACES KEPT BREAKING AND SHE FINISHED EIGHTH.

KERRIGAN SKATED WELL ENOUGH TO GET A MEDAL, BUT LOST GOLD BY THE SLIMMEST OF MARGINS.

HARDING PLED GUILTY, BUT ONLY TO "HINDERING PROSECUTION." SHE WAS BANNED FROM AMATEUR SKATING FOR LIFE.

DEATH AND THE DIET DOCTOR

MARCH 10, 1980.

JEAN HARRIS, THE 57-YEAR-OLD HEAD-MISTRESS OF AN EXCLUSIVE GIRLS' SCHOOL HAD DRIVEN 400 MILES TO THE HOME OF HER LOVER IN THE WEALTHY SUBURB OF PURCHASE, NEW YORK.

SHE ARRIVED AT THE HOME OF 69-YEAR-OLD HERMAN TARNOWER, PHYSICIAN TO THE UPPER CRUST--AND AUTHOR OF THE BESTSELLING *COMPLETE SCARSDALE MEDICAL DIET*.

TARNOWER WAS A WORLD-CLASS SNOB WHO WENT THROUGH WOMEN THE WAY HE WENT THROUGH FOIS GRAS.

HE'D BEEN SEEING HARRIS FOR 14 YEARS -- AS WELL AS ABOUT 30 OTHER WOMEN.

WHAT HAPPENED IN TARNOWER'S BEDROOM THAT NIGHT DEPENDS ON WHICH STORY YOU BELIEVE. EITHER...

DAMN YOU, HI! YOU'VE ALREADY DESTROYED MY LIFE, NOW LET ME DIE!

DON'T BE A FOOL, JEAN! NOW GIVE ME THAT GUN BEFORE--

BANG

--AAAA! JEAN, YOU SHOT ME!

OH DEAR GOD! WHAT HAVE I DONE?

OR...

EAT LEAD, TARNOWER!

BLAM BLAM BLAM

-UUUNNNGH!-

THE DEATH MADE NATIONAL HEADLINES, FASCINATING THE PUBLIC WITH THE TAWDRY EXPLOITS OF THE ULTRA-STUFFY EAST COAST ESTABLISHMENT.

TARNOWER'S DEMISE WAS THE DEATH OF AN AMERICAN DREAM. HE WAS RAISED ON THE STREETS OF BROOKLYN, THE SON OF JEWISH IMMIGRANTS.

I'M GONNA GET OUTTA DIS DUMP BY BECOMIN' A FANCY-PANTS DOCTOR!

HE WORKED CEASELESSLY AT HIS PROFESSION, BUT HIS TRUE PASSION WAS SOCIAL CLIMBING.

MISS VANDERBILT'S BIOPSY AT 3:30. GOLF GAME AT 4:00. QUAIL HUNTING AT 5:00. COCKTAIL PARTY AT...

AND OF COURSE, WOMEN.

MAY I INTEREST YOU IN A '63 VINTAGE CHATEAU D'OR, FOLLOWED BY A LITTLE NOOKIE, MY DEAR?

BY MIDDLE AGE, HE WAS FIRMLY ENTRENCHED IN WESTCHESTER SOCIETY. HE HOSTED ELEGANT DINNER PARTIES FOR SOCIALLY PROMINENT GUESTS.

AS I LEARNED FROM MY RECENT REREADING OF HERODOTUS, BLAH BLAH BLAH BLAH BLAH...

HE'S SO ERUDITE!

THE CHICKS DIG HIM!

WHAT A POMPOUS ASS!

ALWAYS ON A QUEST FOR RESPECTABILITY, HE TOOK UP WITH REFINED, DIGNIFIED -- AND GENTILE -- JEAN HARRIS.

LIKE A GOOD WASP, SHE KEPT A STIFF UPPER LIP THROUGH HIS FREQUENT AFFAIRS.

I AM LUCKY TO HAVE SUCH A GENTLEMAN FRIEND. IF ONLY HE WOULD MARRY ME!

FAT CHANCE. BY THE LATE 70s, HE OPENLY TWO-TIMED HARRIS WITH HIS ATTRACTIVE OFFICE ASSISTANT, LYNNE TRYFOROS.

YOU'RE THE MAN OF MY DREAMS, HI!

THAT'S MY KIND OF GAL!

69

HE WAS ALSO REVELING IN HIS SUDDEN CELEBRITY.

MY GUEST IS DR. HERMAN TARNOWER, AUTHOR OF THE RUNAWAY BESTSELLER, *THE COMPLETE SCARSDALE MEDICAL DIET.*

HARRIS DETESTED BOTH THE PUBLICITY AND TARNOWER'S ENJOYMENT OF IT.

HOW TERRIBLY COMMON!

WHILE HARRIS GREW INCREASINGLY OBSESSED WITH TARNOWER, HE BEGAN AVOIDING HER.

ANSWER THE PHONE, HI!

RING

IT'S THAT DAMN JEAN! TELL HER I'M BUSY!

PUSHED TO THE LIMIT, HARRIS FIRED OFF A LETTER TO TARNOWER, EXPRESSING HER OPINION OF HIS OTHER MISTRESS.

PSYCHOTIC SLUT! WHORE!

AT HER HIGHLY PUBLICIZED TRIAL, HARRIS SWORE SHE INTENDED TO KILL ONLY HERSELF.

JEAN, YOU'RE CRAZY! GO TO BED!

BUT THE JURY WONDERED WHY, IF TARNOWER DIED TRYING TO SAVE HER FROM HERSELF, HE WAS SHOT FOUR TIMES.

MOST OF ALL, HARRIS CONVICTED HERSELF, OFTEN UNLEASHING HER TEMPER ON THE STAND.

THIS IS A TRAVESTY OF JUSTICE!

HER ANGRY LETTER TO TARNOWER WAS THE COUP DE GRACE.

THE PUBLIC SAW HARRIS AS A CLASSIC WRONGED WOMAN, DRIVEN TO DESPAIR BY HER UNFEELING LOVER. SHE'D SERVED 12 YEARS OF A 15-TO-LIFE SENTENCE WHEN NEW YORK GOV. MARIO CUOMO GRANTED HER CLEMENCY.

Jimmy Swaggart in HELL

IN THE 80's HEYDAY OF TELEVANGELISM, JIMMY SWAGGART WAS THE FIERCEST, FIERIEST PREACHER OF THEM ALL.

HOMOSEXUALITY LUST ADULTERY ROCKANROLL SATAN ARR! ARRR!!!

AND HIS MINISTRY WAS THE MOST LUCRATIVE, PULLING IN $150 MILLION PER YEAR.

THANK YOU JESUS!

JIMMY TRULY LOVED THE LORD. BUT HE HAD AT LEAST ONE OTHER INTEREST.

HE REALLY ENJOYED WATCHING WOMEN MASTURBATE.

OOHAAHOOOOOOHHH

SISTER (GULP!) YOU ARE TRULY A LAMB OF GOD!

HIS PERFORMERS OF CHOICE WERE TRASHY HOOKERS WHO HE'D MEET IN CHEAP MOTEL ROOMS.

TEN BUCKS FOR A LITTLE LOOKY-LOOKY?

WHAT KIND OF GIRL DO YOU THINK I AM?

MAKE IT 20!

ONE DAY, ONE OF THE GALS RECOGNIZED JIMMY AS HE WAS, SEEMINGLY, ANTICIPATING THE ACTIVITIES TO COME.

SAY, AIN'T YOU JIMMY SWAGGART? I WATCH-- OH MY LORD!

SWAGGART? (HEH HEH) DON'T KNOW ANY-ONE BY THAT NAME!

BUT HE KEPT GOING BACK TO THE SAME MOTEL.

WORD OF JIMMY'S SORDID SOJOURNS REACHED RIVAL PREACHER MARVIN GORMAN. JIMMY HAD EARLIER ACCUSED GORMAN OF ADULTERY--AND RUINED HIM. NOW IT WAS PAYBACK TIME.

SMILE, BROTHER JIMMY!

POP!

FACED WITH EXPOSURE, JIMMY WENT ON TV AND SUMMONED UP ALL OF HIS THEATRICAL SKILLS FOR A TEARFUL CONFESSION.

I DO NOT INTEND TO (SOB!) WHITEWASH MY SIN!!

OF COURSE, HE DIDN'T SAY WHAT IT WAS HE WAS CONFESSING ABOUT.

HIS CHURCH, ASSEMBLIES OF GOD, BANNED HIM FROM THE PULPIT, AND FROM TV, FOR A YEAR.

SEEK COUNSELING, BROTHER JIMMY!

SOME SPECULATED THAT JIMMY, LIKE MANY SINNERS, **CRAVED** PUNISHMENT. JUST NOT THAT **MUCH** PUNISHMENT. WITH HIS MINISTRY LOSING MILLIONS, HE DEFIED THE CHURCH AND RETURNED TO PREACHING JUST A FEW MONTHS LATER.

HALLELUJAH LORD!

I'M BACK!

HE WAS DEFROCKED AND NEVER REALLY REGAINED HIS FOLLOWING.

FACTOID BOOKS

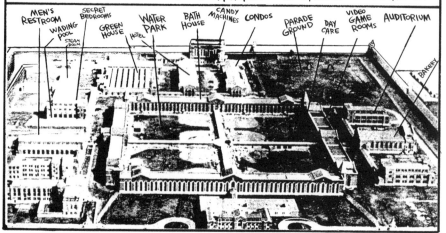

HE HAPPILY TOLD COHORTS HOW HE AND TAMMY "SPICED UP" THEIR SEX LIFE WITH **MARITAL AIDS** -- AND HE ENCOURAGED **OTHERS** TO DO THE SAME.

BUZZZ

IF GOD DIDN'T WANT US TO USE VIBRATORS, HE WOULDN'T HAVE CREATED BATTERIES!

PRAISE THE LORD!

HIS ESCAPADES WEREN'T LIMITED TO HIS **WIFE**, HOWEVER. HE HAD A **HOT TUB** INSTALLED IN HIS OFFICE.

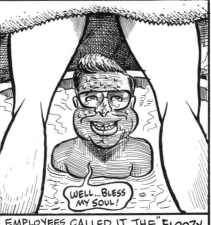

WELL... BLESS MY SOUL!

EMPLOYEES CALLED IT THE "FLOOZY JACUZZI."

NOR, REPORTEDLY, WERE THEY LIMITED TO **WOMEN.** HIS FREQUENT "BACK-RUBS," SOME ASSOCIATES SAID, OFTEN ENDED UP IN HOMO-SEXUAL ROMPS...

BROTHER, YOU'RE DOIN' TH'.... *AAAAAHH!* LORD'S WORK!

...A SERIOUS OFFENSE FOR A PENTECOSTAL MINISTER.

TAMMY FAYE, UNDERSTANDABLY, FELT **NEGLECTED.** SHE TOOK UP WITH BORN-AGAIN SINGER **GARY PAXTON**, BEST KNOWN FOR SINGING THE 60'S NOVELTY HIT "ALLEY OOP."

HEH-HEH! I'M TAKIN' YOU HOME T'MEET MAMA-- TOMORROW!

ON TV, THEY WERE STILL THE PERFECT CHRISTIAN COUPLE -- BEGGING FOR MONEY. THE JIM AND TAMMY SPECIALTY: WEEPING AT WILL!

SNIFF

GIVE WHAT YOU CAN, FRIENDS... OR... *SOB* THIS MINISTRY WILL GO OFF THE AIR!

JIM AND I HAVE *WAAAAHH!* GIVEN EVERYTHING WE HAVE TO KEEP THE MINISTRY ALIVE!!

I'LL BE DANGED IF I'LL LET THAT HAPPEN!

WELL... NOT **QUITE** EVERYTHING. AS PTL FLOUNDERED, JIM AND TAMMY HELD ONTO ENOUGH TO BUY A **ROLLS-ROYCE...**

A FELLA NEEDS A CAR!

... A MILLION-DOLLAR HOME IN THE CALIFORNIA **DESERT...**

IT'S A MARVELOUS HIDEAWAY... IT'S NOT REALLY A SECRET...

...ENOUGH **CLOTHES** TO STOCK TAMMY'S 30-FOOT-DEEP WALK-IN "CLOSET":..

SO MANY DRESSES--

--AND ONLY ONE ME!

... AND ALSO, SOME **REAL** EXTRAVAGANCES -- ALL THE WHILE PLEADING **POVERTY** TO THEIR DEVOTED TV FLOCK.

THEY BEGGED THEIR FOLLOWERS TO DONATE TO PTL'S "OVERSEAS MISSIONS" IN **BRAZIL** AND ELSEWHERE BUT USED THE MONEY FOR DOMESTIC EXPENDITURES, PROMPTING AN **FCC** INVESTIGATION.

♪ I GO TO RIO DE JANIERO! ♪

JIM CAME UP WITH A SCHEME TO RAISE EVEN **MORE** MONEY. HE'D GIVE THREE NIGHTS AND FOUR DAYS PER YEAR IN HIS HERITAGE U.S.A. CONDOS TO **ANYONE** WHO DONATED $1,000 TO **PTL**.

...SO, JIM... IT'S LIKE A TIME SHARE...?

NONSENSE! WE'LL CALL THEM "LIFETIME **PARTNERSHIPS!**"

THERE WASN'T ENOUGH SPACE IN THE CONDOS TO ACCOMMODATE ALL 150,000 "**PARTNERS**" WHO FORKED OVER A GRAND, BUT BAKKER KEPT ON SELLING.

IN DECEMBER, 1984, AN ANONYMOUS FEMALE PHONED **CHARLES SHEPARD**, A REPORTER FOR THE *CHARLOTTE OBSERVER*. A VETERAN OF THE PTL STORY, HE PLAYED A HUNCH.

...IS YOUR NAME **JESSICA HAHN**...?

Y-YES... THAT'S ME... I--I...JUST DON'T WANT TO BE HURT ANYMORE...

THIS NEW YORK CHURCH SECRETARY TOLD A **SORDID** TALE...

...WHICH BEGAN WITH A CALL FROM A LONGTIME ACQUAINTANCE, EVANGELIST **JOHN WESLEY FLETCHER**.

...JESSICA... I'M IN FLORIDA WITH SOMEONE **VERY** SPECIAL I'D LIKE YOU TO MEET... IT'S **JIM BAKKER!**

OH GAWD! I'M SOOOOO NERVOUS!

SHE IDOLIZED BAKKER AND FLEW TO **FLORIDA** TO MEET HIM IN HIS MOTEL.

I NEVER KNEW WOMEN FROM NEW YORK WERE SO BEAUTIFUL. I WISH MY WIFE HAD...UHH... **HAIR** LIKE YOURS!

THE WAY **JESSICA** TOLD IT, FLETCHER THEN LEFT THE ROOM SAYING...

JESSICA... YOU'RE GONNA BE DOING SOMETHIN' **TREMENDOUS** FOR GOD...

Vaseline Intensive Care LOTION

I NEED TO FEEL LIKE I'M STILL A **MAN**, JESSICA.

...MY WIFE-- SHE RIDICULES ME! ONLY **YOU** CAN HELP ME...

BY HELPING THE **SHEPHERD**, JESSICA...

...YOU'RE HELPING THE **SHEEP!**

THE YOUNG **OBSERVER** REPORTER WENT TO HIS EDITORS WHO TOOK THE HIGH ROAD.

LOOK, SHEP... WE'RE NOT RUNNING A **SEX** STORY UNLESS THERE WAS SO ME KIND OF **FINANCIAL MISDEED!**

IT TOOK UNTIL 1987 FOR SHEPARD TO NAIL DOWN THE **FINANCIAL** ANGLE... -- **HUSH MONEY** TO HAHN.

P.T.L. WILL SET UP A $265,000 FUND FOR YOU, JESSICA...

...JUST KEEP YO' MOUTH **SHUT!**

SHEPARD LATER WON THE **PULITZER PRIZE** FOR HIS DILIGENT *P.T.L.* REPORTING.

ON MARCH 18, 1987, WITH THE SCANDAL ABOUT TO BLOW **WIDE OPEN,** BAKKER ABRUPTLY ABDICATED THE PTL **THRONE** -- THOUGH HE WASN'T EXACTLY **APOLOGETIC.**

...I CAN NO LONGER DEFEND MYSELF AGAINST THE CHARLOTTE OBSERVER WHICH HAS ATTACKED US INCESSANTLY...

EH?

HIS ACCOUNT OF THE **JESSICA HAHN** INCIDENT WAS, TO SAY THE LEAST, **SELF-SERVING.**

I WAS WICKEDLY MANIPULATED BY FORMER FRIENDS WHO VICTIM-IZED ME WITH A FEMALE CONFEDERATE.

I KNEW IT! HE'S A DAMN YANKEE!! STILL TIME TO STOP PAYMENT ON THAT CHECK!

ZING

EEYOUR!

HE ENTRUSTED THE PTL TO "MORAL MAJORITY" LEADER **REVEREND JERRY FALWELL,** WHO PROMPTLY BANISHED THE BAKKERS FROM THEIR OWN KINGDOM.

GO FORTH!

...AND ASK THE LORD FOR FORGIVENESS!

TODAY'S SPEAKER REV. JERRY F.

JIM AND TAMMY'S ROCKY MARRIAGE WASN'T HELPED BY THE SEX-AND-CASH SCANDAL. BUT THEY STUCK TOGETHER AS TAMMY TRIED TO KICK A NASTY PRESCRIPTION PILL HABIT.

IT WAS A ROUGH ERA FOR TELEVISION EVANGELISTS. FIRST, **ORAL ROBERTS** MADE A FOOL OF HIMSELF ON NATIONAL TELEVISION...

FRIENDS... IF I DON'T RAISE AT LEAST A MILLION DOLLARS, GOD WILL...HE'LL... **KILL** ME!!

...GOD WOULDN'T DO A THING LIKE THAT!

TELEVANGELIST **JIMMY SWAGGART,** ACCUSED BY BAKKER OF PLOTTING AGAINST HIM, LATER GOT CAUGHT IN HIS **OWN** SEX SCANDAL.

HOW ABOUT $25--AND I DON'T **KISS** YOU?

THE SCANDALS HURT **ALL** TV MINISTRIES. DONATIONS DROPPED SHARPLY.

LORD, WHAT DID **I** EVER DO TO OFFEND THEE?

BUT THE **BAKKERS'** PROBLEMS WERE JUST **BEGINNING.** IN 1988, JIM BAKKER WAS INDICTED ON 24 COUNTS OF **FRAUD** AND CONSPIRACY FOR HIS "LIFETIME PARTNERSHIP" SCHEME.

YO' IN A HEAP O' TROUBLE NOW, BOY...

GUILTY

HEH HEH HEH HEH

AS FOR **JESSICA HAHN,** SHE GAVE A TELL-ALL INTERVIEW TO **PLAYBOY** MAGAZINE. SHE ALSO POSED NUDE, SAYING THAT SHOWING HER BODY, FINALLY ALLOWED HER TO FEEL "GOOD" ABOUT HERSELF.

SAY "CHEESE," SWEETIE...

C'MON... WHEN DO WE GET TO THE INTERVIEW?

NOT GOOD **ENOUGH,** APPARENTLY. SHE LATER UNDERWENT BREAST IMPLANTS AND HAD A NOSE JOB, THEN POSED FOR **PLAYBOY AGAIN,** TO SHOW OFF HER **NEW** ASSETS.

HOW'S THIS?

MAYBE WE OUGHTTA WAIT TILL YOUR NOSE HEALS...

SHE ALSO DID A BRIEF STINT AS A MUSIC-VIDEO **SEX KITTEN.**

BAKKER'S 1988 TRIAL WAS ROUGH ON HIM. ONE DAY, HE CURLED UP IN **THE FETAL POSITION** UNDER HIS LAWYER'S DESK AND WENT INTO **HYSTERICS.**

UHHH...MR. BAKKER?

WAAAHHH! DON'T LET THEM **DO** THIS TO ME!

HE HAD **ANOTHER** BREAKDOWN WHEN HE WAS CONFRONTED BY A GAGGLE OF REPORTERS AS HE WAS BEING LED TO A SQUAD CAR. HE HALLUCINATED, SEEING THEM AS GIANT **ANTS.**

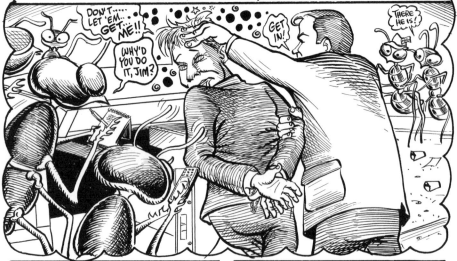

DON'T..... LET 'EM.... GET... ME!!

WHY'D YOU DO IT, JIM?

GET IN!

THERE HE IS!

DESPITE HIS "PANIC ATTACK," BAKKER WAS DEEMED **FIT** TO STAND TRIAL. THINGS ONLY GOT **WORSE.**

GUILTY!

AH HEREBY SENTENCES YOU TO 45 YEARS IN PRISON..!!

AS IF **THAT** WASN'T BAD ENOUGH, TAMMY FINALLY **DIVORCED** JIM-- AND MARRIED HIS BEST FRIEND, **ROSS MESSNER,** A MILLIONAIRE BUILDER OF CHURCHES.

ON APPEAL, HIS SENTENCE WAS **REDUCED.** HE WAS **FREED** IN 1991. HE NEVER RECLAIMED HIS MINISTRY. BUT HE **DID** WRITE A **BOOK,** WHICH HE TITLED FITTINGLY...

I WAS WRONG

JIM BAKKER

FACTOID BOOKS

WHEN THE HEIR TO THE PULITZER PUBLISHING FORTUNE WED A FORMER CHEERLEADER FROM UPSTATE NEW YORK 21 YEARS YOUNGER THAN HE WAS, THE PALM BEACH UPPER CRUST SHOULD HAVE KNOWN THEY WERE IN FOR A SORDID TALE OF...

SEX, DRUGS, & ROX

THE FIVE-YEAR MARRIAGE OF HERBERT ("PETER") AND ROXANNE PULITZER WAS A WHIRLWIND OF DRUGS AND KINKY SEX.

I'M ALMOST READY, LADIES!

INEVITABLY, THE RELATIONSHIP DEGENERATED INTO A CROSSFIRE OF ACCUSATIONS: INCEST, LESBIANISM, ADDICTION, OCCULTISM.

THE LATTER CHARGE CAME FROM ROXANNE'S HABIT OF HOLDING SEANCES, AT LEAST ONE OF WHICH INVOLVED A TRUMPET.

SPIRITS! SPEAK THROUGH ME! OR AT LEAST THROUGH THIS FUNKY BRASS INSTRUMENT.

SOMEHOW, THE STORY GOT OUT THAT SHE WAS TAKING THIS TRUMPET TO BED WITH HER.

I DO NOT NOW, NOR HAVE I EVER ENGAGED IN CONJUGAL RELATIONS WITH A TRUMPET. IF THAT'S EVEN POSSIBLE.

IN THEIR SPECTACULAR 1982 DIVORCE TRIAL, HERBERT ACCUSED ROXANNE OF A LESBIAN AFFAIR WITH THE YOUNG WIFE OF SEPTUAGENARIAN KLEENEX MAGNATE JIM KIMBERLY, JACQUIE, WHO RESPONDED...

HERBERT'S A —! HONK! DEGENERATE!

ROXANNE FIRED BACK, ALLEGING THAT HERBERT AND HIS DAUGHTER BY A PREVIOUS MARRIAGE, LIZA, WERE INCESTUOUS LOVERS. LIZA RESPONDED...

ACTUALLY, ROX WANTED TO DO IT WITH ME.

HERBERT SUBPOENAED DOZENS OF PALM BEACH SOCIALITES--WHO PROMPTLY SPLIT TOWN, DUCKING THE TRIAL'S INTENSE PUBLICITY.

DANG IT, MARTHA! WHERE'S ALL THEM RICH FOLKS WE CAME DOWN HERE TO GET A LOOK AT?

IN THE END, HERBERT GOT THE ESTATE AND THE KIDS.

ROXANNE SCANDALIZED PALM BEACH FURTHER WITH A TELL-ALL BOOK, RECOUNTING GROUP SEX PARTIES AND FISHBOWLS OF COCAINE.

IN 1992 ROXANNE DUMPED HER FRENCH NOBLEMAN BOYFRIEND TO MARRY A SPEEDBOAT RACER-- OVER THE OBJECTIONS OF HIS SOCIALITE MOTHER.

YOU'LL NEVER GET MY SON, YOU-- YOU-- STRUMPET WITH A TRUMPET!!

CYRIL BURT: THE INTELLIGENCE MAN

SMART KIDS

EVERYBODY ELSE

CYRIL BURT WAS A TOWERING INTELLECTUAL FIGURE, THE FIRST PSYCHOLOGIST TO EARN KNIGHTHOOD.

HIS VIEWS ON THE NATURE OF HUMAN INTELLIGENCE SHAPED THE BRITISH EDUCATIONAL SYSTEM.

INTELLECTUAL ABILITY IS *INHERITED*, NOT DUE TO TEACHING OR TRAINING.

BURT'S IDEAS HAD BROAD IMPLICATIONS FOR SOCIETY.

INCOME LEVELS ARE LARGELY AN EFFECT, NOT OF CIRCUMSTANCE, BUT OF THE WIDE INEQUALITY IN INNATE INTELLIGENCE.

HE SUPPORTED HIS IDEAS WITH STUDIES OF HARD-TO-FIND SETS OF SEPARATED-AT-BIRTH IDENTICAL TWINS.

THEIR INTELLIGENCE, IT SEEMS TO ME, IS EQUAL. THIS PROVES IT'S ALL HEREDITARY.

BURT'S "INNATE INTELLIGENCE" THEORIES WERE A HIT WITH BRITAIN'S RICH AND POWERFUL, PROVIDING A "SCIENTIFIC" BASIS FOR THE COUNTRY'S RIGID CLASS SYSTEM.

LOVE TO HELP THE LITTLE BLIGHTERS, BUT THERE'S NOTHING WE CAN DO FOR THEM. BURT'S PROVED IT.

JOLLY GLAD *WE* WERE BORN WITH A BIT OF THE OLD INNATE INTELLIGENCE, DON'T YOU KNOW?

WHILE KNOWN AS A GENEROUS AND HELPFUL MAN, HE COULD ALSO BE ECCENTRIC, AUTOCRATIC, AND INTOLERANT OF OTHER VIEWPOINTS.

WE KNOW INTELLIGENCE IS HEREDITARY-- BECAUSE I SAY SO.!!

HE WAS AN ELOQUENT SPEAKER, BUT THERE WERE WHISPERED SUSPICIONS ABOUT HIS PROFESSIONAL INTEGRITY. A FRIEND ONCE SAID...

I DON'T BELIEVE A WORD THE OLD ROGUE SAYS, BUT BY GOD, I ADMIRE THE WAY HE SAYS IT!

NONETHELESS, BURT RETAINED THE IMMENSE RESPECT OF HIS PEERS AND BRITISH SOCIETY, WORKING CEASELESSLY UNTIL HIS DEATH IN 1971.

WITH THE IMPOSING BURT NOW GONE, OTHER SCHOLARS BEGAN TO SCRUTINIZE THE TWIN STUDIES THAT WERE THE FOUNDATION OF HIS IDEAS. AMONG THE FIRST WAS PRINCETON PSYCHOLOGY PROFESSOR LEON KAMIN.

BURT'S SAMPLES CHANGE, BUT HIS RESULTS REMAIN THE SAME TO THE *THIRD DECIMAL!* STATISTICALLY, THAT'S VIRTUALLY IMPOSSIBLE!

KAMIN REACHED AN UNTHINKABLE CONCLUSION.

BURT'S FINDINGS CAN ONLY BE DUE TO *SCIENTIFIC FRAUD!*

ALSO, BURT'S NUMBERS OF RARE SEPARATED-AT-BIRTH TWIN PAIRS KEPT MYSTERIOUSLY GROWING, EVEN WHEN THERE WAS NO WAY HE COULD HAVE GONE OUT AND FOUND NEW ONES.

TWINS! TWINS! I NEED MORE TWINS!

AND BURT'S CITED COLLABORATORS WERE TWO WOMEN WHO APPARENTLY DIDN'T EXIST-- OR AT LEAST HADN'T BEEN SEEN FOR DECADES.

WHO'S HE TALKING TO?

MISS CONWAY! MISS HOWARD! HAVE YOU CORRELATED OUR LATEST DATA YET?

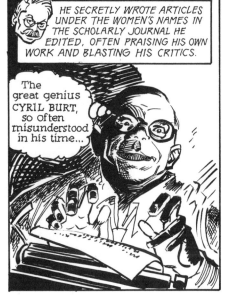

HE SECRETLY WROTE ARTICLES UNDER THE WOMEN'S NAMES IN THE SCHOLARLY JOURNAL HE EDITED, OFTEN PRAISING HIS OWN WORK AND BLASTING HIS CRITICS.

The great genius CYRIL BURT, so often misunderstood in his time...

THE *SUNDAY TIMES* RAN A BURT EXPOSÉ AND THE SCANDAL WENT WORLDWIDE, SHAKING UP THE SCIENTIFIC *AND* POLITICAL ESTABLISHMENTS.

DAMN SHAME ABOUT BURT. DON'T THINK BRITAIN'S GOING TO ABANDON THE CLASS SYSTEM, THOUGH.

SUNDAY TIMES

DEFENDERS OF THE INHERITED-INTELLIGENCE POSITION TRIED LAMELY TO DEFEND BURT-- NOTED BERKELEY PSYCHOLOGIST ARTHUR JENSEN AMONG THEM.

BURT MAY HAVE MADE A FEW *CARELESS MISTAKES* -- BUT HIS CRITICS HAVE *POLITICAL MOTIVES!*

THOUGH BURT WAS DISCREDITED, HIS CENTRAL THEME--THAT SOCIETY CAN'T HELP ITS UNDERPRIVILEGED BECAUSE THEY'RE JUST "INNATELY" STUPIDER THAN THE REST OF US--IS ENJOYING RENEWED POPULARITY.

CHAPPA

THAT MAY BE THE REAL SCANDAL.

THE NEW YORK TIMES BESTSELLER! THE BELL CURVE

79

The King
and Mrs Simpson

ON JANUARY 20, 1936, FOLLOWING THE DEATH OF GEORGE V, ALL OF BRITAIN CHEERED THE ASCENSION OF ITS YOUNG, HANDSOME CHARISMATIC NEW KING, EDWARD VIII.

WHAT THE PUBLIC DIDN'T KNOW WAS THAT BEHIND THE SCENES THE NEW KING WAS BORED SILLY WITH HIS REGAL DUTIES.

HE SIMPLY DIDN'T DO THE THINGS A KING IS SUPPOSED TO. HE WOULDN'T EVEN MEET WITH OTHER KINGS.

YOUR MAJESTY! KING CAROL OF ROMANIA REQUESTS AN AUDIENCE.

TELL HIM I'M BUSY, WOULD YOU?

IN ADDITION TO HIS NATURAL DISIN-CLINATION TO WORK, THE KING HAD A MAJOR DISTRACTION: AN AMERICAN SOCIALITE NAMED WALLIS SIMPSON.

OH, WALLIS, MY LOVE! I'D SIMPLY DIE WITHOUT YOU!

AS A POTENTIAL WIFE OF THE KING OF ENGLAND, WALLIS HAD A FEW DRAWBACKS. NOT ONLY WAS SHE AMERICAN, SHE WAS DIVORCED-- A SCANDAL IN ITSELF IN THOSE DAYS-- AND EVEN WORSE, SHE WAS MARRIED AGAIN.

WALLIS REMAINED A WELL-KEPT SECRET UNTIL THE KING TOOK HER ON HIS SUMMER HOLIDAY--A RAUCOUS EUROPEAN CRUISE ABOARD A CHARTERED LUXURY YACHT.

HI HO!

TALBOT.97

STOPPING THROUGHOUT EUROPE FOR OFFICIAL FUNCTIONS, THE KING AND WALLIS CREATED AN INTERNATIONAL SCANDAL.

OUR KING HAS THE GOOD SENSE TO LEAVE HIS MISTRESS HOME WHEN HE TRAVELS!

THE BRITISH PRESS REMAINED DISCREET, PRINTING NOT A WORD OF THE ROYAL AFFAIR. BUT THE AMERICAN PRESS WENT WILD. WORRIED, WALLIS ATTEMPTED TO EXTRICATE HERSELF FROM THE RELATIONSHIP.

"I AM SURE YOU AND I WOULD ONLY CREATE DISASTER TOGETHER. ISN'T IT BEST FOR ME TO STEAL QUIETLY AWAY?"

BALTIMORE

ENGLISH KING IN DIVORCEE LOVE TRYST

MONARCH TAKES A MISTRESS

San Francisco Examiner

A YANKEE QUEEN?

SCANDAL KING

EDW OV

THE KING, HOWEVER, HAD A SECRET PLAN OF HIS OWN-- A PLAN THAT OUTRAGED THE PRIME MINISTER, STANLEY BALDWIN.

IT HAS ALWAYS BEEN OUR INTENTION TO *MARRY MRS. SIMPSON!*

WITH ALL RESPECT, YOUR MAJESTY-- *OVER MY DEAD BODY!*

THE KING OFFERED SOME HALF-HEARTED SOLUTIONS TO THE GROWING CRISIS.

PERHAPS I COULD MARRY HER-- BUT NOT MAKE HER QUEEN!

SORRY, KING, OLD CHAP! CAN'T ALLOW IT!

BY EARLY DECEMBER, FLEET STREET COULD HOLD BACK NO LONGER. THE SCANDAL WENT PUBLIC--AND WALLIS BECAME BRITAIN'S MOST HATED WOMAN.

MRS SIMPSON PINCHED OUR KING!

YANKEE GO HOME!

SHE FLED THE COUNTRY.

THE MONARCHY AND THE GOVERNMENT ITSELF WAS THREATENED. THE KING ALWAYS KNEW WHAT HE HAD TO DO.

I HAVE FOUND IT IMPOSSIBLE TO CARRY THE HEAVY BURDEN OF BEING KING WITHOUT THE WOMAN I LOVE.

HIS BROTHER BECAME GEORGE VI, THE NEW KING. THE EX-KING RECEIVED THE TITLE "DUKE OF WINDSOR", BUT NOT MUCH ELSE. HIS FAMILY CUT HIM OFF.

SORRY, OLD SPORT, WE SIMPLY CAN NEVER SPEAK AGAIN.

THE DUKE'S MOTHER, QUEEN MARY, ALWAYS HATED WALLIS AND NOW SENT HER OWN SON INTO EXILE.

NEVER RETURN TO ENGLAND AS LONG AS YOU'RE WITH *THAT WOMAN!*

MARRIED IN JUNE, 1937, BUT BANISHED FROM BRITAIN, THE DUKE AND WALLIS (NOW DUCHESS) TRAVELED THE WORLD-- SOMETIMES SHOWING NO BETTER JUDGMENT IN THEIR NEW FRIENDS THAN THEY HAD IN THEIR ROMANCE.

30 YEARS LATER, HIS FAMILY FINALLY SOFTENED. QUEEN ELIZABETH II GRANTED HIS REQUEST FOR BURIAL IN THE ROYAL PLOT.

HE RETURNED TO ENGLISH SOIL FOR GOOD IN 1972 AND WALLIS FOLLOWED HIM A FEW YEARS AFTER.

EVERYONE CALLED IT A "FAIRY TALE WEDDING"! AND WHY NOT? DOESN'T EVERY YOUNG GIRL DREAM OF MARRYING A PRINCE? FOR **LADY DIANA** SPENCER, A SHY 20-YEAR-OLD FROM AN ARISTOCRATIC-THOUGH-FRACTURED FAMILY, THE DREAM CAME TRUE ON JULY 29TH, 1981! SHE WED **CHARLES**, PRINCE OF WALES-- ENGLAND'S FUTURE KING!

NOW SHE WAS THE PROUD NATION'S FUTURE QUEEN. OR SO IT SEEMED AT THE TIME...

Charles & Diana

FOR YEARS, THE BRITISH PUBLIC INDULGED, EVEN ENJOYED THE "ACTION MAN" LIFESTYLE OF ITS MONARCH-IN-WAITING. CHARLES DATED A PARADE OF GORGEOUS WOMEN...

...FLEW FIGHTER JETS IN THE ROYAL AIR FORCE...

...AND, OF COURSE, PLAYED PLENTY OF POLO!

ONE IS HAVING A SIMPLY **SMASHING** TIME!

LESS WIDELY KNOWN WAS THAT CHARLES HAD PLANNED TO MARRY THREE DIFFERENT WOMEN. EVERY ONE NIXED HIM.

I SAY, I WONDER... WOULD YOU....?

HEY, I DON'T NEED THE AGGRAVATION!

I'M TERRIBLY SORRY...

SORRY, CHARLIE!

LADY JANE WELLESLEY

AMANDA KNATCHBULL

ANNA WALLACE

HE SETTLED ON **LADY DI**. BUT HE DROPPED HINTS THAT HE WAS **SETTLING**. AT THE ENGAGEMENT PRESS CONFERENCE...

CHARLES, ARE YOU IN LOVE WITH DIANA?

UM, YES-- WHATEVER THAT MAY MEAN!

THERE WERE STRONGER HINTS OF TROUBLE TO COME. A FEW MONTHS EARLIER, A WOMAN WAS SPOTTED BOARDING CHARLES' TRAIN ONE NIGHT-- AND STAYING SEVERAL HOURS!

TEN DAYS LATER, THE STORY HIT THE PAPERS -- IDENTIFYING THE WOMAN AS NONE OTHER THAN THE SUPPOSEDLY VIRGINAL DIANA.

A BIG SCANDAL! BUT IT WASN'T HER.

THE WOMAN'S TRUE IDENTITY WOULD HAVE CAUSED AN EVEN BIGGER SCANDAL. SHE WAS THE PRINCE'S LONGTIME MISTRESS AND TRUE LOVE, A MARRIED WOMAN NAMED CAMILLA PARKER-BOWLES!

BACK THEN, FEW KNEW ABOUT THE PRINCE'S DECADE-LONG FLING WITH CAMILLA, OR ABOUT HIS COOLNESS TOWARD HIS YOUNG WIFE. THE PUBLIC, DELIGHTED WITH THE FAIRY TALE, FELL IN LOVE WITH DIANA.

CHARLES WASN'T ACCUSTOMED TO HIS NEW STATUS AS PUBLIC ICON #2!

NOR WAS HE KEEN TO SURRENDER THE LIFESTYLE OF HIS BACHELOR DAYS, WHICH DIANA FOUND TIRESOME AND ABSURD.

DIANA WAS EVEN MORE ANNOYED WITH CHARLES' DEVOTION TO THE REAL LADY IN HIS LIFE: THE QUEEN!

BARELY OUT OF HER TEEN YEARS, DIANA FELT STIFLED BY THE RIGIDITY OF ROYAL ROUTINE. HER OUTLET: BREAKFAST CEREAL!

SHE DOWNED MOUNDS OF THE STUFF!

SHE DEVELOPED A NASTY CASE OF BULIMIA TO COMPLEMENT HER CEREAL BINGES.

THEN CAME THE NEWS THAT, THE ROYAL FAMILY HOPED, WOULD TURN DIANA'S BLACK MOOD AROUND. SHE WAS PREGNANT.

NATURALLY, ONE IS ABSOLUTELY DELIGHTED...

PREGNANCY DIDN'T DO THE TRICK. AT ONE POINT SHE TUMBLED DOWN SOME STAIRS, LANDING AT THE FEET OF H.R.H. THE QUEEN MOTHER!

DIANA LATER CLAIMED IT WAS A SUICIDE ATTEMPT. IF SO, IT WAS A LAME ONE. SHE WAS UNHURT (AS WAS THE BABY).

THOUGH DELIGHTED TO BE A MOTHER, SHE REMAINED TEMPERAMENTAL. SHORTLY AFTER THE BIRTH, SHE REFUSED TO ATTEND A ROYAL FUNCTION!

I'M TIRED! YOU TRY CARRYING A KID AROUND FOR NINE MONTHS!

THIS--THIS IS UN-ROYAL!!

THEN, AFTER HER CHAIR HAD BEEN DISCREETLY REMOVED TO DISGUISE HER ABSENCE, SHE COMPOUNDED THE FAUX PAS BY SHOWING UP ANYWAY.

HELLO... WHAT ARE YOU ALL STARING AT?

THE QUEEN, ESPECIALLY, WAS SOURED ON HER DAUGHTER-IN-LAW AFTER THE INCIDENT.

THESE ARE THE SORTS OF THINGS THAT THE ROYALS WORRY ABOUT.

BY THE MID 1980s, DESPITE A SECOND CHILD, CHARLES AND DI HAD DRIFTED FAR APART. THEY GAVE UP TRYING TO DISPLAY AFFECTION (ALWAYS A DIFFICULT PROPOSITION FOR THE FAMOUSLY STIFF CHARLES).

DIANA TRIED SUICIDE AGAIN.

THIS IS MY ONLY ESCAPE!

SLEEPO SNOOZE PILLS Queen size

SHE CHANGED HER MIND JUST IN TIME, VOMITING UP THE PILLS SHE'D SWALLOWED.

WHEN HE GOT MARRIED, CHARLES SWORE OFF SLEEPING WITH CAMILLA PARKER-BOWLES. NOW HE RETURNED TO HER.

OH CHARLES! IT'S BEEN SO LONG!

SORRY, MY LOVE! MARRIED LIFE AND ALL THAT...

IN 1986, DIANA FOUND A FRIEND! CHARLES' YOUNGER BROTHER PRINCE ANDREW, DUKE OF YORK, MARRIED A FUN-LOVING GIRL NAMED SARAH FERGUSON. SUCH WAS THE INFLUENCE OF "FERGIE" THAT DIANA WAS ONCE HEARD TO SAY...

COME ON—LET'S GET DRUNK!

WHEN THE PRESS REPORTED THE REMARK, SHE MADE A SPEECH ASSURING THE PUBLIC THAT SHE HAD NO PLANS TO BECOME AN ALCOHOLIC.

THE ANDREW-SARAH MARRIAGE WAS NO BED OF ROSES EITHER. HE SPENT MOST OF IT AT SEA WITH HIS NAVAL UNIT. SHE CAVORTED AROUND LONDON WITH A TEXAS OIL MILLIONAIRE.

THIS HERE'S MAH WOMAN!

THIS HERE'S MY FINANCIAL ADVISOR!

WHILE THE PUBLIC OBSESSED ON CHARLES AND DIANA'S WOES, THE OTHER ROYAL MARRIAGE BLEW UP. IN EARLY 1992, AFTER ANDREW FOUND PHOTOS OF FERGIE AND HER TEXAN ON VACATION, BUCKINGHAM PALACE ANNOUNCED THEIR SEPARATION.

WHAT THE BLOODY HELL..!?

GOOD GOD! THIS CHAP'S SUCKING FERGIE'S TOES! YUCH!!

THE Sun

FERGIE'S BARE-CHESTED BEACH ROMP HORROR!

INSIDE PHWOAR! IT'S BINGO!

EXCLUSIVE PHOTOS—PAGES 2, 3, 4, 5, 7, 8, 10, 15—24, 27, 30

THEN THE ROYAL FAMILY WAS DISGRACED WHEN A TABLOID PUBLISHED TOPLESS PICTURES OF FERGIE ON A BEACH. THE FAMILY OSTRACIZED HER.

BUT 1992 WAS JUST GETTING STARTED! NEXT CAME A BOOK, ORCHESTRATED BY DIANA, THAT PORTRAYED HER AS A MARTYR!

SNIFF THE POOR DEAR! I KNOW JUST HOW SHE FEELS!

MEN ARE BRUTES!

Diana Her True Story

IT REVEALED HER BULIMIA AND SUICIDE ATTEMPTS.

A MONTH LATER, MYSTERIOUSLY, TAPES SURFACED OF A PHONE CALL BETWEEN DIANA AND LIQUOR HEIR JAMES GILBEY. THE TAPES CAPTURED GILBEY UTTERING THE IMMORTAL WORDS...

OH SQUIDGY! I LOVE YOU!

SQUIDGY??!

PUBLIC EVIDENCE OF THE CHARLES-DI RIFT HAD APPEARED EARLIER WHEN DIANA TURNED HER BACK ON HIM AS HE TRIED TO GIVE HER A CEREMONIAL KISS AFTER A POLO MATCH.

?

THE ROYAL FAMILY HOPED A NOVEMBER TOUR OF SOUTH KOREA BY THE COUPLE--THEIR FIRST JOINT TRIP IN A LONG TIME-- WOULD LEAD TO RECONCILIATION.

THE PLAN DIDN'T WORK.

THE BOOK, THE TOUR, THE "SQUIDGY" TAPES — THE FAIRY-TALE MARRIAGE WAS CLEARLY FINISHED. THE QUEEN ASKED PRIME MINISTER JOHN MAJOR TO ANNOUNCE...

THE PRINCE AND PRINCESS OF WALES HAVE DECIDED TO SEPARATE!

1992 WAS SO DISASTROUS THAT IN HER CHRISTMAS ADDRESS, THE QUEEN CALLED IT...

...MY ANNUS HORRIBILIS!

WOT?

I DUNNO... SOMETHING ABOUT PILES?

THE SEPARATION DIDN'T PUT A STOP TO THE SCANDALS. A TAPE OF CHARLES AND CAMILLA SURFACED IN JANUARY, 1993.

I'D LIKE TO COME BACK AS YOUR TAMPAX!

OH... WHAT A WONDERFUL IDEA...

PRETTY EMBARRASSING STUFF-- BUT ALSO THE FIRST PUBLIC CONFIRMATION OF THE PRINCE'S 20-YEAR-LONG AFFAIR.

I WANT TO FEEL MY WAY UP AND DOWN YOU-- AND IN AND OUT!

IN THE NEXT COUPLE OF YEARS IN SEPARATE INTERVIEWS, THEY BOTH ADMITTED...

I HAVE BEEN UNFAITHFUL IN MY MARRIAGE.

THE QUEEN EARLIER BELIEVED THAT DIVORCE THREATENED THE EXISTENCE OF THE MONARCHY. BUT WITH THE MARRIAGE NOW ONE GIANT CONTINUOUS SCANDAL, SHE SAW DIVORCE AS THE ONLY HOPE!

OH, FORGET IT! END THIS THING ALREADY!

YOU SAID THE MAGIC WORDS, MOTHER!

DIANA CALLED IT "THE SADDEST DAY OF MY LIFE." CHARLES CELEBRATED WITH A CHEERFUL PHONE CALL TO CAMILLA.

THE FAIRY TALE ENDED IN AUGUST OF 1996 WHEN THE DIVORCE WENT THROUGH.

BUT DIANA—A CHILD OF DIVORCE HERSELF—REMAINED A DEVOTED MOTHER TO HER TWO BELOVED SONS, WILLIAM AND HARRY, HEIRS TO THE THRONE AFTER CHARLES.

SHE WAS DETERMINED TO GIVE THEM WHAT THEIR **REGALLY ALOOF** FATHER NEVER KNEW— A TASTE OF "NORMAL" LIFE. SHE EVEN TOOK THEM TO M^CDONALD'S—AND MADE THEM WAIT IN LINE LIKE EVERYONE ELSE!

BUT LIFE FOR THE WORLD'S MOST FAMOUS WOMAN COULD NEVER BE NORMAL. PHOTOGRAPHERS SHADOWED DIANA'S EVERY MOVE—

THE PRESS IS FEROCIOUS! ANY SANE PERSON WOULD HAVE LEFT BRITAIN LONG AGO! BUT I CAN'T. I HAVE MY SONS...

VALIANTLY, SHE USED HER STATUS TO CALL ATTENTION TO MANY HUMANITARIAN CAUSES.

WE MUST RID THE WORLD OF THE EVIL OF LAND MINES, WHICH MAIM AND KILL OUR CHILDREN!

SHE BECAME KNOWN AS "THE PEOPLE'S PRINCESS"!

BUT MOSTLY, THE CAMERAS MADE HER LIFE MISERABLE. SHE COULDN'T EVEN VACATION WITH HER CHILDREN IN PEACE.

PLEASE!! GIVE US SOME SPACE!!!

FINALLY, IN AUGUST OF 1997, IT SEEMED DIANA WAS ON THE VERGE OF HAPPINESS. SHE'D FOUND A NEW BEAU: EGYPTIAN PLAYBOY **DODI AL FAYED.**

THE PRESS WENT **WILD!**

JUST AFTER MIDNIGHT, AUGUST 31ST —DIANA AND DODI WERE LEAVING THE RITZ HOTEL IN PARIS. PHOTOGRAPHERS WERE IN HOT PURSUIT.

HAHAA! CATCH ME IF YOU CAN!

THEIR CHAUFFEUR WAS REPORTEDLY **DRUNK!**

ACCORDING TO REPORTS, THE CAR WAS SPEEDING AT OVER 100 mph WHEN IT ENTERED A NARROW TUNNEL AND...

THE FAIRY-TALE PRINCESS — THE QUEEN OF HEARTS—WAS DEAD. THE BRITISH- AND WORLD- PUBLIC ERUPTED IN AN INCREDIBLE SPONTANEOUS OUTPOURING OF GRIEF, AND 1.5 MILLION PEOPLE LINED THE ROUTE OF HER FUNERAL PROCESSION IN LONDON.

THE PAPARAZZI WHO FOLLOWED HER CAUSED FRESH SCANDAL WHEN THEY SNAPPED THE DYING DIANA, WHILE CHARLES AND THE ROYAL FAMILY WERE FORCED BY PUBLIC OPINION TO DISCARD MUCH OF THEIR RIGID ROYAL PROTOCOL. FOLLOWING THE DEATH OF THE PEOPLE'S PRINCESS, BRITAIN COULD WELL BE IN FOR THE BIGGEST SCANDAL YET AS HER MONARCHY CRUMBLES AWAY.

FACTOID BOOKS

O.J.'s FINAL RUN

JUNE 12, 1994.
A COOL EVENING
IN WEST L.A.

OWWWWOOOOOOOO

ON A NORMALLY QUIET STREET, A DOG HOWLS.

A LITTLE AFTER MIDNIGHT, OFFICER ROBERT RISKE RESPONDS TO A CALL ON SOUTH BUNDY DRIVE IN BRENTWOOD. A COUPLE HAS FOUND THE TROUBLED DOG -- AND IT LED THEM TO A TERRIBLE DISCOVERY.

POLICE

OFFICER RISKE RETRACED THE DOG'S STEPS.

OH, BROTHER!

HE TURNED TO HIS RIGHT.

GOD!

A GRUESOME DOUBLE MURDER.

AT THE DEAD MAN'S FEET, RISKE SPOTTED A BLACK CAP, A WHITE ENVELOPE, AND ONE LEATHER GLOVE.

THE HOUSE WAS OPEN. RISKE WENT IN AND NOTICED...

IT'S...IT'S O.J. SIMPSON!

O.J. SIMPSON. FOOTBALL SUPERSTAR. IN THE 60s, HE WAS THE GREATEST RUNNER THE COLLEGE GAME HAD EVER SEEN.

IN THE 70s, AS A PRO, HE SMASHED ALL NFL RUSHING RECORDS. HE WAS THE GREATEST RUNNER EVER.

BLESSED WITH CHARISMA--ACCENTUATED BY A CAREFULLY CRAFTED PUBLIC IMAGE-- O.J. PARLAYED HIS GRIDIRON GREATNESS INTO ALL-AROUND CELEBRITY. HE BUILT A MOVIE CAREER, WITH SUCH FILMS AS *THE TOWERING INFERNO*.

ENDORSEMENTS ROLLED IN. HE STARRED IN A CLASSIC SERIES OF COMMERCIALS FOR HERTZ RENT-A-CAR.

HE WAS NOT ONLY A HUGE STAR, HE WAS OBVIOUSLY BUT SIGNIFICANTLY A HUGE **BLACK** STAR. BUT RACIAL ISSUES DIDN'T INTEREST HIM. HE ONCE DECLARED,...

I'M NOT BLACK! I'M O.J.!!

NOR WAS HE INTERESTED IN ISSUES OF MARITAL FIDELITY. IN 1977, WHILE STILL HITCHED TO HIS HIGH SCHOOL SWEETHEART AND MOTHER OF HIS KIDS, HE MET 18-YEAR-OLD WAITRESS NICOLE BROWN.

HEY, HEY, BABY! WANNA SEE MY HEISMAN?

O.J. RETIRED FROM FOOTBALL AND GOT DIVORCED IN 1979. IN 1985 HE MARRIED NICOLE, WHO WAS PREGNANT WITH THEIR FIRST CHILD.

BUT ALL WAS FAR FROM WELL. ONE NIGHT IN 1985, POLICE WERE CALLED TO O.J.'s BRENTWOOD ESTATE FOR A DOMESTIC DISTURBANCE.

SHE'S MY WIFE AND SHE'S FINE! THERE'S NO TROUBLE HERE!

THE PATROLMAN WHO ANSWERED THE CALL WAS NAMED MARK FUHRMAN.

DO YOU WANT TO FILE A REPORT, MRS. SIMPSON?

N--NO. -'SNIFF!'-

BY 1994, FUHRMAN WAS AN EXPERIENCED HOMICIDE DETECTIVE. A PHONE CALL WOKE HIM AT 1 A.M., JUNE 13.

WE'VE GOT A DOUBLE HOMICIDE. ONE OF THE VICTIMS MIGHT BE O.J. SIMPSON'S WIFE.

OKAY. —YAWN—

THE OTHER WAS RON GOLDMAN, A FRIEND OF NICOLE'S.

FUHRMAN ARRIVED AT 2:10 A.M. HE WAS THE 17TH POLICE OFFICER AT THE MURDER SCENE.

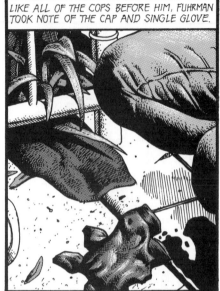

LIKE ALL OF THE COPS BEFORE HIM, FUHRMAN TOOK NOTE OF THE CAP AND SINGLE GLOVE.

HE WAS ALSO SHOWN SPLASHES OF BLOOD LEADING AWAY FROM THE MURDER SCENE.

THE GLOVE IS LEFT-HANDED, SO IT LOOKS LIKE THE KILLER'S LEFT HAND WAS CUT IN THE STRUGGLE.

DETECTIVES TOM LANGE AND PHIL VANNATTER SHOWED UP, ASSIGNED TO TAKE CHARGE OF THE CASE.

HEADQUARTERS WANTS O.J. NOTIFIED BEFORE THE MEDIA GETS THE STORY, THEY DON'T WANT ANOTHER BELUSHI SITUATION.

ANYBODY KNOW WHERE O.J. LIVES?

I WAS THERE ONCE YEARS AGO. I THINK I CAN FIND IT.

THINGS WERE AMISS AT THE SIMPSON HOMESTEAD.

HEY, THERE'S BLOOD ON THIS VEHICLE!

SOMEONE COULD BE HURT IN THE HOUSE! WE'D BETTER GO IN!

FINDING THE MAIN HOUSE EMPTY, THEY CHECKED THE GUEST COTTAGES OUT BACK. THERE FUHRMAN ENCOUNTERED BRIAN "KATO" KAELIN.

NOTICE ANYTHING UNUSUAL TONIGHT?

AS A MATTER OF FACT...

"...I WAS ON THE PHONE AT ABOUT 10:45 WHEN I HEARD A LOUD THUMP!"

THUMP

YIPES! AN EARTHQUAKE!

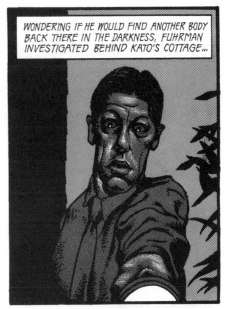

WONDERING IF HE WOULD FIND ANOTHER BODY BACK THERE IN THE DARKNESS, FUHRMAN INVESTIGATED BEHIND KATO'S COTTAGE...

...WHERE HE FOUND...

WHAT THE...??!!

...A BLOODY GLOVE!

THINGS WEREN'T LOOKING GOOD FOR O.J.; IN ADDITION TO THE BLOODY GLOVE IN HIS BACK YARD, THERE WERE BLOOD DROPS LEADING AWAY FROM THE MURDERS, ON HIS BRONCO, AND LASTLY, IN THE ENTRY-WAY TO HIS HOUSE -- A TRAIL OF BLOOD.

THAT'S IT. SEAL OFF THE HOUSE!

THE DETECTIVES DISCOVERED THAT O.J. HAD TAKEN A REDEYE FLIGHT TO CHICAGO. THEY CALLED HIM AT HIS HOTEL.

OH MY GOD! NICOLE IS KILLED? OH MY GOD! SHE'S DEAD?

THE GRIDIRON GREAT'S RESPONSE TROUBLED DETECTIVE RON PHILIPS...

FUNNY. I'VE TOLD HUNDREDS OF PEOPLE THEIR LOVED ONES HAVE BEEN KILLED. THEY ALWAYS ASK WHAT HAPPENED. BUT O.J. NEVER ASKED.

AROUND NOON, SIMPSON ARRIVED BACK AT HIS BRENTWOOD COMPOUND, NOW CRAWLING WITH POLICE.

O.J., A BLOOD TRAIL LED FROM THE MURDER SCENE TO YOUR HOUSE.

OH, MAN! OH, MAN! OH, MAN!

THERE WAS SOMETHING ELSE. O.J. HAD A DEEP GASH ON HIS MIDDLE FINGER-- HIS *LEFT* MIDDLE FINGER.

OH, MAN! OH, MAN!

O.J. AGREED TO GO DOWN TO THE STATION FOR QUESTIONING.

HOW DID YOU GET THE INJURY ON YOUR HAND?

I DON'T KNOW. I RECALL BLEEDING AT MY HOUSE. IT WAS NO BIG DEAL. I BLEED ALL THE TIME.

FOR SOME REASON--THOUGH O.J. *ADMITTED* BLEEDING AT THE TIME HIS WIFE WAS BEING KILLED (QUITE A COINCIDENCE!) AND HAD *NO EXPLANATION* FOR HOW HE'D BEEN CUT--THE DETECTIVES LET HIM GO AFTER *A HALF HOUR.* NOT MUCH OF AN INTERROGATION.

LATER, L.A. DISTRICT ATTORNEY GIL GARCETTI MADE A SOLEMN ANNOUNCEMENT...

MR. SIMPSON IS OUR SUSPECT. HE HAS 48 HOURS TO TURN HIMSELF IN.

WHY A SUSPECTED DOUBLE MURDERER WOULD BE ALLOWED TWO DAYS TO LOUNGE AROUND WAS NOT EXPLAINED.

NOT SURPRISINGLY, WHEN FRIDAY MORNING CAME...

I WONDER WHERE O.J. IS.

BEATS ME. HE SAID HE'D BE HERE.

BY NOW, THE MEDIA--FASCINATED BY THE SPECTACLE OF A BELOVED STAR TURNED MURDER SUSPECT--WERE SATURATING THE AIRWAVES WITH COVERAGE OF...

O.J.!

O.J.!

O.J.!

FINALLY, THE POLICE TRACKED O.J. TO THE MANSION OF HIS BEST FRIEND, ROBERT KARDASHIAN. O.J.'S CELEBRITY LAWYER ROBERT SHAPIRO WAS THERE.

HEH HEH. O.J. SEEMS TO HAVE -- WELL, TO MAKE A LONG STORY SHORT-- *DISAPPEARED!*

AT ABOUT 6:30 P.M., O.J. WAS SPOTTED. HE WAS IN A BRONCO DRIVEN BY HIS LONGTIME FRIEND AND FORMER TEAMMATE AL COWLINGS ON A FREEWAY ABOUT 60 MILES FROM HIS HOME. THE POLICE KEPT THEIR DISTANCE BECAUSE...

...O.J. WAS IN THE BACK SEAT THREATENING TO KILL HIMSELF.

I JUST WANT TO *LEAVE!* I WANT TO *GO WITH NICOLE!*

HE'D EVEN LEFT A SELF-PITYING "SUICIDE" NOTE WHICH KARDASHIAN READ TO THE MEDIA AFTER SIMPSON FLED.

"AT TIMES I'VE FELT LIKE A BATTERED HUSBAND OR BOYFRIEND. BUT I LOVED HER..."

THE "SLOW SPEED CHASE" (AS IT CAME TO BE KNOWN) WAS AN INSTANT RATINGS HIT, BROADCAST ON ALL THE NETWORKS AND, THANKS TO CNN, AROUND THE WORLD.

IN A GHOULISH SPECTACLE, THE BRONCO ATTRACTED CHEERING CROWDS, DRAWN BY THE SATURATION TV COVERAGE -- AS IF O.J.'s MACABRE DRIVE WERE JUST ANOTHER FOOTBALL GAME.

We ♡ U O.J.!

SAVE THE JUICE!

O.J.'s GETAWAY WAS AN EERIE RE-MINDER OF NEW YEAR'S, 1989, WHEN POLICE, FOR THE NINTH TIME, RE-SPONDED TO A DOMESTIC VIOLENCE CALL AT HIS HOME.

THIS IS A FAMILY MATTER! WHY ARE YOU ARRESTING ME?

BUT WHEN THE COP GAVE O.J. TIME TO CHANGE CLOTHES, "THE JUICE" TOOK OFF.

HEY!

POLICE GAVE CHASE, BUT JUST LIKE ON THE FOOTBALL FIELD, O.J. OUTRAN THEM.

NOT SO IN 1994. O.J. GAVE UP ON KILLING HIMSELF AND SURRENDERED AT HIS HOME, APOLOGIZING TO THE POLICE.

I'M SORRY FOR CAUSING YOU GUYS SO MUCH TROUBLE.

LITTLE OF THE EVIDENCE AGAINST O.J. HAD BEEN REVEALED, SO THE PUBLIC DIDN'T KNOW WHAT TO MAKE OF THE SCANDAL. MYTH-MAKING GOT UNDERWAY FAST.

HE'S AN AMERICAN HERO!

...A HERO!

O.J.'s *MY* HERO!

...A HERO TO THE KIDS!

O.J. BRASHLY DETERMINED TO HANG ON TO HIS "HEROISM" IN THE FACE OF DISGRACE. BY JULY 22 HE'D PULLED HIMSELF TOGETHER AND PLEADED...

ABSOLUTELY 100% *NOT GUILTY!*

BUT THE SCANDAL WAS JUST GETTING STARTED.

ABSOLUTELY ONE HUNDRED PERCENT NOT GUILTY!

DESPITE HIS DEFIANT DECLARATION OF INNOCENCE, THERE WAS A MOUNTAIN OF EVIDENCE AGAINST O.J. SIMPSON. BUT INSTEAD OF AN OPEN-AND-SHUT CASE, HIS TRIAL TURNED INTO...

CIRQUE du O.J.

SIMPSON HIRED A TEAM THAT FEATURED NOT ONE, BUT FOUR LAWYERS FAMOUS FOR THEIR HIGH-PROFILE CASES AND CELEBRITY CLIENTS:

ROBERT SHAPIRO

JOHNNY COCHRAN

ALAN DERSHOWITZ

F. LEE BAILEY

THEY SQUARED OFF AGAINST A PROSECUTION TEAM SPEARHEADED BY DEPUTY DISTRICT ATTORNEYS MARCIA CLARK AND CHRISTOPHER DARDEN.

THE MAN IN CHARGE: JUDGE LANCE ITO.

HEY! I'M ON TV!!

EASILY SWAYED BY THE LAWYERS, ITO LET THEM BOMBARD PROSPECTIVE JURORS WITH A 302-QUESTION FORM.

THE PROSECUTION ASSERTED THAT O.J. BEAT NICOLE REPEATEDLY AND ULTIMATELY KILLED HER. NICOLE TOLD HER MOTHER...

HE'S FOLLOWING ME AGAIN, MOMMY. I'M SCARED! HE'S GOING TO KILL ME!

THE DEFENSE STRATEGY, WHICH SHAPIRO LEAKED TO JEFFREY TOOBIN OF THE NEW YORKER MAGAZINE, HAD LITTLE TO DO WITH THE FACTS OF THE CASE.

WE'RE GONNA SAY THAT FUHRMAN PLANTED THAT GLOVE. HE'S A BAD COP, A RACIST COP.

THE GLOVE, FOUND BY FUHRMAN ON SIMPSON'S PROPERTY, WAS FAR FROM THE ONLY EVIDENCE AGAINST O.J., BUT IT WAS EXTREMELY DAMNING.

I'LL BE A SON OF A...

IT HAD BLOOD FROM NICOLE, RON GOLDMAN, AND O.J., FIBER FROM RON'S SHIRT, STRANDS OF NICOLE'S HAIR, AND FIBER FROM O.J.'S BRONCO. ALONE, IT CONVICTED O.J. SIMPSON.

BUT *PLANTED*--? THE SCENARIO SEEMED PATENTLY ABSURD.

THERE'S GOTTA BE SOMETHING HERE I CAN USE TO *FRAME O.J.!*

FUHRMAN WAS THE 17TH OFFICER AT THE MURDER SCENE.

NO ONE SAW MORE THAN ONE GLOVE THERE. BUT SUPPOSEDLY--

WHAT A STROKE OF LUCK! A SECOND GLOVE THAT *NOBODY* NOTICED!

NOW I'LL JUST PLANT THIS ON O.J.'S PROPERTY... BUT WAIT! FOR ALL I KNOW, O.J. HAS AN IRONCLAD ALIBI! HE COULD EVEN BE OUT OF THE COUNTRY!

THEN IT WOULD BE OBVIOUS THAT I *PLANTED* EVIDENCE! I COULD GO TO *JAIL*. IN FACT, BECAUSE THIS IS A HOMICIDE CASE, I COULD GET THE *GAS CHAMBER!*

AAAAA, WHAT THE HECK! IT'S *WORTH THE RISK TO FRAME O.J.!*

NEEDLESS TO SAY, THE PLANTED-GLOVE "THEORY" WAS, SHALL WE SAY, IMPLAUSIBLE.

NOT TO MENTION *IMPOSSIBLE*. FUHRMAN WAS NEVER ALONE AROUND ANY OF THE EVIDENCE.

BUT SIMPSON'S LAWYERS DID HAVE SOME EVIDENCE THAT FUHRMAN WAS A BIGOT. A WOMAN CLAIMED THAT ABOUT 10 YEARS EARLIER HE'D SAID...

I'D LIKE TO GET ALL THE *NIGGERS* TOGETHER AND *BURN THEM!*

DARDEN, THE ONLY BLACK PROSECUTOR, MADE AN EMOTIONAL PLEA FOR ITO TO DISALLOW USE OF "THE N WORD" IN FRONT OF THE MOSTLY-BLACK JURY...

IT'S A DIRTY, FILTHY WORD. IT WILL BLIND THIS JURY. IT WILL *AFFECT THEIR JUDGMENT.*

DARDEN'S PLEA PRACTICALLY INVITED A GRANDSTANDING FLOURISH FROM COCHRAN...

I AM *ASHAMED* THAT MR. DARDEN WOULD ALLOW HIMSELF TO BECOME AN *APOLOGIST* FOR MARK FUHRMAN.

...WHICH WORKED ON ITO.

SURE, I'LL ALLOW IT! WHY NOT? WE'RE ON *TV!*

F. LEE BAILEY CROSS-EXAMINED FUHRMAN AND MILKED THE N WORD FOR ALL IT WAS WORTH.

HAVE YOU, DETECTIVE FUHRMAN, AT ANY TIME IN THE PAST 10 YEARS ADDRESSED A BLACK PERSON AS A...

...*NIGGER?!*

TO WHICH FUHRMAN COOLLY ANSWERED...

NOT THAT I RECALL, NO.

SO MUCH FOR A TRIAL BASED ON THE EVIDENCE.

IN A CITY WHERE THE POLICE BEATING OF RODNEY KING WAS STILL FRESH IN THE PUBLIC MIND, SIMPSON'S LAWYERS TURNED THIS RELATIVELY SIMPLE MURDER TRIAL INTO A REFERENDUM ON LAPD RACISM.

THE O.J. TRIAL DOMINATED THE AIRWAVES, WITH SHOWS SUCH AS *LARRY KING LIVE* GOING ALMOST 100% O.J.. COUNTLESS COMMENTATORS WERE HAPPY TO ENTERTAIN VIRTUALLY ANY THEORY.

SECOND KILLER!

COLOMBIAN DRUG DEALERS!

BLAH BLAH BLAH!

FORGED EVIDENCE!

THE PROSECUTORS OFTEN MADE THINGS EASY FOR THE DEFENSE. DARDEN HAD AN INSPIRATION.

LET'S HAVE O.J. TRY ON THE GLOVES!

THE JUICE TOOK THE BALL AND RAN WITH IT.

UNNNGGH! GRRNNT! RRRRGGH! THEY DON'T FIT!

COCHRAN SEIZED THAT OPPORTUNITY, TOO. HE COINED A LITTLE SLOGAN FOR THE JURORS.

IF IT DOESN'T FIT, YOU MUST ACQUIT!

BUT STILL THE FACT REMAINED THAT O.J.'S BLOOD WAS ON THE GLOVE...AND AT THE MURDER SCENE...AND IN HIS HOUSE... IT SEEMED O.J.'S BLOOD WAS EVERYWHERE!

HEH HEH. OOPS.

THE LAWYERS CAME UP WITH AN ANSWER THAT, TO MOST OBSERVERS, MAY HAVE INDICATED THAT THEY'D BEEN SMOKING SOMETHING.

IT WAS ALL A BIG CONSPIRACY, MAN!

BLOOD SMEARS, LATER DETERMINED TO BE SIMPSON'S BLOOD, WERE FOUND ON THE BACK GATE TO NICOLE'S TOWNHOUSE.

CLEAR EVIDENCE THAT SIMPSON WAS THE KILLER.

SEVERAL POLICE TESTIFIED THAT THEY SAW THE BLOOD ON THE GATE THE NIGHT OF THE MURDERS.

YEP. I SAW IT.

ME TOO.

IT WAS BLOOD ALL RIGHT.

THE DEFENSE NEVER CHALLENGED THEIR TESTIMONY, BUT STILL CLAIMED...

THE POLICE PLANTED THAT BLOOD!

COCHRAN PINNED IT ALL ON LEAD DETECTIVE PHILIP VANNATTER AND, OF COURSE, FUHRMAN. HE DUBBED THEM...

THE TWIN DEVILS OF DECEPTION!

VANNATTER HAD NEVER MET FUHRMAN BEFORE. BUT ACCORDING TO COCHRAN'S CONSPIRACY THEORY, THE TWO INSTANTLY CONCOCTED A SINISTER PLOT.

NICE TO MEET YA! WANNA JOIN MY *CONSPIRACY?*

SURE!

COCHRAN CLAIMED THAT VANNATTER "SPRINKLED BLOOD" ON SIMPSON'S PROPERTY FROM A SAMPLE SIMPSON GAVE VOLUNTARILY

THEY'LL NEVER CATCH ME!

SPRINKLE SPRINKLE

VANNATTER DID BRING THE SAMPLE TO SIMPSON'S HOUSE WHERE HE HANDED IT IMMEDIATELY TO AN LAPD CRIMINALIST-- UNDER THE WATCHFUL EYE OF SWARMING MEDIA.

GUYS, THIS BLOOD-SPRINKLING IS *OFF THE RECORD!*

EVENTUALLY, THE DEFENSE GOT THE EVIDENCE THEY'D BEEN WAITING FOR! NOT A SIMPSON ALIBI OR PROOF OF A "REAL KILLER." INSTEAD THEY FOUND TAPE RECORDINGS OF MARK FUHRMAN SAYING...

NIGGER! NIGGER! NIGGER! NIGGER! NI...

AND SO ON. ALL IN ALL, FUHRMAN USED THE HATED WORD 41 TIMES.

FUHRMAN MADE THE TAPES WHILE COLLABORATING ON A SCREENPLAY. HE SAID HE WAS "IN CHARACTER" THE WHOLE TIME, TRYING TO BE THE TOUGH, CYNICAL COP HOLLYWOOD LOVES.

DOESN'T *EVERYONE* IN L.A. HAVE A SCREENPLAY?

THE LAST TAPE OF FUHRMAN UTTERING "N" WAS IN 1988. BUT THAT WAS "IN THE LAST 10 YEARS," SO WHEN HE WAS RECALLED AS A WITNESS HE SAID...

I WISH TO ASSERT MY FIFTH AMENDMENT PRIVILEGE.

THAT PRETTY MUCH DID IT. AFTER A YEARLONG TRIAL, THE JURY DELIBERATED FOR JUST FOUR HOURS.

I GUESS THAT COVERS EVERYTHING! WE'RE OUTTA HERE!

THE JURY'S VERDICT:

NOT GUILTY!

NOT ALL OF O.J.'s LAWYERS WERE HAPPY. ROBERT SHAPIRO QUICKLY DECLARED...

WE PLAYED THE RACE CARD AND DEALT IT FROM THE *BOTTOM* OF THE DECK.

OF COURSE, IT WAS HIS IDEA IN THE FIRST PLACE.

THE MEDIA SEEMED TO CONFIRM THE RACIAL DIVIDE, CONTRASTING THE REACTION OF AFRICAN-AMERICANS TO THE VERDICT...

ALL RIGHT! GO O.J.! YEAH!

...WITH THE WHITE RESPONSE.

YOU'VE GOT TO BE KIDDING!

HOW COULD THE JURY HAVE REACHED THIS ONCE-UNTHINKABLE VERDICT? THE JURORS ATTEMPTED TO EXPLAIN THEMSELVES.

HOW DO YOU EXPLAIN AWAY O.J.'s BLOOD AT THE MURDER SCENE, FOUND HOURS BEFORE HIS BLOOD SAMPLE WAS TAKEN?

WE CAN'T EXPLAIN IT AWAY. THAT WAS NOT ONE OF THE ISSUES.

SORRY. IF YOUR BLOOD'S AT A MURDER SCENE AND YOU'RE NOT A VICTIM-- YOU'RE THE KILLER! IT'S AN ISSUE.

ANOTHER JUROR ACTUALLY SAID...

IF THE CUT ON O.J.'s HAND WAS REALLY BAD, HIS BLOOD SHOULD HAVE BEEN ON THE GLOVE. BUT IT WASN'T!

WHAT TRIAL WAS SHE WATCHING? (IT WAS.)

AS FOR O.J. ...

I VOW TO DEVOTE MY LIFE TO FINDING THE *REAL KILLERS!* ...*FORE!*

THE CIRCUS CONTINUED AS NEARLY EVERYONE REMOTELY CONNECTED TO THE CASE WROTE A BOOK.

JOHNNY COCHRAN, AUDACIOUSLY, TITLED HIS BOOK *JOURNEY TO JUSTICE.*

WHEN THE BROWN AND GOLDMAN FAMILIES SUED O.J. FOR "WRONGFUL DEATH," THAT JURY FOUND O.J. "LIABLE" AND HIT HIM WITH A STAGGERING $33.5 MILLION IN DAMAGES.

THE KILLER OF RON AND NICOLE REMAINS AT LARGE.

CHAPTER THREE

POLITICS AS USUAL

We've seen how the twin lusts for fame and social status have their little drawbacks. But the lust for *power* may be even more fertile ground for corruption—and hence, scandal. No wonder then that the political world provides some of our tawdriest tales. What could be more distasteful than Ted Kennedy's pursuit of self-justification after leaving ill-fated Mary Jo Kopechne trapped in a submerged Oldsmobile? How about Richard Nixon's paranoia pushing the U.S. republic to the breaking point? Or Ronald Reagan, taking a nap as his underlings set up their own secret government? Most of the political scandals in this section, however, deal with matters of far less gravity. Some have to do with nothing more than politicians who can't keep their pants zipped and their bottles corked. But when you have to answer to the voters, sleaze doesn't sell.

SUDDENLY THE TAX CODE WASN'T AS MUCH FUN. MILLS SHOWED UP AT A STRIP JOINT CALLED THE SILVER SLIPPER, NO LONGER SHY ABOUT ATTRACTING ATTENTION.

I'M CONGRESSMAN WILBUR MILLS AND THE DRINKS ARE ON ME!

HE TOOK A SHINE TO ONE "DANCER," ANNABELLA BATTISTELLA, AKA FANNE FOXE, "THE ARGENTINE FIRECRACKER."

ANNA STOPPED DANCING, BUT RETURNED TO THE CLUB OFTEN AS MILLS' DATE. HE ONCE SPENT $1,700 IN AN EVENING THERE.

ANOTHER BOTTLE OF DOM PERIGNON FOR US AND ANOTHER ROUND FOR ALL MY FRIENDS!

IT ALL FELL APART FOR MILLS IN THE EARLY MORNING HOURS OF OCT. 7, 1974, WHEN HIS CAR WAS PULLED OVER BY WASHINGTON, D.C. POLICE.

THEY IMMEDIATELY NOTICED THAT FANNE HAD TWO BLACK EYES AND WILBUR'S EYEGLASSES HAD BEEN SMASHED.

WITHOUT WARNING, FANNE SUDDENLY LEAPT OUT OF THE CAR--

ANNA, GET BACK HERE!

GOTTA GET AWAY!

-- AND FELL INTO THE POTOMAC RIVER.

SPLASH

SHE WAS RESCUED. MILLS' CAREER SANK.

ONCE WASHINGTON'S LEAST LIKELY CANDIDATE FOR A SEX SCANDAL, MILLS BLAMED HIS DOWNFALL ON ALCOHOLISM.

I, ER, SHOULDN'T DRINK CHAMPAGNE. IT GOES TO MY HEAD QUICKLY.

THE $106,000 IN ILLEGAL CAMPAIGN FUNDS HE'D COLLECTED WAS ANOTHER STORY.

WE DID DAMN WELL BY EACH OTHER, DIDN'T WE, WILBUR? HAVE A NICE RETIREMENT!

FANNE WENT BACK TO STRIPPING, AND MILLS FLEW UP TO BOSTON TO CATCH HER ACT.

NEVER ONE FOR COMEDY, HE RETIRED A LAUGHINGSTOCK. HE DIED IN 1992.

the proFumo Affair

THE SCANDAL THAT SHOOK THE BRITISH GOVERNMENT BEGAN IN SUITABLY SORDID FASHION.

DEC. 14, 1962, ON THE STREET OUTSIDE A LONDON FLAT ...

CHRISTINE! CHRISTINE!

MANDY RICE-DAVIES ANSWERED THE CALLER--BUT IT WAS HER ROOMMATE, CHRISTINE KEELER, HE WANTED TO SEE...

CHRISTINE'S NOT 'ERE!

I KNOW YOU IN DERE, CHRISTINE!

'E'S NOT GOING AWAY, CHRISTINE. YOU'D BETTER SPEAK TO 'IM.

CHRISTINE! WHY YOU DO DIS TO ME?

JOHNNY, PLEASE GO-- OH, GOD!

BLAM BLAM BLAM

YOU BITCH!!!!

BRITISH WAR MINISTER JOHN PROFUMO DIDN'T HEAR THOSE SHOTS AS THEY FLEW PAST CHRISTINE KEELER'S HEAD, BUT HE WOULD FEEL THEM. THE INCIDENT TOOK PLACE AT THE HOME OF AN ACQUAINTANCE, SOCIETY DOCTOR STEPHEN WARD. AND...

TERRIBLY SORRY TO TROUBLE YOU, MINISTER, BUT THEY'RE LINKING YOU TO THE SHOWGIRL WHO WAS SHOT AT, MISS KEELER.

I SAY! THAT'S RIDICULOUS!

BUT IT WASN'T. THE CONSERVATIVE WAR MINISTER HAD, IN FACT, CARRIED ON AN AFFAIR WITH THE PROMISCUOUS SHOWGIRL.

AND THE STORY ONLY GOT WORSE.

AT THE CENTER OF THE SCANDAL WAS STEPHEN WARD, THE SOCIETY OSTEOPATH WHO MANIPULATED THE BONES OF BRITAIN'S WEALTHY AND FAMOUS.

READY FOR YOUR RE-ALIGNMENT, DEAR?

OH, YESS!

WARD, HOWEVER, CONSIDERED HIS TRUE OCCUPATION TO BE HAVING A GOOD TIME. HE THREW CONSTANT PARTIES. YOUNG WOMEN ALWAYS LIVED AT HIS FLAT.

WARD WAS ALSO A CONFIRMED SOCIAL CLIMBER. A PATIENT, LORD ASTOR, GRANTED WARD THE "COTTAGE" ON HIS VAST ESTATE.

A POUND PER YEAR, OLD BOY, AND SHE'S YOURS!

SMASHING!

WARD MET CHRISTINE KEELER AT THE CLUB WHERE SHE "DANCED." HE TOOK HER UNDER HIS WING.

ON JULY 8, 1961 -- THE HOTTEST DAY OF THE YEAR -- WARD HAD A PARTY AT ASTOR'S COTTAGE. ASTOR ALSO HELD A PARTY AT THE MAIN HOUSE. PROFUMO ATTENDED ASTOR'S FUNCTION, WHILE CHRISTINE TURNED UP AT WARD'S SOMEWHAT WILDER SOIREE. THEY CROSSED PATHS AT THE POOL.

I SAY!

OOOOO!

ALSO AT WARD'S PARTY WAS YEGNEVY IVANOV -- A SOVIET DIPLOMAT AND, UNBEKNOWNST TO THE PARTYGOERS, A SPY.

CHRISTINE ENTERTAINED THEM BOTH AT WARD'S FLAT.

I SAY, CHRISTINE! DID I HEAR VOICES?

NO, JACK! WHAT EVER MAKES YOU SAY SUCH A THING?

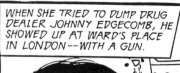

CHRISTINE'S SEX LIFE WAS ALWAYS COMPLICATED. AFTER A MONTH-LONG FLING WITH PROFUMO, SHE TOOK UP WITH TWO WEST INDIAN DRUG DEALERS WHO FOUGHT OVER HER.

WHEN SHE TRIED TO DUMP DRUG DEALER JOHNNY EDGECOMB, HE SHOWED UP AT WARD'S PLACE IN LONDON--WITH A GUN.

BLAM BLAM

EEEEEE!

THE STORY HIT THE TABLOIDS. CHRISTINE FLED FOR SPAIN. BUT NOT BEFORE CONFIDING IN FRIENDS...

IVANOV ASKED ME TO GET NUCLEAR SECRETS FROM JACK PROFUMO!

EDGECOMB WENT ON TRIAL. BUT ONE CRUCIAL WITNESS WAS MISSING.

WHERE IS MISS KEELER?

RUMOR HAD IT THAT PROFUMO HAD ARRANGED FOR CHRISTINE'S FLIGHT. HE MADE A STATEMENT TO PARLIAMENT.

I HAVE NOTHING TO DO WITH MISS KEELER'S ABSENCE AND THERE WAS NO IMPROPRIETY IN MY ACQUAINTANCE WITH HER.

CHRISTINE TURNED UP IN SPAIN.

I'M FRIGHTFULLY SURPRISED AT ALL THE FUSS!

SUDDENLY, PROFUMO-- ONCE A PROSPECT FOR PRIME MINISTER-- RESIGNED.

UM, THAT THING I SAID ABOUT "NO IMPROPRIETY." WELL, ER, IT WASN'T PRECISELY-- HOW SHOULD I PUT THIS ?-- TRUE.

CHRISTINE SOLD HER MEMOIRS TO A TABLOID, REVEALING HER DUAL AFFAIR WITH PROFUMO AND THE SPY IVANOV, WHOM SHE DESCRIBED AS...

...A BIG HUGGY BEAR OF A MAN!

COR BLIMEY!

THE OUT-OF-CONTROL RUMOR MILL HAD CHRISTINE DISPENSING HER FAVORS TO A PARADE OF PROMINENT MEN.

NEXT!

NEWS REPORTS TOLD OF UPPER-CLASS DEBAUCHERY, INCLUDING ONE DINNER PARTY WHERE THE "WAITER" WAS SAID TO BE A MAN "ON EXTREMELY FRIENDLY TERMS WITH THE QUEEN."

HIT HARD BY THE SCANDAL, THE CONSERVATIVE GOVERNMENT NEEDED A SCAPEGOAT. IT FOUND ONE IN STEPHEN WARD.

BUT I'VE TOLD ALL I KNOW TO BRITISH INTELLIGENCE!

HE WAS CHARGED-- FALSELY--WITH PIMPING. THE GOVERNMENT INQUISITOR, LORD DENNING, BLAMED THE WHOLE SCANDAL ON HIM.

...IMMORAL, WICKED, THE EMBODIMENT OF EVIL...

THE DISGRACE WAS TOO MUCH FOR WARD TO BEAR.

IT'S BETTER THIS WAY-- FOR EVERYONE.

HE DOWNED A HANDFUL OF SLEEPING PILLS AND NEVER WOKE UP.

ALMOST IMMEDIATELY, FALTERING PRIME MINISTER HAROLD MACMILLAN WENT ON TV TO ANNOUNCE HIS "COMEBACK."

BEING PRIME MINISTER IS SOMETIMES TOUGH, BUT IT'S A WON- DERFUL JOB!

HE RESIGNED A FEW MONTHS LATER.

LORD DENNING'S REPORT WHITEWASHED EVERYTHING.

IT'S ALL WARD'S FAULT, REALLY. HE WAS BOTH A PERVERT AND A COMMUNIST.

DENNING INQUIRY

IN A BITTER IRONY, 20 YEARS LATER, BRITISH INTELLIGENCE ADMITTED WARD WAS ITS AGENT IN A PLOT TO TRAP IVANOV.

WE FELT RATHER SORRY FOR THE POOR CHAP AT THE END OF THE DAY.

CHRISTINE TRAVERSED A STORMY SERIES OF RELATIONSHIPS. BY THE '80s SHE WAS NEARLY BROKE AND LIVING IN A COUNCIL FLAT. HER MEMORY OF THE SCANDAL--?

IT WAS SO SILLY! SILLY STEPHEN! SILLY PROFUMO! SILLY ME!

X-RATED CONGRESS

WASHINGTON, D.C., 1975.

WOW! OUR NATION'S CAPITAL! WHAT A PLACE FOR A 25-YEAR-OLD TEXAS GIRL LIKE ME!

THE NEW GIRL LEARNED THE LESSONS OF CAPITOL HILL QUICKLY.

AND WHAT'S YOUR NAME, SWEETHEART?

UH, RITA, SIR.

WELL, RITA, I'M A UNITED STATES CONGRESSMAN. HOW'D YOU LIKE TO GO TO THE VIRGIN ISLANDS WITH ME? WE'LL LIE NUDE IN THE SAND ALL DAY AND MAKE LOVE ALL NIGHT.

THIS GUY'S A CREEP-OLA!

A YEAR LATER, RITA CARPENTER AND JOHN JENRETTE WED IN A SMALL BUT ROMANTIC CEREMONY.

DO YOU, JOHN, TAKE RITA TO BE...

BEEP BEEP

HOLD ON! THAT'S MY BEEPER!

THEIR WEDDING NIGHT WAS EVEN MORE ROMANTIC.

MY CRONIES IN SOUTH CAROLINA WANT TO HEAR ABOUT MY WEDDING, SO I'M OUTTA HERE! HAVE A NICE NIGHT!

AND THEIR MARRIAGE MORE MAGICAL STILL.

WHO THE @#$% IS THAT?!

-HIC- OH. HI, HONEY.

CONGRESSMAN JENRETTE HAD A REPUTATION TO UPHOLD-- A REPUTATION AS A LIQUORED-UP SLEAZEBAG. HIS AFFAIRS WERE TOO NUMEROUS TO COUNT.

RITA, FOR HER PART, GOT NOTICED AS ONE OF WASHINGTON'S MOST PRIZED TROPHY WIVES.

HEY HEY, BABY! WANNA SIT ON MY COMMITTEE?

WHEN JOHN GOT CAUGHT BY THE FBI IN THE "ABSCAM" BRIBERY SCANDAL, HOWEVER, THEIR WORLD CAME CRUMBLING DOWN.

RITA TOOK DECISIVE ACTION. SHE POSED NUDE IN *PLAYBOY.*

HEF PROMISED ME TWICE WHAT BO DEREK GOT! I'M ONLY DOING IT TO RAISE MONEY FOR JOHN'S DEFENSE.

HER NUDE PICTURES SCANDALIZED WASHINGTON-- BUT NOT AS MUCH AS HER TELL-ALL REVELATIONS, INCLUDING HER STORY OF HOW SHE AND JOHN ONCE HAD SEX ON THE CAPITOL STEPS.

THIS IS WHAT I CALL THE PURSUIT OF HAPPINESS!

SHE ALSO TOLD OF WILD SEX ORGIES AMONG THE WASHINGTON ELITE, INCLUDING ONE WHERE A PROMINENT LEGISLATIVE AIDE TRIED TO FORCE HIMSELF ON HER WITH THE HELP OF AMYL NITRATE.

JOHN! FOR GOD'S SAKE WAKE UP AND GET THIS CREEP OFFA ME!

SLOBBER DROOL SLURP

SSSSNORE!

SHE ALSO SPILLED THE BEANS ABOUT THOSE "FISHING TRIPS" THAT JOHN AND HIS FELLOW CONGRESSMEN LOVED SO MUCH.

CATCH ANYTHING, JENRETTE?

I'M WORKIN' ON IT! HA HA HA!

RITA SHOCKED THE NATION WITH HER PORTRAIT OF CONGRESS AS "A WORLD OF THIRSTS THAT CAN'T BE QUENCHED."

THE DRUG HABITS, DRINKING PROBLEMS, MISTRESSES, AND BROKEN HOMES ATTEST TO THAT.

AFTER RITA DID IT, OTHER "WOMEN OF WASHINGTON" COULDN'T WAIT TO GET THEIR CLOTHES OFF FOR *PLAYBOY'S* CAMERAS. YOUNG LOBBYIST PAULA PARKINSON, FOR EXAMPLE.

RRRRRIP

I OWN THE WORLD LAND SPEED RECORD FOR GETTING NAKED.

SOON AFTER PAULA'S *PLAYBOY* APPEARANCE, A NEWSPAPER REVEALED HER AFFAIR WITH REPUBLICAN CONGRESSMAN TOM EVANS-- IMPLYING THAT EVANS HAD SWAPPED HIS VOTE FOR SEX.

SO HOW 'BOUT VOTIN' AGAINST THAT CROP INSURANCE BILL, BIG BOY?

GULP!

SHAMELESSLY, PARKINSON *OFFERED* TO MAKE VIDEOTAPES OF HERSELF IN BED WITH VARIOUS CONGRESSMEN. BOTH *PLAYBOY* AND *PENTHOUSE* NIXED HER.

I DON'T UNDERSTAND WHY NO ONE WANTS TO WATCH ME HAVE SEX WITH PAUNCHY MIDDLE-AGED POLITICIANS.

STRANGELY, PARKINSON'S NAME CAME UP AGAIN IN THE 1988 PRESIDENTIAL CAMPAIGN, LINKED TO VICE-PRESIDENTIAL CANDIDATE DAN QUAYLE. THERE WAS NOTHING TO IT, BUT THE STORY ELICITED A CLASSIC QUAYLE-ISM.

THERE OUGHT TO BE SOME RESPECT AND DIGNITY FOR THINGS I DIDN'T DO.

A SEX SCANDAL HAD ALREADY MARRED THAT CAMPAIGN.

CANDIDATE AND SENATOR GARY HART WAS DISGRACED WHEN HE WAS CAUGHT IN A TRYST WITH BRAINY BEAUTY QUEEN DONNA RICE.

AS FOR THE QUEEN OF CAPITOL HILL SEX, RITA FINALLY DIVORCED JOHN JENRETTE. SHE REACHED A BREAKING POINT WHEN SHE SHOWED HIM HER *PLAYBOY* PICTURES.

YOU'RE A LITTLE OLD FOR THIS, RITA. I MEAN, YOU'RE NO RAQUEL WELCH.

AFTER ENDURING HIS UNENDING AFFAIRS, SHE COULDN'T PUT UP WITH HIS DEGRADING REMARKS.

THEN SHE FOUND $25,000 HE'D STASHED IN A SHOEBOX.

I'LL TAKE THAT S-O-B FOR EVERYTHING HE'S GOT!

HER HUSBAND WAS CONVICTED OF TAKING A $50,000 BRIBE. RITA DECIDED TO MOVE ON.

I'M SICK OF BEING THOUGHT OF AS A BIMBO! I WANT A CAREER OF MY OWN!

AFTER A BITTER DIVORCE, RITA STRUCK OUT FOR HOLLYWOOD. HER SCREEN HIGHLIGHT: *ZOMBIE ISLAND MASSACRE.*

SHE GAVE UP ACTING, THEN FOUND SOME SUCCESS AS AN AUTHOR OF POTBOILER NOVELS.

FACTOID BOOKS

THEY ALWAYS SAID NELSON ROCKEFELLER COULDN'T WIN THE BIG ONE. HE WAS THE "PUBLIC" ROCKEFELLER, GROOMED FOR THE PRESIDENCY HE NEVER ATTAINED. BUT WHEN IT CAME TO THE END OF THE LINE FOR THE MAN THEY CALLED --

ROCKY

--HE WENT OUT LIKE A CHAMP... SO TO SPEAK.

THOUGH OBVIOUSLY RAISED IN PRIVILEGE, ROCKY TOOK NO CRAP, AS A FAMOUS NEWSPAPER PHOTO REVEALED.

ROCKY FIGHT'S BAC

FOUR TIMES ELECTED NEW YORK GOVERNOR, HE WAS APPOINTED VICE-PRESIDENT BY GERALD FORD, IN THE WAKE OF WATERGATE.

I, NELSON ROCKEFELLER...

HE RETIRED FROM POLITICS TO WORK ON HIS TRUE PASSION: ART HISTORY. HE PUBLISHED SEVERAL BOOKS-- WITH THE HELP OF AN ATTRACTIVE 25-YEAR-OLD AIDE, MEGAN MARSHACK.

THESE LOOK INTERESTING, GOVERNOR.

LATE IN THE EVENING, JANUARY 26, 1979, MARSHACK AND ROCKY WERE (SUPPOSEDLY) WORKING, WHEN --

COME QUICKLY!! I THINK GOVERNOR ROCKEFELLER'S HAD A HEART ATTACK!!

HE HAD INDEED. BUT MARSHACK HADN'T CALLED 911. SHE CALLED A FRIEND (WHO THEN DIALED 911). A FAMILY SPOKESMAN DEALT WITH THE MEDIA.

THE GOVERNOR WAS WITH HIS CHAUFFEUR WHEN HE DIED. SO BACK OFF!

THE LIE FUELED THE VERY SUSPICIONS THE FAMILY TRIED TO QUELL. MARSHACK HAD BEEN SPOTTED.

AND THERE WAS FOOD AND WINE ON THE TABLE -- BUT NO "WORK."

MARSHACK NEVER TALKED.

MISS MARSHACK! JUST A QUICK -- OH, NEVER MIND.

THE PUBLIC WAS LEFT WITH AN IMPRESSION OF THE 70-YEAR-OLD ROCKY'S FINAL HOURS THAT WAS EITHER SCANDALOUS...OR HEROIC, DEPENDING ON YOUR POINT OF VIEW.

FACTOID BOOKS

from Camelot to CHAPPAQUIDDICK

JOSEPH P. KENNEDY MADE A FORTUNE IN BOOTLEGGING. BUT HE DREAMED OF FAR MORE THAN MONEY. HE SAW HIMSELF AS THE PATRIARCH OF A POLITICAL DYNASTY.

HE RAISED HIS ELDEST SON, JOE JR., WITH ONE PURPOSE: TO BECOME PRESIDENT. THOSE DREAMS WERE BLOWN TO SMITHEREENS ALONG WITH JOE JR.'s PLANE IN WORLD WAR II.

THE MANTLE FELL TO THE SECOND SON, JACK--WHO *WAS* ELECTED PRESIDENT IN 1960. WITH HIS GLAMOROUS WIFE JACKIE, HIS YOUTH AND ENERGY WON AMERICA'S HEARTS.

THEY CALLED HIS ADMINISTRATION "CAMELOT."

ON NOV. 22, 1963 AN ASSASSIN'S BULLETS BROUGHT CAMELOT CRASHING DOWN.

SOMETHING HAS HAPPENED IN THE MOTORCADE!!

BUT THE KENNEDY DREAM DID NOT DIE. IN 1968 THE THIRD BROTHER, BOBBY, RAN AND LOOKED LIKE A WINNER.

NOW, ON TO CHICAGO!

ONCE AGAIN, VIOLENCE CRUELLY SHATTERED THE KENNEDY HOPES.

THERE WAS ONE BROTHER LEFT.

TEDDY. BORN 17 YEARS AFTER HIS OLDEST BROTHER AND THE YOUNGEST OF NINE KENNEDY CHILDREN, EDWARD M. KENNEDY WAS FUN-LOVING AND SLIGHTLY RECKLESS.

LIKE A GOOD KENNEDY, HE ENTERED POLITICS. IN 1962, WITH NOTHING MORE THAN AN ASSISTANT DISTRICT ATTORNEY'S JOB ON HIS RESUME, HE WAS ELECTED SENATOR FROM MASSACHUSETTS.

BOBBY'S DEATH SENT TED INTO A DEEP DEPRESSION. AFTER MONTHS IN SECLUSION, HE EMERGED WITH A NEW, IF UNSPOKEN, SENSE OF PURPOSE.

TED'S TIME HAD ARRIVED. OR SO IT SEEMED.

ON JUNE 18, 1969, TED RELAXED BY RACING IN REGATTA OFF MARTHA'S VINEYARD. HE DIDN'T WIN, BUT WAS AN AFFABLE LOSER.

HERE'S TO THE CHAMPIONS!

A SMALL PARTY FOLLOWED IN A COTTAGE ON A TINY MASSACHUSETTS ISLAND CALLED BY ITS TRADITIONAL NATIVE AMERICAN NAME: CHAPPAQUIDDICK.

AROUND 11:30, TED WAS READY TO LEAVE.

I'M GOING BACK TO THE FERRY. WHERE'S THE KEYS TO THE OLDS?

A PRETTY 29-YEAR-OLD WHO HAD WORKED AS SECRETARY ON BOBBY'S PRESIDENTIAL CAMPAIGN, MARY JO KOPECHNE, WAS A LITTLE TIPSY.

COULD I CATCH A RIDE WITH YOU, SENATOR?

HEY, SURE!!

TED WAS ALWAYS AN ERRATIC DRIVER, BUT THIS WRONG TURN WAS EXTREME EVEN FOR HIM. INSTEAD OF THE FERRY, HE HEADED IN THE EXACT OPPOSITE DIRECTION-- TOWARD THE BEACH.

ABOUT A HALF-MILE DOWN THE ROAD ROSE AN OLD WOODEN BRIDGE BENDING OFF SLIGHTLY TO THE LEFT.

TED DIDN'T SEE THE BEND.

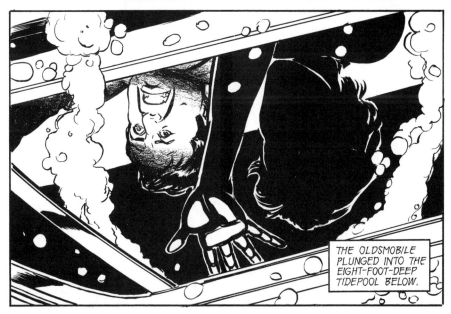

THE OLDSMOBILE PLUNGED INTO THE EIGHT-FOOT-DEEP TIDEPOOL BELOW.

SOMEHOW TED ESCAPED. BUT MARY JO WAS TRAPPED. SO WHAT DID TED KENNEDY DO?

UNFORTUNATELY, NOTHING.

HE DIDN'T CALL POLICE UNTIL 10 HOURS LATER. BY THAT TIME MARY JO WAS LONG DEAD.

WHEN THEY FOUND MARY JO, HER FACE WAS PRESSED AGAINST THE FLOOR OF THE UPSIDE-DOWN VEHICLE, AS IF SHE'D BEEN BREATHING FROM A SMALL AIR POCKET, HOPING DESPERATELY FOR THE RESCUE THAT NEVER CAME.

THOUGH BADLY SHAKEN AND DISTRAUGHT, TED WAS ACUTELY AWARE OF HIS RESPONSIBILITY AS A KENNEDY.

FOR A WEEK, HE HUDDLED WITH FAMILY ADVISORS, PLOTTING HOW TO MINIMIZE DAMAGE TO HIS POLITICAL CAREER.

HE RETURNED TO FACE A CHARGE OF "LEAVING THE SCENE OF AN ACCIDENT." TO WHICH HE PLEADED...

GUI...G...GUILTY.

THE SAME NIGHT, TED MADE A MEA CULPA-- LIVE ON ALL THREE NETWORKS.

I REGARD AS INDEFENSIBLE THE FACT THAT I DID NOT REPORT THE ACCIDENT IMMEDIATELY.

HE THEN TURNED THE SCANDAL INTO A REFERENDUM ON HIS POLITICAL FUTURE.

IF THE CITIZENS OF MASSACHUSETTS LACK CONFIDENCE IN THEIR SENATOR, I WILL RESIGN.

IF THE CITIZENS OF MASSACHUSETTS LACK CONFIDENCE IN THEIR SENATOR, I WILL RESIGN.

POLITICALLY, THE SPEECH WAS A SUCCESS.

CHEER UP, TED! HERE'S 100,000 CARDS AND LETTERS URGING YOU TO KEEP YOUR SENATE SEAT!

BUT HIS VAGUE EXPLANATIONS FAILED TO QUELL THE RUMORS. HAD TED BEEN DRUNK?

COME ON! I'LL BE FINE ONCE I GET BEHIND THE WHEEL!

HIS TELEVISED DENIAL ONLY FUELED THAT SPECULATION.

SAME WITH THE VERY MARRIED TED'S DENIAL OF "IMMORAL CONDUCT" WITH MARY JO.

FORGET THE FERRY, DOLL! WE'RE HEADED FOR THE BEACH!

THOUGH THAT WOULDN'T BE A CRIME.

BUT CONTINUING SUSPICION THAT TED HAD COMMITTED *SOME* CRIME BESIDES "LEAVING THE SCENE" LED THE DISTRICT ATTORNEY TO ANNOUNCE...

...AN *INQUEST* INTO THE DEATH OF MARY JO KOPECHNE!

IN THE END, JUDGE JAMES BOYLE FOUND...

...SENATOR KENNEDY'S NEGLIGENT DRIVING CONTRIBUTED TO MISS KOPECHNE'S DEATH.

TED COULD HAVE BEEN ARRESTED, BUT WASN'T. ALLEGATIONS OF COVER-UP NOW COMPOUNDED THE SCANDAL.

THE SPECTRE OF CHAPPAQUIDDICK HAUNTED TED KENNEDY. ONCE A SURE-FIRE PRESIDENTIAL CANDIDATE, HE CHOSE NOT TO RUN IN 1972 OR IN 1976.

IT APPEARED THAT CAMELOT WAS GONE FOR GOOD.

A DECADE WENT BY. AND THEN...

CARTER CAN BE BEATEN!

INFLATION! THE HOSTAGES! AMERICA NEEDS THE *KENNEDY MAGIC!*

CAMELOT RISES AGAIN!

IN A NATIONALLY TELEVISED INTERVIEW TED PROVED, SADLY, THAT HE HAD NEVER RECOVERED FROM THAT NIGHT.

ON THAT, THERE'S -- THE PROBLEM IS -- FROM THAT NIGHT -- I... I FOUND THE BEHAVIOR ALMOST, SORT OF, BEYOND BELIEF MYSELF.

NEITHER HAD THE VOTERS.

YOU KILLED THAT GIRL, KENNEDY!

STAY AWAY FROM *MY* DAUGHTER, YOU MURDERING COWARD!

JOE SR. DIED JUST SIX MONTHS AFTER CHAPPAQUIDDICK. IT WAS A GOOD THING HE WASN'T AROUND TO SEE TED'S PATHETIC BID TO RECLAIM THE KENNEDY LEGACY.

YOU LET ME DOWN, TEDDY.

EVEN TODAY, TED-KENNEDY-THE-SCANDAL EATS AWAY AT TED KENNEDY.

HOW DO YOU FEEL ABOUT WHAT YOU DID TO THAT WOMAN?

MA'AM. THAT'S WITH ME EVERY DAY OF MY LIFE.

THE CONFIRMATION HEARING OF A NOMINEE TO THE SUPREME COURT IS USUALLY A SOLEMN, DIGNIFIED EVALUATION, BUT IN THE CASE OF CLARENCE THOMAS, IT DEGENERATED INTO A NASTY GAME OF...

HE SAID, SHE SAID!

THURGOOD MARSHALL WAS THE SUPREME COURT'S ONLY BLACK JUSTICE AND STAUNCHEST LIBERAL. IN 1991, EMBITTERED BY THE COURT'S RIGHTWARD TILT, HE RETIRED.

POWER, NOT *REASON*, IS THE NEW CURRENCY OF THIS COURT'S DECISION-MAKING!

PRESIDENT BUSH SAW THE OPPORTUNITY TO NOMINATE A **CONSERVATIVE** BLACK JUDGE IN CLARENCE THOMAS.

HE'S THE MOST *QUALIFIED* MAN FOR THE JOB!

THOMAS HAD SERVED JUST TWO YEARS ON THE FEDERAL BENCH.

BUSH ADDED, GRATUITOUSLY...

THE FACT THAT HE'S BLACK HAD *NOTHING TO DO* WITH THIS!

THOMAS WAS AN OKAY JUDGE, BUT OBVIOUSLY NEITHER STATEMENT WAS TRUE. INADVERTENTLY, BUSH HAD DRAWN THE BATTLE LINES.

AT HIS CONFIRMATION, DEMOCRATIC SENATORS STARTED OFF BY GRILLING THOMAS ON HIS HARD-RIGHT IDEOLOGY, BUT THOMAS PLAYED COY, EVEN ON THE NATION'S MOST VOLATILE ISSUE.

WHAT IS YOUR VIEW ON... *ABORTION??!!*

I REALLY HAVE NO OPINION, SENATOR.

OKLAHOMA LAW PROFESSOR ANITA HILL WORKED FOR THOMAS AT THE EQUAL EMPLOYMENT OPPORTUNITY COMMISSION, THE AGENCY THAT MONITORS SEXUAL HARASSMENT COMPLAINTS. SHE CONFIDED IN A FRIEND...

I WAS *SEXUALLY HARASSED* BY CLARENCE THOMAS.

SOMEHOW THE RUMOR SPREAD THROUGHOUT WASHINGTON, REACHING COMMITTEE CHAIRMAN SENATOR JOSEPH BIDEN.

THIS IS A BOMBSHELL!

SENATE AIDES PUSHED HILL.

NO, I--I DON'T WANT TO COME FORWARD WITH THIS!

THE REPUBLICANS WENT ALL-OUT TO DISCREDIT HILL. THEY DESIGNATED SENATOR ARLEN SPECTER, A FORMER PHILADELPHIA PROSECUTOR, AS THEIR POINT MAN.

ANITA HILL MAY HAVE COMMITTED *PERJURY!*

THEY PORTRAYED HER AS MENTALLY UNSTABLE, SEXUALLY OBSESSED WITH THOMAS.

IT IS POSSIBLE MISS HILL SUFFERS FROM *EROTOMANIA!*

SHE MUST!

OH, DEFINITELY!

THEY BROUGHT IN A ONETIME ACQUAINTANCE OF HILL'S NAMED JOHN DOGGETT TO PROVE THEIR POINT.

OH, YEAH. ANITA WAS OBSESSED WITH ME. SHE FANTASIZED ABOUT ME ALL THE TIME.

BUT AS HE KEPT TALKING, DOGGETT HIMSELF TURNED OUT TO BE THE WEIRDO.

OF COURSE, WOMEN FIND ME IRRESISTIBLE. LAST NIGHT THIS WOMAN SAID TO ME, "HEY, JOHN! PUT YOUR PENIS BACK IN YOUR PANTS!"

DESPITE ATTEMPTS TO PAINT HILL AS A LONE NUT, THERE WERE FOUR OTHER WOMEN READY TO TESTIFY ABOUT THOMAS' INAPPROPRIATE BEHAVIOR.

CLARENCE IS NOT THE MAN HE SAYS HE IS!

MYSTERIOUSLY, THEY WERE NEVER CALLED.

HILL LEFT WASHINGTON-- AND FOUND SHE'D ACQUIRED THE NOTORIETY SHE'D ORIGINALLY FEARED.

YOU LITTLE WITCH!

THOMAS SURVIVED. THE SENATE CONFIRMED HIM 58-42 -- THE CLOSEST MARGIN EVER FOR A SUPREME COURT NOMINEE.

- HARRUMPH! -

REPORTERS DUG UP NEW EVIDENCE OF THOMAS' CRAVING FOR PORNOGRAPHY.

SURE, I REMEMBER THE GUY... FROM BACK *THERE!*

MUST BE OVER 18

BEFORE THE STORY BROKE, THE WHITE HOUSE HAD THOMAS SWORN IN -- MORE THAN A WEEK EARLY.

BUT THE SCANDAL PRODUCED A BACKLASH AGAINST MALE-DOMINATED WASHINGTON. IN 1992 A RECORD NUMBER OF WOMEN WON CONGRESSIONAL SEATS. BILL CLINTON DEFEATED GEORGE BUSH LARGELY WITH WOMEN'S VOTES.

THE EEOC ONCE HEADED BY CLARENCE THOMAS RECORDED A 50% JUMP IN SEXUAL HARASSMENT COMPLAINTS.

121

IN 1994, PRESIDENT BILL CLINTON ACQUIRED THE DUBIOUS DISTINCTION OF BECOMING THE FIRST PRESIDENT SUED FOR SEXUAL MISCONDUCT. THE INCIDENT ALLEGEDLY OCCURRED WHILE CLINTON WAS STILL GOVERNOR OF ARKANSAS.

UH, WANNA KISS IT?

BUT THERE HAVE BEEN PLENTY OF OTHER...

PANTS-FREE PRESIDENTS

WHILE HE WAS ENGAGED TO MARTHA, GEORGE WASHINGTON HAD A FLING WITH A WOMAN NAMED SALLY FAIRFAX.

I CANNOT TELL A LIE. I DID IT WITH MY BEST FRIEND'S WIFE.

WELL-KNOWN AS A PLAYBOY, JAMES GARFIELD IS THE FIRST PRESIDENT KNOWN TO HAVE CHEATED ON HIS WIFE.

I'M PAVING THE WAY FOR FUTURE CHIEF EXECUTIVES, MY DARLING!

IN THE 1884 PRESIDENTIAL CAMPAIGN, THE PRESS HAMMERED GROVER CLEVELAND FOR SIRING AN ILLEGITIMATE CHILD.

THE DAILY POST

I WANT MY PA!

IDENT CLEVEL

IT WAS A MAJOR SCANDAL, BUT CLEVELAND WON ANYWAY.

SKIP AHEAD TO THE 20TH CENTURY, WHEN WARREN G. HARDING FROLICKED IN A WHITE HOUSE CLOSET WITH HIS MISTRESS, NAN BRITTON, AS HIS WIFE RAGED AND HIS CORRUPT ADMINISTRATION CRUMBLED AROUND HIM...

KA-THUMPA-THUMPA-THUMP!

...AND FRANKLIN ROOSEVELT, DESPITE POLIO THAT CONFINED HIM TO A WHEELCHAIR, CARRIED ON AFFAIRS WITH A SECRETARY AND, POSSIBLY, THREE OTHER WOMEN.

WE HAVE NOTHING TO FEAR BUT--- MY WIFE!

THEN THERE WAS JACK KENNEDY, THE MOST PROLIFIC PHILANDERER OF ALL.

WHAT A MAN!

MORE THAN JUST A MAN-- A PRESIDENT!

WHICH BRINGS US BACK TO CLINTON, WHOSE ALLEGED MISTRESS GENNIFER FLOWERS PUBLICLY REVEALED SUCH DETAILS AS CLINTON'S APTITUDE FOR ORAL SEX.

HE DID IT LIKE A CHAMP!

D'OH!

WATERGATE

The scandal that lent its suffix to all other political scandals had roots as far back as 1969, shortly after Richard M. Nixon took office as president.

It was a time of high tension. With the Vietnam disaster abroad and massive protests at home, the already-paranoid Nixon felt immediately under siege.

With their boss's tacit blessing, top aides to the new, Republican President drew up a list of the administration's "enemies."

WE'RE GONNA SCREW ALL THESE SOBs.

Then on June 13, 1971, The New York Times started publishing "The Pentagon Papers," a top secret document revealing massive government deception about the war.

WHO THE ☆!◎!!! LEAKED THIS I☆!#!!!

THE SECRET HISTORY OF VIETNAM

"The Plumbers" were born, ostensibly to "plug leaks." Their top operatives were CIA agent Howard Hunt and former FBI and CIA man G. Gordon Liddy. Their real function: covert operations.

They burglarized the office of a psychiatrist who'd treated Pentagon Papers leaker Daniel Ellsberg, among other illegal activities.

June 17, 1972. In the midst of Nixon's re-election campaign, the Plumbers targeted the famed Watergate complex.

Their supposed mission: to bug the sixth-floor headquarters of the Democratic National Committee.

Exactly why they did it remains murky to this day.

What is clear is that, as undercover cops burst into the DNC headquarters, the Plumbers had botched the job.

FREEZE!

GEEZ! THESE BURGLARS ARE BETTER-DRESSED THAN WE ARE!

At his court arraignment, burglar James McCord mumbled a startling admission.

I, UM, USED TO WORK FOR THE —AHEM— CIA.

GOLLY JEEPERS!

Washington Post cub reporter Bob Woodward knew he had a big story.

June 19. Woodward and partner Carl Bernstein reported that McCord was also a paid security man for Nixon's re-election committee.

#@!O!!$!!!!!

The scandal was on.

Woodward later claimed to have a high-level secret source who met him in parking garages and whom he called, evocatively, "Deep Throat."

FOLLOW THE MONEY.

GEE WHILLIKERS! YOU BET I WILL!

Follow it he did. Woodward and Bernstein discovered that a check from a Nixon campaign contributor went straight to a Watergate burglar.

HOW THE @!¥⚡†!! DID THOSE !$‡*O!! GET THIS?

Washington Post
Check For Nixon Went to Burglar

With Deep Throat's help, they traced the scandal to its roots.

by Bob Woodward and Carl Bernstein

The Watergate bugging stemmed from a massive campaign of political spying and sabotage on behalf of the President. Fu...

Even worse, a cover-up was underway. On June 23, Nixon ordered his chief of staff, H.R. "Bob" Haldeman, to coax the CIA into thwarting the FBI's investigation.

THIS INVOLVES THE CUBANS, HUNT AND A LOT OF HANKY-PANKY. TELL THEM IT COULD BLOW THE WHOLE BAY OF PIGS THING.

In reality, Nixon was blowing his presidency.

But why would the CIA be scared to "blow the whole Bay of Pigs thing"? Years later, Haldeman speculated:

HE WAS REFERRING TO THE KENNEDY ASSASSINATION. IN A CHILLING PARALLEL TO THE WATERGATE COVER-UP, THE CIA ERASED ANY CONNECTION BETWEEN ITSELF AND THE JFK ASSASSINATION.

The Senate formed a Watergate committee, headed by folksy North Carolina Democrat Sam Ervin, who dug up various sordid details.

IT APPEA-YUHS THAT THE PREZ'DENT HAS BEEN DODGIN' HIS TAXES ALL THESE YEA-YUHS!

But the cover-up held as all the President's men took the bullet for their boss.

WHAT DID THE PRESIDENT KNOW AND WHEN DID HE KNOW IT?

I HAVE NO RECOLLEC-TION — OF ANYTHING.

Until July 13, 1973 — Friday the 13th — when minor White House aide Alexander Butterfield revealed to committee staffers:

THERE'S A RECORD-ING SYSTEM IN THE PRESIDENT'S OFFICE. EVERYTHING WAS TAPED.

When Watergate special prosecutor Archibald Cox demanded the tapes, Nixon fired him and several other officials. The press dubbed it "The Saturday Night Massacre."

THOSE TAPES'LL NEVER SEE THE LIGHT O' DAY!

The scandal was now a full-blown constitutional crisis.

Bowing to the inevitable, Nixon released some tapes. One important tape contained an ominous 18-minute "gap," for which Nixon's loyal secretary took the blame.

I'M SUCH A KLUTZ!

But at least a week earlier, Deep Throat told Woodward:

AT LEAST ONE OF THE TAPES CONTAINS DELIBERATE ERASURES.

JIMINY CRICKET!

When the tape of his June 23, 1972, chat with Haldeman came out, the game was over. It was the "smoking gun" proving Nixon ordered the cover-up, that he'd been lying all along.

IT'S THAT WHOLE BAY OF PIGS THING.

On August 9, 1974, Nixon resigned rather than face impeachment. Most of his loyal lieutenants went to jail. But incoming President Gerald Ford issued Nixon a full pardon. He never faced charges and died 20 years later.

The IRAN-CONTRA SCANDAL

PROLOGUE: 1979. U.S. FOREIGN POLICY SUFFERS TWO SEVERE BLOWS. POPULAR REVOLUTIONS IN NICARAGUA AND IRAN DEPOSE BRUTAL, U.S.-BACKED DICTATORS.

VIVA LA REVOLUCION!!

NICARAGUA'S SANDINISTAS, SNUBBED BY THE U.S., BECOME INCREASINGLY MARXIST AND LOOK TO THE SOVIET UNION FOR BACKING.

THE NEW ISLAMIC-FUNDAMENTALIST GOVERNMENT OF IRAN IS ANTI-AMERICAN FROM THE START.

IN NOVEMBER, "STUDENTS" SEIZE THE U.S. EMBASSY IN TEHRAN, TAKING EVERYONE HOSTAGE FOR 444 DAYS, NOT RELEASING THEM UNTIL JAN. 20, 1981 -- THE DAY AMERICA INAUGURATES ITS NEW PRESIDENT, RONALD REAGAN.

GETTING RID OF THE SANDINISTAS BECAME AN OBSESSION FOR THE FIERCELY ANTI-COMMUNIST REAGAN ADMINISTRATION. USING THE CIA, THE REAGANITES FUNNEL AID TO THE "CONTRA" REBELS.

...AND IF YOU EVER NEED ANYTHING, JUST DIAL 1-800-CIA-CASH!

BUT IN 1983 CONGRESS PASSES THE "BOLAND AMENDMENT," BANNING U.S. EFFORTS TO DEPOSE THE SANDINISTAS.

DON'T WORRY ABOUT CONGRESS AND ITS FOOLISH LAWS. WE DON'T.

A WORLD AWAY, IN WAR-TORN BEIRUT, REAGAN SENDS U.S. MARINES AS "PEACEKEEPERS." IN OCTOBER, 1983, 241 MARINES DIE WHEN TERRORISTS BOMB THEIR COMPOUND.

BBBAMM

INTELLIGENCE REVEALED THAT THE BOMBING WAS BACKED BY IRAN.

MARCH, 1984: IRANIAN-BACKED TERRORISTS KIDNAP THE CIA'S BEIRUT STATION CHIEF, WILLIAM BUCKLEY. SIX OTHER AMERICANS ARE TAKEN OVER THE NEXT YEAR.

THE SCANDAL: IN PUBLIC, REAGAN'S TOUGH-ON-TERRORISTS POLICY WAS UNCOMPROMISING.

LET ME MAKE IT PLAIN TO THE ASSASSINS IN BEIRUT AND THEIR ACCOMPLICES -- AMERICA WILL *NEVER* MAKE CONCESSIONS TO *TERRORISTS!*

BEHIND THE SCENES, THINGS WERE A LITTLE DIFFERENT. ON SEPT. 15, 1985, THE U.S. -- WITH ISRAEL AS COURIER -- SECRETLY DELIVERED 408 TOW MISSILES TO IRAN.

THE SAME DAY, HOSTAGE BENJAMIN WEIR WAS GRANTED FREEDOM.

WELCOME HOME

THE ARMS-FOR-HOSTAGES PLAN ORIGINATED WITH SHADOWY IRANIAN ARMS MERCHANT MANUCHER GHORBANIFAR.

I HAVE HIGH-LEVEL CONTACTS AMONG "MODERATE" IRANIAN FACTIONS.

THEY WILL RELEASE THE HOSTAGES IF YOU SELL THEM ARMS.

IRAN DESPERATELY NEEDED WEAPONS FOR ITS INTERMINABLE AND GORY BORDER WAR WITH IRAQ.

BUT BECAUSE IRAN WAS DESIGNATED A "TERRORIST STATE," U.S. ARMS SALES THERE WERE ILLEGAL -- AND HYPOCRITICAL!

NATIONAL SECURITY ADVISOR ROBERT "BUD" McFARLANE ASKED REAGAN TO APPROVE THE ARMS-FOR-HOSTAGES DEAL.

WELL, IT SURE WOULD BE GREAT TO GET THOSE HOSTAGES BACK. OKAY, GO AHEAD.

REAGAN ALSO CHARGED McFARLANE WITH KEEPING THE CONTRAS IN BUSINESS.

KEEP THEM ALIVE *BODY AND SOUL,* BUD. THEY REMIND ME OF OUR OWN FOUNDING FATHERS.

EXCEPT MOST OF OUR FOUNDING FATHERS WEREN'T FORMER MEMBERS OF A DESPOTIC DICTATOR'S SECRET POLICE.

IN CHARGE OF BOTH THE CONTRA SUPPLY PROGRAM *AND* THE ARMS-FOR-HOSTAGES DEAL: FORMER MARINE OLIVER NORTH. ONE DAY...

SAY, I'VE GOT A *NEAT* IDEA!!

HE DECIDED TO TAKE SOME OF THE MILLIONS IN "RESIDUAL FUNDS" FROM THE IRAN ARMS SALES AND PASS IT ON TO THE CONTRAS.

- HEH-HEH - THIS IS *NEAT!*

THE DEALS WERE HANDLED BY "THE ENTERPRISE", A SECRET ORGANIZATION HEADED BY RETIRED AIR FORCE GENERAL RICHARD SECORD AND FINACIER ALBERT HAKIM.

AT THIS POINT, NORTH AND FRIENDS HAD BECOME A GOVERNMENT UNTO THEMSELVES, PAYING NO HEED TO U.S. LAWS -- WITH REAGAN'S OKAY. THE CONTRA RESUPPLY WAS ILLEGAL; THE IRAN ARMS SALES WERE ILLEGAL. NOW THE GOVERNMENT WAS BEING ILLEGALLY CHEATED OF REVENUE FROM THOSE ILLEGAL ARMS SALES.

AND IT WAS ALL BEING DONE BY A SECRET CABAL OF ADMINISTRATION OFFICIALS, MERCENARIES, AND BUSINESSMEN.

I PREFER TO CALL IT AN "OFF-THE-SHELF OPERATION."

ANYWAY, BY APRIL, 1986, OVER 1,000 MISSILES HAD PRODUCED JUST ONE HOSTAGE. McFARLANE AND NORTH WERE LOSING PATIENCE WITH THEIR MIDDLEMAN, GHORBANIFAR.

JUST A FEW MORE MISSILES, GENTLEMEN!

McFARLANE AND NORTH VISITED TEHRAN THEMSELVES. THEY BROUGHT, AS A PEACE OFFERING, A CHOCOLATE CAKE.

AACCH! PHOOEY!

A BAD GIFT TO GIVE IN THE MIDDLE OF RAMADAN, THE ISLAMIC HOLY MONTH, DURING WHICH MUSLIMS MUST FAST ALL DAY EVERY DAY.

THEN, ON OCT. 5, 1986, DISASTER FOR NORTH AND THE ENTERPRISE. THE SANDINISTAS SHOOT DOWN A CONTRA RESUPPLY PLANE, CAPTURING CIA-CONNECTED MERCENARY EUGENE HASENFUS.

THE JIG WAS UP. CIA DIRECTOR WILLIAM CASEY, A FANATICAL CONTRA BACKER, ORDERED THE OPERATION SHUT DOWN.

DAMMIT, NORTH! YOU'VE SCREWED UP EVERYTHING!

I GUESS I'M GONNA BE THE FALL GUY.

THE REAGAN-LOVING PRESS CORPS JUST DIDN'T GET IT. IT TOOK A *LEBANESE* PAPER TO BREAK THE ARMS-FOR-HOSTAGES STORY.

WHY THE #%@&& DIDN'T *WE* HAVE THIS?

C'MON, CHIEF! *PRESIDENT REAGAN* WOULD NEVER BARGAIN WITH TERRORISTS! WOULD HE?

SOME REPORTERS AT LEAST ASKED REAGAN ABOUT IT ON NOVEMBER 6, 1986.

WE NEVER SOLD ARMS TO IRAN!

GREAT! GLAD TO HEAR IT! WHAT A RELIEF!

A WEEK LATER, THE PRESIDENT MODIFIED THE LIE.

THE CHARGE THAT THE U.S. SHIPPED ARMS FOR HOSTAGES IS UTTERLY FALSE.

IT *CAN* BE DONE

A WEEK LATER, REAGAN ADDED MORE PREVARICATIONS.

NO ARMS WERE SHIPPED BEFORE JANUARY, 1986 AND WE WEREN'T INVOLVED WITH ISRAEL IN THIS DEAL.

ALL THE INSIDERS KNEW THAT THE IRAN AND CONTRA OPERATIONS WERE TOO CLOSELY TIED. REAGAN'S ATTORNEY GENERAL AND OLD FRIEND ED MEESE LAUNCHED A PREEMPTIVE STRIKE.

CERTAIN MONIES RECEIVED IN TRANSACTIONS BETWEEN ISRAEL AND IRAN WERE MADE AVAILABLE TO FORCES OPPOSED TO THE SANDINISTA GOVERNMENT.

AAAW! WHAT'D YOU GO AND TELL US THAT FOR? NOW WE'RE GONNA HAVE TO DO SOME *WORK!*

TO AVOID THE APPEARANCE OF A COVER-UP (EVEN THOUGH ONE WAS WELL UNDERWAY) MEESE CALLED FOR A SPECIAL PROSECUTOR. LAWRENCE WALSH, FORMER JUDGE AND DIPLOMAT, GOT THE JOB.

THE PRESIDENT APPOINTED A SPECIAL INVESTIGATING COMMITTEE, HEADED BY REPUBLICAN SENATOR JOHN TOWER.

CONGRESS SET UP ITS OWN COMMITTEES, WITH SPLASHY TELEVISED HEARINGS. THE FIRST WITNESS, LT. COL. OLIVER NORTH, WHO PUT HIS UNIFORM BACK ON FOR THE OCCASION.

I SWEAR TO TELL THE TRUTH, THE WHOLE TRUTH...

TO THE CONGRESSMEN'S MORTIFICATION, THE EARNEST, BOYISHLY HANDSOME NORTH PROVED HUGELY TELEGENIC.

THE AMERICAN PEOPLE MUST UNDERSTAND THAT THIS IS A DANGEROUS WORLD AND THIS NATION IS AT RISK!

AVERAGE AMERICANS, FED UP WITH THE COMPLEXITIES AND PRETENSIONS OF WASHINGTON INSIDER POLITICS, LOVED THE COLONEL.

THE GUY'S AN AMERICAN HERO! -BUUURRPP!-

NORTH'S GORGEOUS AND MELLIFLUOUSLY NAMED SECRETARY, FAWN HALL, TESTIFIED THAT SHE HELPED HER BOSS DESTROY CRUCIAL DOCUMENTS.

SOMETIMES YOU HAVE TO GO ABOVE THE WRITTEN LAW.

THE IMAGE OF OLLIE AND FAWN, ALONE, SHREDDING DOCUMENTS WELL INTO THE NIGHT, LED TO RUMORS. BUT WHEN NORTH DECLARED...

THERE WAS NO HANKY-PANKY!

...EVERYONE WHO KNEW THE RAMROD-STRAIGHT EX-MARINE BELIEVED HIM.

THE IRAN-CONTRA SCANDAL, AS IT WAS NOW CALLED, OPENED A PANDORA'S BOX OF ILLEGAL COVERT OPERATIONS. SENATOR JOHN KERRY DISCOVERED:

SOME PLANES CARRYING WEAPONS TO THE CONTRAS CAME BACK LOADED WITH COCAINE. DRUG PROFITS MAY HAVE HELPED FUND THE CONTRAS.

NO ONE ELSE WANTED TO TOUCH THAT ONE -- LEAST OF ALL THE PRESS.

THE 1988 PRESIDENTIAL ELECTION ROLLED AROUND, WITH VICE-PRESIDENT GEORGE BUSH VYING TO SUCCEED REAGAN--AND FACING A GRILLING ABOUT HIS OWN IRAN-CONTRA ROLE.

I TOLD YA, DAN! I WAS OUT OF THE LOOP!!

IT WAS A BALDFACED LIE. RECORDS PROVED THAT BUSH HAD ATTENDED NUMEROUS KEY MEETINGS ABOUT THE IRAN AND CONTRA OPERATIONS, INCLUDING ONE WHERE SECRETARY OF STATE GEORGE SCHULTZ WAS DESCRIBED AS "APOPLECTIC" ABOUT THE ARMS-FOR-HOSTAGES SWAP.

THAT'S THE STUPIDEST !#@$% PIECE OF FOREIGN POLICY I'VE EVER HEARD!!!

BUSH WON THE ELECTION ANYWAY, BRUSHING OFF THE CONSTITUTIONAL SUBVERSION OF IRAN-CONTRA AND RUNNING ON SUCH ISSUES AS PRISON FURLOUGHS, THE ACLU, AND...

I PLEDGE ALLEGIANCE TO THE FLAG...

BUSH WASN'T THE ONLY LIAR. THE PRESIDENT TOLD HIS OWN TOWER COMMISSION...

I DIDN'T KNOW THAT ANYONE ON THE NATIONAL SECURITY COUNCIL WAS HELPING THE CONTRAS.

EVEN THOUGH NSC HEAD JOHN POINDEXTER (McFARLANE'S SUCCESSOR) SAID...

I BRIEFED THE PRESIDENT ON MOST ALL ASPECTS OF ALL THE PROJECTS COLONEL NORTH WAS INVOLVED WITH.

IN 1989, WALSH BROUGHT NORTH TO TRIAL. ON THE STAND, NORTH ADMITTED TO AIDING THE CONTRAS WHEN CONGRESS PROHIBITED IT, SHREDDING DOCUMENTS, FALSIFYING RECORDS, USING GOVERNMENT TRAVELER'S CHECKS FOR HIMSELF AND FABRICATING PAYMENT RECORDS FOR A SECURITY SYSTEM HE'D ACCEPTED FROM SECORD. BUT, HE PROTESTED...

I DON'T BELIEVE I EVER DID ANYTHING CRIMINAL.

NORTH WAS CONVICTED ON THREE COUNTS. ON APPEAL, THE VERDICTS WERE THROWN OUT ON TECHNICALITIES.

GOD, I LOVE THIS COUNTRY!

HE RAN FOR U.S. SENATE AS AN ULTRA-CONSERVATIVE REPUBLICAN. HE LOST NARROWLY.

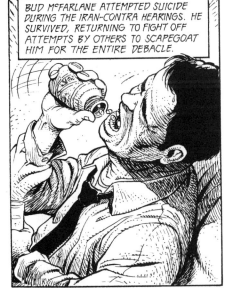

BUD McFARLANE ATTEMPTED SUICIDE DURING THE IRAN-CONTRA HEARINGS. HE SURVIVED, RETURNING TO FIGHT OFF ATTEMPTS BY OTHERS TO SCAPEGOAT HIM FOR THE ENTIRE DEBACLE.

GEORGE BUSH LOST THE 1992 ELECTION. IN HIS FINAL MONTH AS A LAME DUCK, HE RELEASED A "POLITICAL DIARY" HE'D BEEN HIDING SINCE 1986. THEN HE PARDONED REAGAN DEFENSE SECRETARY CASPER WEINBERGER, McFARLANE, AND FOUR OTHERS.

We the People

READ MY LIPS! THE COVER-UP CONTINUES!

IT WAS THE FIRST TIME A PRESIDENT ISSUED A PARDON FOR A PERSON WHO MIGHT HAVE CALLED *HIM* AS A WITNESS.

FACTOID BOOKS

THE WRONG ARM OF THE LAW

JUST THE FACTS, MA'AM.

ONE-ADAM-12, ONE-ADAM-12!

THE LOS ANGELES POLICE DEPARTMENT, THE CLEANEST, MOST EFFICIENT POLICE DEPARTMENT IN THE UNITED STATES.. AT LEAST, THAT WAS ITS IMAGE FOR DECADES, PROMOTED BY TV SHOWS LIKE *DRAGNET* AND *ADAM 12*. THE DEPARTMENT MOTTO: "TO PROTECT AND TO SERVE."

THE IMAGE WAS UPHELD BY A SERIES OF NO-NONSENSE POLICE CHIEFS. THE TOUGHEST OF ALL: DARRYL GATES.

WHEN HE TOOK OVER IN 1978, GATES HAD ALREADY HELPED CREATE THE LAPD'S SWAT TEAM --

-- SPAWNING *ANOTHER* TV SHOW.

TO BE SURE, GATES WAS CONTROVERSIAL. HE GOT IN TROUBLE FOR SUCH UTTERANCES AS...

CASUAL DRUG USERS OUGHT TO BE TAKEN OUT AND SHOT!

MORE TELLINGLY, TRYING TO EXPLAIN WHY 12 BLACKS HAD DIED IN POLICE CHOKE-HOLDS, HE MUSED...

WE MAY BE FINDING THAT IN SOME BLACKS, VEINS OR ARTERIES DO NOT OPEN UP AS FAST AS THEY DO IN *NORMAL* PEOPLE.

CLEARLY, THE LAPD HAD SERIOUS PROBLEMS. IN 1980, TWO OFFICERS GUNNED DOWN A WOMAN DISTRAUGHT OVER HER ELECTRIC BILL, KILLING HER -- JUST *TWO MINUTES* AFTER THEY ARRIVED AT HER HOME.

BLAM BLAM

BASEBALL SUPERSTAR JOE MORGAN WAS ROUGHED UP BY OFFICERS WHO INSISTED HE WAS A DRUG DEALER.

IN 1990 ALONE, THE CITY PAID A WHOPPING *$11 MILLION* IN POLICE BRUTALITY CLAIMS.

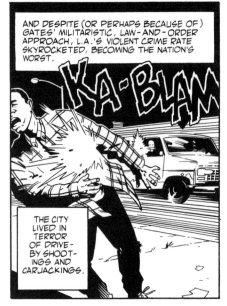

AND DESPITE (OR PERHAPS BECAUSE OF) GATES' MILITARISTIC, LAW-AND-ORDER APPROACH, L.A.'S VIOLENT CRIME RATE SKYROCKETED, BECOMING THE NATION'S WORST.

KA-BLAM

THE CITY LIVED IN TERROR OF DRIVE-BY SHOOTINGS AND CARJACKINGS.

YET NOTHING FAZED GATES. AS LONG AS PRESIDENTS PRAISED HIM, THE LAPD'S NATIONAL REPUTATION AS THE NATION'S FINEST FORCE SUFFERED NOT A DENT.

DARRYL'S A *GOOD* MAN.

HE'S GOOD!

HE'S GOOD!

ON THE EARLY MORNING OF MARCH 3, 1991, THE OFFICERS PURSUING A SPEEDING HYUNDAI HAD NO WAY OF KNOWING THAT THEIR NEXT ACTIONS WOULD FOREVER DESTROY THE LAPD'S TREASURED REPUTATION AND LEAD TO THE DOWNFALL OF LEGENDARY CHIEF DARRYL GATES.

RRRRRAAAAOOOWW

DRIVING THE HYUNDAI, A FRIGHTENED YOUNG BLACK MAN NAMED RODNEY KING.

RODNEY, WHAT YOU DOIN'? PULL OVER, MAN!

WHEN KING FINALLY PULLED OVER, NO LESS THAN 23 LAPD OFFICERS WERE ON THE SCENE. MOST OF THEM SHOWED UP AFTER KING STOPPED. AT LEAST 10 DREW THEIR GUNS AND AIMED AT KING.

THE SERGEANT IN CHARGE: 15-YEAR VETERAN OF THE L.A. STREETS STACEY KOONS.

EVERYBODY-- BACK!

KOONS SHOT THE FALLEN KING WITH A TASER. 50,000 VOLTS ROCKED KING'S BODY.

JJRRRZZZAAPP!!

AND THEN IT BEGAN . . .

BAM THUD

CRACK

CRUNCH

KING HEARD SGT. KOONS SHOUT . . .

YOU BETTER RUN, NIGGER! WE'RE GONNA KILL YOU!

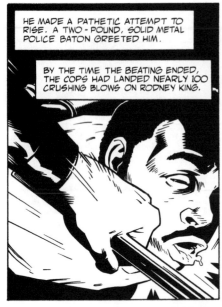

HE MADE A PATHETIC ATTEMPT TO RISE. A TWO-POUND, SOLID METAL POLICE BATON GREETED HIM.

BY THE TIME THE BEATING ENDED, THE COPS HAD LANDED NEARLY 100 CRUSHING BLOWS ON RODNEY KING.

WHAT THE OFFICERS DIDN'T KNOW WAS THAT, AMONG THE HORRIFIED CROWD OF ONLOOKERS ACROSS THE STREET WAS A MAN WITH A HOME VIDEO CAMERA.

WHIRRRR

THE FOLLOWING DAY, AND FOR WEEKS TO COME, THE TAPE PLAYED OVER AND OVER ON NEWSCASTS ACROSS THE NATION, TO THE HORROR OF EVERYONE...

MY GOD! THIS DOESN'T LOOK LIKE *DRAGNET!*

DARRYL GATES, HOWEVER, WAS UNDAUNTED...

THIS INCIDENT WAS AN *ABERRATION!*

THE OFFICERS WERE TRIED FOR THE BEATING. THE VIDEO PROOF SEEMED TO MAKE IT AN OPEN AND SHUT CASE. BUT IN APRIL 1992, AN ALL-WHITE JURY FOUND THEM *NOT GUILTY,* AND L.A.'S BLACK COMMUNITY ERUPTED INTO THE WORST RIOT IN AMERICAN HISTORY.

AT THE EPICENTER OF THE RIOT, THE LAPD WAS STRANGELY ABSENT.

WE'RE DOIN' THIS FOR *RODNEY KING!!*

LAUNDROMAT

GATES HAD SURVIVED A WITHERING REPORT AFTER THE BEATING THAT UNCOVERED SYSTEMATIC LAPD RACISM, INCLUDING HUNDREDS OF "INAPPROPRIATE" MESSAGES IN THE POLICE COMPUTER.

"MONKEY SLAPPING TIME"?

BUT EVEN GATES COULDN'T EXPLAIN WHY HIS DEPARTMENT DID NOTHING WHILE L.A. BURNED.

YOU LET ME DOWN, GATES. YOU LET US ALL DOWN.

HE STEPPED DOWN, TAKING THE MYTH OF THE LAPD WITH HIM.

THE LAPD HAD A NEW REPUTATION -- AS A CADRE OF BIGOTS AND THUGS. IT WAS A BITTER LEGACY WITH SOME BIZARRE CONSEQUENCES.

WE FIND THE DEFENDANT, O.J. SIMPSON, *NOT GUILTY!*

FACTOID BOOKS

THIS IS THE STORY OF THE GREATEST BANK HEIST IN HISTORY--A TRILLION DOLLAR HAUL

The GREAT S&L ROBBERY

NEIGHBORHOOD SAVINGS + LOAN

AND THE ROBBERS PULLED IT OFF WITHOUT GUNS OR MASKS, IN FACT, THEY WORE SUITS.

BANKER AND ANTI-PORN CRUSADER CHARLES KEATING GOT RICH WHILE HIS LINCOLN SAVINGS AND LOANS LOST $600 MILLION -- WITH TAX-PAYERS PICKING UP THE TAB.

PICTURES OF NAKED WOMEN ARE IMMORAL.

HUSTLER

SWINDLING RETIREES OUT OF ALL THEIR MONEY IS BASICALLY OKAY.

NEIL BUSH, THE PRESIDENT'S YOUNGEST SON, CUT SWEETHEART DEALS THAT HELPED HIS SILVERADO SAVINGS AND LOAN GO BELLY-UP.

GOSH, THIS FINANCIAL STUFF IS WAY OVER MY HEAD. BUT IT SURE LOOKS FUN!

ATTABOY NEIL!

THE STORY OF THE BIGGEST FINANCIAL SCAM IN HISTORY BEGAN WITH CONGRESSMAN FERNAND ST. GERMAIN, CHAIRMAN OF THE HOUSE BANKING COMMITTEE.

GOD, I LOVE THE BANKING BUSINESS!

ST. GERMAIN ENJOYED THE BENEFITS OF HIS OFFICE, AND HE KNEW HOW TO LOOK AFTER HIS FRIENDS.

THESE DEPRESSION-ERA S&L REGULATIONS ARE STRANGLING OUR INDUSTRY, FERNAND.

JUST LEAVE IT TO ME!

ON OCTOBER 15, 1982, PRESIDENT REAGAN SIGNED THE GARN-ST. GERMAIN BILL WHICH RELAXED MANY OF THE 40-YEAR-OLD S&L REGULATIONS.

ALL IN ALL, I THINK WE'VE HIT THE JACKPOT!

RONNIE

YEAH. BUT WHO'S "WE"?

THE FDR-ERA REGULATIONS WERE DESIGNED TO HELP WORKING-CLASS FAMILIES. THE GOVERNMENT INSURED DEPOSITS UP TO $40,000 WHILE S&Ls COULD INVEST ONLY IN SINGLE-FAMILY MORTGAGES, ALLOWING LOTS OF PEOPLE TO PURCHASE THEIR OWN HOMES.

WALL St

THE REAGAN-ERA CHANGES RAISED THE INSURANCE CEILING TO $100,000 AND LET S&Ls INVEST IN NEARLY ANYTHING. "THRIFTS," AS THEY WERE QUAINTLY CALLED, BECAME A FAST BUCK TOOL FOR HIGH-ROLLING SPECULATORS, LIKE KEATING.

KEEP OUT!

KEATING HAD NEVER BEEN CITED BY REGULATORS OVER HIS INVOLVEMENT IN ANOTHER BANK. NOW HE WAS DEEMED THE TYPE OF VISIONARY THE S&L INDUSTRY NEEDED. HE PURCHASED LINCOLN, A MODEST, FAMILY-RUN S&L IN IRVINE, CALIFORNIA, FROM DONALD CROCKER.

HOW'S $51 MILLION SOUND?

FINE. JUST DON'T MAKE TOO MANY CHANGES AROUND HERE.

HIS PROMISES TO RETAIN LINCOLN'S MANAGEMENT AND STICK TO HOME MORTGAGES WERE QUICKLY FORGOTTEN.

THERE SHE IS, GENTLEMEN. OUR OWN PERSONAL MINT.

SHREWDLY, HE HELD NO OFFICIAL POSITION AT LINCOLN. INSTEAD, HE MADE THE BANK PART OF HIS LAND DEVELOPMENT FIRM, AMERICAN CONTINENTAL CORPORATION.

HEY, I DON'T WANT ANY TROUBLE.

MOST HIGH-INTEREST INVESTMENTS ARE ALSO HIGH-RISK, BUT NOT S&Ls. AFTER REAGAN'S REFORMS, THEY WERE INSURED -- WITH TAXPAYER MONEY. HIGH YIELD, NO RISK. WALL STREET LOVED IT. BIG INVESTMENT FIRMS BECAME THE S&Ls' TOP DEPOSITORS.

ABANDONING THE STRUGGLING HOMEOWNERS, KEATING PULLED IN WALL STREET MONEY AND FUNNELED IT OUT INTO HIGH RISK INVESTMENTS.

SAY, YOU KNOW WHAT WE NEED? MORE JUNK BONDS!

MEANWHILE, IN WASHINGTON, CHIEF BANK REGULATOR, ED GRAY WAS TIPPED OFF TO SOMETHING AMISS BY AN ANONYMOUSLY MAILED VIDEOTAPE.

HMM... WHAT COULD THIS BE?

THE VIDEO SHOWED ROWS AND ROWS OF DILAPIDATED CONDO COMPLEXES -- BAD INVESTMENTS OF A MAJOR TEXAS S&L.

I THINK I'M GONNA BE SICK!

AND THAT WAS JUST ONE S&L OF THE DOZENS THAT WERE GOING UNDER, EACH COSTING TAXPAYERS HUNDREDS OF MILLIONS.

GRAY CRACKED DOWN ON THE S&L OWNERS' FAST BUCK SCHEMES, EARNING HIMSELF THE WRATH OF NUMEROUS THRIFT-BACKED CONGRESSMEN.

YOU'LL NEVER WORK IN THE BANKING BUSINESS AGAIN, GRAY!

I HOPE YOU LIKE SLEEPING ON HEATING GRATES!

KEATING, WITH THE SKILL OF A STREET HUSTLER, ESPECIALLY WANTED GRAY OFF HIS BACK. HE WORKED A SERIES OF FINANCIAL SCHEMES TO DISGUISE LINCOLN'S MASSIVE LOSSES.

FIND THE QUEEN! FIND THE LADY!

KEATING SOLD $250 MILLION IN LINCOLN JUNK NOTES, MOSTLY TO SENIOR CITIZENS WHO STAKED THEIR PENSIONS. HIS SALESMEN TOLD THEM...

YOU CAN'T LOSE! THESE NOTES ARE FEDERALLY INSURED!

THEY WEREN'T.

KEATING KNEW HOW THE WASHINGTON GAME WAS PLAYED. HE FUNNELED HUGE BACK-DOOR CONTRIBUTIONS TO DOZENS OF POLITICIANS. HE CALLED IN FIVE PRESTIGIOUS SENATORS TO LEAN ON GRAY.

WE GOT A MESSAGE FROM OUR FRIEND AT LINCOLN SAVINGS AND LOAN!

THE MESSAGE IS-- LAY OFF!

THE SENATORS DENIED ANY CONNECTION BETWEEN THEIR MEETING WITH GRAY AND THE THOUSANDS THEY TOOK FROM KEATING.

IT'S OUTRAGEOUS THAT ANYONE SHOULD MAKE SUCH A SUGGESTION.

THE SENATORS, ALAN CRANSTON, JOHN GLENN, DONALD RIEGLE, DENNIS De CONCINI, AND JOHN McCAIN, RECEIVED ANYWHERE FROM $34,000 TO $112,000 FROM KEATING AND CO. CRANSTON ALSO BENEFITED FROM ALMOST A MILLION DOLLARS IN BACK-DOOR MONEY FROM KEATING TO SEVERAL "GET OUT THE VOTE" GROUPS.

LATER, ASKED IF HE THOUGHT HIS CONTRIBUTIONS INFLUENCED THE SENATORS, KEATING SAID...

I CERTAINLY HOPE SO!

KEATING BOUGHT AN EXTRA YEAR TO BLEED LINCOLN FURTHER. IN 1989, THE GOVERNMENT FINALLY TOOK IT OVER. KEATING FACED FRAUD CHARGES -- AND SOME OF THE ANGRY RETIREES HE'D BILKED. ONE GOT CLOSE ENOUGH TO SLUG HIM.

KEATING, YOU #$@&!! THIEF! LIAR!

WHUMP!

S&Ls WERE FAILING ALL OVER THE COUNTRY. THE GOVERNMENT CLOSED DENVER'S SILVERADO S&L ON NOV. 9, 1988, ONE DAY AFTER THE PRESIDENTIAL ELECTION.

SEIZED BY U.S. GOVERNMENT

THE TIMING WAS CRUCIAL. UNTIL HE WAS SAFELY ELECTED, GEORGE BUSH DIDN'T NEED ANY SCANDALS DISTRACTING VOTERS FROM THE IMPORTANT ISSUES.

AND MOST OF ALL, I'D LIKE TO THANK-- WILLIE HORTON!

WHAT A SCANDAL IT WOULD HAVE BEEN. BUSH'S SON NEIL-- SEEKING TO STAKE HIS OWN CLAIM IN THE BUSINESS WORLD-- PLAYED A KEY ROLE IN SILVERADO'S COLLAPSE.

GOTTA GET MY PIECE O' THE PIE!

THE GOOD-NATURED NEIL WAS SHORT ON SUCCESS. HE TRIED TO TAKE AFTER HIS DAD IN THE OIL BUSINESS, BUT CAME UP DRY.

IT'S GOTTA BE DOWN THERE SOMEWHERE!

NEIL TOOK A SPOT ON SILVERADO'S BOARD OF DIRECTORS, AN UNPAID BUT PRESTIGIOUS (AND ADVANTAGEOUS) POSITION.

ALL RIGHT! NOW I'M GETTIN' SOMEWHERE!

NEIL!

NEIL VOTED TO APPROVE LOANS AND CREDIT TO KENNETH GOOD AND WILLIAM WALTERS, BOTH HIS OWN BUSINESS PARTNERS IN OTHER VENTURES. THE PAIR ENDED UP STIFFING SILVERADO FOR $130 MILLION, DRIVING A LARGE NAIL INTO THE S&L'S COFFIN.

WOW! I'VE GOT SO MANY FRIENDS I DON'T HAVE ENOUGH HANDS TO SHAKE WITH!

GOOD HAD ONCE "LOANED" NEIL $100,000 -- WITH NO REQUIRE-MENT THAT IT BE PAID BACK.

I KNOW IT LOOKS A LITTLE FISHY.

THE PRESIDENT DIDN'T HAVE MUCH TO SAY ABOUT HIS WAYWARD SON.

THIS SORTA THING, VERY PAINFUL, VERY BAD.

PRESIDENT OF DA UN

STILL, THE BUSH ADMINISTRATION TIMED MAJOR ANNOUNCEMENTS TO DIVERT ATTENTION FROM NEIL'S PLIGHT.

WASHINGTON POST

WHITE HOUSE ANNOUNCES S&L BAILOUT

NEIL BUSH CALLS LOAN "FISHY"

THE REGULATOR RESPONSIBLE FOR SILVERADO TOLD A CONGRESSIONAL COMMITTEE...

I WAS ORDERED BY WASHINGTON NOT TO CLOSE IT DOWN UNTIL AFTER THE ELECTION.

NEIL WAS EVENTUALLY ORDERED TO PAY MILLIONS TO THE GOVERNMENT, BUT IT WAS DOUBTFUL ANY OF THE MONEY WOULD COME FROM HIS OWN POCKET.

WELL, ON TO MY NEXT ADVENTURE!

CHARLES KEATING WAS CONVICTED AND WENT TO JAIL. IN 1996 HIS CONVICTIONS WERE THROWN OUT ON TECHNICALITIES.

OF THE "KEATING FIVE," ONLY ALAN CRANSTON WAS SCOLDED BY THE SENATE ETHICS COMMITTEE.

NONE OF THE FIVE WERE PUNISHED.

THE S&L SCANDAL EVENTUALLY FADED FROM THE HEADLINES, TOO COMPLEX FOR THE AVERAGE PERSON TO UNDERSTAND-- OR FOR THE MEDIA TO EXPLAIN. BUT WITH THE COST OF THE BAILOUT ZOOMING TOWARD A TRILLION DOLLARS, THE TAXPAYER MIGHT DO WELL TO REMEMBER THE SCANDAL EVERY APRIL 15.

WHERE THE HELL DOES ALL THE MONEY GO?

FACTOID BOOKS

THE "LIBYAN TERRORIST." AMERICA'S ALL-PURPOSE DEMON. BUT WHAT IF THEY WERE TRAINED AND ARMED BY AMERICANS WITH CLOSE CIA TIES? THAT'S EXACTLY WHAT HAPPENED IN...

The WILSON-TERPIL AFFAIR

OCT. 27, 1955. A POOR IDAHO FARM BOY AND EX-MARINE JOIN AN EXCLUSIVE CLUB.

EDWIN P. WILSON, DO YOU SWEAR YOU WILL NEVER REVEAL ANYTHING ABOUT YOUR ACTIVITIES AS AN AGENT OF THE CENTRAL INTELLIGENCE AGENCY?

THIS LOOKS LIKE A PRETTY GOOD RACKET.

SURE.

AFTER A DECADE OF GRUNT WORK, WILSON WAS PUT IN CHARGE OF A "PROPRIETARY"—A "LEGITIMATE" SHIPPING COMPANY THAT WAS REALLY A CIA FRONT.

THE CIA PICKED UP THE TAB FOR HIS OFFICE, STAFF, AND AMPLE EXPENSE ACCOUNT AS WILSON'S COMPANY SENT ARMS, EXPLOSIVES, AND HIGH-TECH SPY EQUIPMENT TO SOUTH AMERICA, ASIA, AFRICA, AND THE MIDDLE EAST—— ANYWHERE THE CIA WAS COOKING UP TROUBLE.

YOU WANT GUNS? WE GOT GUNS! YOU WANT BOMBS? HECK, WE GOT 'EM TOO!

WHILE UNCLE SAM COVERED HIS COSTS, WILSON POCKETED HUGE PROFITS. THE CIA THOUGHT THAT WAS GREAT. IT MADE HIM LOOK MORE LEGITIMATE.

I KNEW THIS SPY BIZ WAS A GOOD RACKET!

A BURLY, AFFABLE GUY, WILSON KNEW THE IMPORTANCE OF WELL-PLACED FRIENDS. HE HUNG AROUND WITH CIA OFFICER THOMAS CLINES, WHO CONTINUALLY HIT WILSON UP FOR MONEY.

I WILL GLADLY PAY YOU TUESDAY...

HE GREW CLOSE TO CLINES' BOSS, THE AGENCY'S TOP COVERT OPERATIONS MAN, TED SHACKLEY—— THE MYSTERIOUS "BLONDE GHOST."

YEARS LATER, MERELY KNOWING ED WILSON WOULD CAUSE THE LEGENDARY SHACKLEY'S DOWNFALL.

WILSON'S CIA BOSSES LOVED HIM AND HE WAS GETTING RICH. HE BOUGHT THE FIRST PIECE OF WHAT WOULD GROW INTO A VAST ESTATE IN RURAL VIRGINIA.

SOMEDAY, ALL THIS LAND WILL BE MINE!

IN 1970, THINGS CHANGED. PRESIDENT NIXON BLAMED SHODDY CIA INTELLIGENCE FOR HIS TROUBLES IN VIETNAM. HE ORDERED A TOP-TO-BOTTOM FINANCIAL AUDIT.

THEY'VE GOT 40,000 PEOPLE OVER THERE *READING* NEWSPAPERS!

"PROPRIETARY" COMPANIES LIKE WILSON'S, WITH THEIR OUT-OF--CONTROL COSTS, WERE FIRST TO BE CUT.

THE CIA OFFERED ITS MAN WILSON A KEY ASSIGNMENT. BUT THAT MEANT HE'D BE JUST ANOTHER SPY ON A CIVIL SERVANT'S PAY.

I WILL GLADLY PAY YOU TUESDAY...

NO WAY I'M ENDING UP LIKE *THAT* LOSER!

JUST TWO MONTHS LATER, WILSON JOINED THE NAVY'S ULTRA-SECRET "TASK FORCE 157." THE GROUP'S PURPOSE: TO SPY ON ALL SOVIET SHIPPING ACTIVITY. TO DO IT, THEY NEEDED A NETWORK OF FRONT COMPANIES FOR COVER. WILSON WAS THEIR MAN.

LOOK OUT, WORLD! I'M BACK IN BUSINESS!

WILSON OPENED HIS 1,500-ACRE ESTATE TO NONSTOP PARTIES FOR DIGNITARIES AND OFFICIALS. HE CREATED HIS OWN BACKSLAPPING NETWORK OF POWERFUL CONTACTS.

SLAP

- UNNFF! -

HE THREW HIMSELF INTO THE WEAPONS BUSINESS, SPENDING A LOT OF TIME IN IRAN SELLING ARMS TO THE SHAH--NOT EXACTLY A NAVAL INTELLIGENCE PRIORITY.

CHECK IT OUT. JUST PRESS THIS AND...

POOF

COOL!

HIS NAVAL BOSSES WERE NONE TOO THRILLED.

YOU WERE SUPPOSED TO SET UP 10 OVERSEAS OFFICES WITH AGENTS IN PLACE AND *I* DON'T SEE ONE!

TAKE IT EASY. I'LL GET RIGHT ON IT.

SUSPICIOUS, THE NAVY CHECKED OUT WILSON'S BACKGROUND WITH THE CIA AND COULDN'T BELIEVE THE RESPONSE.

WILSON'S GOT A TRIPLE-A RATING. HE'S TOPNOTCH.

IF HE'S YOUR BEST, I'D HATE TO SEE YOUR WORST!!

FEARING FOR HIS JOB, WILSON PULLED SOME STRINGS AND ARRANGED LUNCH WITH NAVY BOSS ADMIRAL BOBBY RAY INMAN.

YOU NEED FUNDING? I CAN GET IT. I KNOW PEOPLE.

DAMMIT, WILSON! ARE YOU TRYING TO BRIBE ME?

INMAN REPORTED WILSON TO THE FBI, BUT NOTHING HAPPENED.

THAT'S WHY THEY CALL IT THE INTELLIGENCE *COMMUNITY!* WE TAKE CARE OF OUR OWN.

BUT EVEN WILSON'S CONNECTIONS COULDN'T SAVE HIS NAVY JOB.

AS USUAL, WILSON WAS PREPARED. AT A PARTY IN 1975 HE'D MET A COLORFUL EX-CIA OPERATIVE NAMED FRANK TERPIL.

I GOT FRIENDS IN HIGH PLACES-- IN LIBYA! I THINK WE CAN DO BUSINESS WITH 'EM.

TERPIL WASN'T PARTICULAR ABOUT HIS CUSTOMERS OR HIS SALES TECHNIQUES. HE BRAGGED THAT HE'D SOLD A NEW FORM OF POISON TO A TERRORIST BY DEMONSTRATING IT ON AN INNOCENT DINER IN A BEIRUT RESTAURANT.

-- AARRGGGUBBBUUGGHH! --

I TOLD YA THE STUFF WAS GOOD!

TERPIL HAD BEEN KICKED OUT OF THE CIA FOR SMUGGLING. HE HAD TWO ARRESTS FOR GUNRUNNING.

NONE OF THAT BOTHERED WILSON. HE FORMED A NEW COMPANY WITH TERPIL.

THEY TOOK ON A THIRD PARTNER, KEVIN MULCAHY, A CIA LOYALIST WHOSE FATHER WAS A DISTINGUISHED AGENCY OFFICER.

YOU SURE HE'S OKAY--?

DON'T WORRY. HAVING HIM AROUND MAKES US LOOK MORE LEGIT!

MULCAHY, A RECOVERING ALCOHOLIC, GOT INVOLVED IN THINGS WITH WILSON THAT DROVE HIM OFF THE WAGON.

WE NEED TO GET HALF A MILLION OF THESE THINGS TO LIBYA. CAN YOU HANDLE IT?

EXPLOSIVE DETONATORS

I NEED A STIFF DRINK!

UH, ED--? WHY EXACTLY DOES QADDAFI NEED 500,000 DETONATORS?

AH, IT'S NOTHING. HE JUST WANTS TO CLEAR SOME ISRAELI MINES LEFT OVER FROM THE '73 WAR.

BUT THERE *WERE* NO ISRAELI MINES IN LIBYA FROM THE '73 WAR.

WHAT'S MORE, THE DETONATORS WERE TIME-DELAY DEVICES. THEY COULD EASILY BE USED IN BOMBS PLANTED BY *TERRORISTS* -- OF THE TYPE LIBYAN LEADER QADDAFI OPENLY SUPPORTED.

WE WILL BRING THE WEST TO ITS KNEES!

MULCAHY GOT WORRIED. HE HAD REASON TO BE. HE SNUCK INTO WILSON'S FILES AND FOUND THE COMPANY'S SECRET. WILSON AND TERPIL WERE NOT ONLY SELLING EXPLOSIVES TO LIBYA, THEY WERE HIRING GREEN BERETS TO *TRAIN TERRORISTS.*

THESE GUYS *HAVE TO BE* WORKING FOR *THE CIA!* HOW ELSE COULD THEY GET AWAY WITH THIS?

THEY WERE SELLING ALL SORTS OF JAMES BOND-LIKE DEVICES TO LIBYA. ONE NOTABLE ITEM OF INVENTORY: THE EXPLODING ASHTRAY.

I KNEW SMOKING WAS HAZARDOUS TO YOUR HEALTH, BUT THIS IS RIDICULOUS!

STEELING HIMSELF, MULCAHY PHONED THE MAN AT THE CIA WHO WOULD KNOW WHAT WAS GOING ON: TED SHACKLEY.

YOU GOTTA TELL ME, TED! IS THIS A CIA OP?

I'LL CHECK INTO IT.

GUESS WHAT? NOTHING HAPPENED.

NO WONDER. SHACKLEY AND WILSON WERE STILL CLOSE. THEY OFTEN DINED TOGETHER, THOUGH SHACKLEY DEMURRED:

ED WILSON? HE'S JUST A GOOD *INTELLIGENCE SOURCE.*

AROUND THE SAME TIME, WILSON AND TERPIL CONTRACTED WITH A CUBAN CIA VET.

WE'VE GOT A JOB FOR YOU. A *WET JOB!*

IT'S GREAT TO BE WORKING FOR THE AGENCY AGAIN!

BUT HE WASN'T WORKING FOR THE AGENCY.

HE WAS WORKING FOR QADDAFI...

ENEMIES OF THE REVOLUTION MUST DIE!

...WHO'D HIRED WILSON AND TERPIL TO ASSASSINATE A LIBYAN DEFECTOR IN EGYPT.

THE WOULD-BE ASSASSIN HE THOUGHT THE TARGET MIGHT BE THE NOTORIOUS FREELANCE TERRORIST CARLOS "THE JACKAL".

WHEN HE FOUND OUT WHO IT REALLY WAS, HE BACKED OUT OF THE JOB AND REPORTED THE INCIDENT TO THE CIA.

TERPIL LEFT WILSON AND HOOKED UP WITH UGANDAN MADMAN IDI AMIN. HE BOASTED OF TAKING PART IN AMIN'S ATROCITIES.

SEE HOW THE RAT EATS THROUGH HIS BELLY TO ESCAPE! CLEVER, NO?

NICE ONE, IDI!

MULCAHY TOOK HIS INFORMATION TO THE FBI.

WILSON'S A MENACE! YOU'VE GOT TO NAIL HIM!

YEAH, WE'LL GET RIGHT ON IT.

NO ONE WANTED TO PROSECUTE WILSON. HELL, HALF OF WASHINGTON HUNG OUT AT WILSON'S MT. AIRY ESTATE. BUT A TOP LAWYER FOR THE U.S. ATTORNEY LAWRENCE BARCELLA, WAS AN EXCEPTION. HE MADE WILSON HIS PERSONAL CRUSADE.

ONE'A THESE DAYS, WILSON...

WANTED

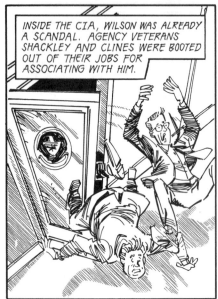

INSIDE THE CIA, WILSON WAS ALREADY A SCANDAL. AGENCY VETERANS SHACKLEY AND CLINES WERE BOOTED OUT OF THEIR JOBS FOR ASSOCIATING WITH HIM.

USING INFORMATION FROM MULCAHY AND THE CUBAN ASSASSIN, BARCELLA INDICTED WILSON, WHO BECAME A FUGITIVE. WHEN WILSON WAS ARRESTED IN MALTA, HE BRIBED HIS WAY TO FREEDOM.

MULCAHY, HOWEVER, ACCUSED BARCELLA OF FOOT-DRAGGING. IN 1981, HE TALKED TO PULITZER PRIZE WINNER SEYMOUR HERSH, WHO WROTE MULCAHY'S STORY FOR THE NEW YORK TIMES MAGAZINE. THE WILSON-TERPIL SCANDAL WAS SUDDENLY TOO HOT TO IGNORE.

The New York Times M
THE QADDAFI CONNE
By Seymour M. Hersh

IN 1982 BARCELLA SET A TRAP, USING AN INTERMEDIARY, TO LURE WILSON OUT OF LIBYA.

THE NATIONAL SECURITY COUNCIL GUARANTEES YOU SAFE HAVEN IN THE DOMINICAN REPUBLIC.

THAT'S GOTTA BE BETTER THAN THIS GODFORSAKEN PLACE!

BUT THE DOMINICANS, AS PLANNED, PUT HIM ON A PLANE TO NEW YORK WHERE, AFTER FOUR YEARS ON THE LAM, WILSON WAS ARRESTED. ALTHOUGH WEALTHY WITH LIBYAN MONEY, EVEN WILSON WASN'T RICH ENOUGH TO POST THE $20 MILLION BAIL.

WARRANT

WILSON'S ARREST WAS THE MEDIA EVENT OF THE YEAR.

THERE ARE THINGS GOING ON HERE NO ONE KNOWS ABOUT.

WITH HIS LAWYERS, WILSON PLOTTED HIS DEFENSE.

THIS WHOLE THING WAS A CIA OPERATION! I'LL TELL THINGS THAT'LL HAVE THE AGENCY SHAKING IN FEAR!

ON OCTOBER 26, 1982, KEVIN MULCAHY WAS FOUND DEAD OUTSIDE HIS MOTEL ROOM. HIS REVELATIONS LED TO WILSON'S DESTRUCTION, BUT HE DIDN'T LIVE LONG ENOUGH TO SEE HIS ARCHENEMY CONVICTED.

THE AUTOPSY SHOWED HE DIED OF PNEUMONIA, BUT WILD RUMORS HELD THAT HE WAS RUBBED OUT BY THE CIA. OR BY WILSON.

OR MAYBE THOSE RUMORS WEREN'T SO WILD. IN PRISON WILSON APPROACHED ANOTHER INMATE WITH HIS PERSONAL "HIT LIST." ON TOP OF THE LIST:

THAT SONUVABITCH BARCELLA! I'LL PAY A QUARTER-MILLION TO WHOEVER WHACKS HIM.

THE MURDER-PLOT CHARGES ONLY ADDED TO THE LIST HE ALREADY FACED...

THEY SET ME UP, GODDAMMIT! I'M INNOCENT!

...INCLUDING SHIPPING 21 TONS OF DEADLY "C4" EXPLOSIVE TO LIBYA. HE WAS CONVICTED ON MOST CHARGES AND SENTENCED TO 52 YEARS--IN EFFECT, LIFE.

AS FOR TERPIL, HE ESCAPED CAPTURE, TAKING REFUGE IN CUBA.

FIDEL, BABY! I LUV YA!

WILSON'S "CIA DEFENSE" FELL FLAT, BUT SERIOUS QUESTIONS REMAINED ABOUT HIS DEALINGS WITH TOP AGENCY SPOOKS, SHACKLEY IN PARTICULAR.

I WAS DUPED BY A FRIEND. I DIDN'T KNOW WHAT WILSON WAS UP TO. SO GET OFF MY BACK!

THE WILSON AFFAIR ECHOED IN THE IRAN-CONTRA SCANDAL (ANOTHER ARMS-TO-TERRORISTS OPERATION). GENERAL RICHARD SECORD, IT TURNED OUT, HAD BEEN A LONGTIME ASSOCIATE OF WILSON'S.

BUT I NEVER TOOK PART IN HIS ILLEGAL DEALS!

A CHILLING FOOTNOTE: ON DEC. 21, 1988 A PAN AM 747 EXPLODED OVER LOCKERBIE, SCOTLAND, KILLING 259, MOSTLY AMERICANS.

THE CAUSE: A TERRORIST BOMB ON A SOPHISTICATED TIMER. THE CHIEF SUSPECTS: TWO LIBYAN INTELLIGENCE AGENTS.

NEW YORK. WORLDWIDE CAPITOL OF FINANCE, MEDIA, AND THE ARTS. HOME TO 10 MILLION PEOPLE OF EVERY RELIGION, RACE, AND NATIONALITY. AND IN THE 1980S, NEW YORKERS WATCHED AS THEIR CITY WAS PLUNDERED AND DISGRACED BY...

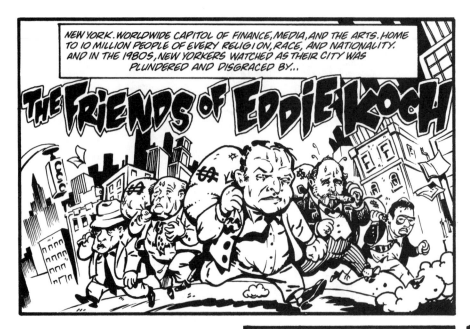

THE FRIENDS OF EDDIE KOCH

NEW YORK HAD A LONG HISTORY OF CORRUPT POLITICAL "BOSSES." THE PROTOTYPE WAS WILLIAM M. "BOSS" TWEED WHO RULED (AND ROBBED) IN THE MID-19TH CENTURY.

TWEED LED A POLITICAL MACHINE KNOWN AS "TAMMANY HALL," THAT LOOTED THE CITY OF MORE THAN $40 MILLION-- UNTIL THE DEVASTATING EDITORIAL CARTOONS OF THOMAS NAST EXPOSED HIM.

STOP THEM DAMN *PICTURES!*

TAMMANY'S STRANGLEHOLD ON THE CITY CONTINUED--UNTIL THE 1930'S, WHEN MAYOR FIORELLO LaGUARDIA WAGED A CAMPAIGN AGAINST CORRUPTION.

SMASH

THE 1950S SAW THE COMEBACK OF TAMMANY HALL. BOSS CARMINE DeSAPIO'S COOL STYLE AND UNDERWORLD CONNECTIONS SUITED THE ERA.

TAMMANY HALL HAS BEEN *UNFAIRLY STIGMATIZED* AS SOMETHING SINISTER AND EVIL.

IN THE EARLY 60s, TAMMANY WAS SWEPT AWAY BY AN IDEALISTIC BAND OF REFORMERS LED BY EDWARD T. KOCH.

VILLAGE INDEPENDENT DEMOCRATS

POLITICS NEED *NOT* BE FULL OF MORAL *LEPERS* WHO'LL SELL THEIR INTEGRITY FOR A *JOB!*

IN 1978, NEW YORKERS ELECTED THE CHARISMATIC KOCH THEIR MAYOR. A LARGER-THAN-LIFE CHARACTER, KOCH LOVED TO ASK...

HOW'M I DOIN'?

HE NEVER DOUBTED THE ANSWER.

HIS LOVABLY ECCENTRIC IMAGE ASIDE, KOCH OWED HIS POWER TO A COALITION OF BACKSTAGE KINGMAKERS-- CHIEF AMONG THEM, QUEENS BOROUGH PRESIDENT DONALD MANES.

ATTABOY, ED!

SLAP!

KOCH THOUGHT HE'D BE MAYOR FOR LIFE. ON NEW YEAR'S DAY, 1986, HE WAS SWORN IN FOR HIS THIRD TERM, WITH NO END IN SIGHT.

HOW'M I DOIN'?!

JUST 10 DAYS AFTER THE INAUGURATION, A CAR SWERVED CRAZILY ON THE GRAND CENTRAL PARKWAY. POLICE PULLED IT OVER.

RRRRAOOOOWW!!

POLICE

THE OFFICERS FOUND THE DRIVER DRENCHED IN HIS OWN BLOOD. AND MORE SHOCKING...

THAT'S-- THAT'S DONALD MANES!!

THE BIZARRE ATTACK ON THE CITY'S SECOND-MOST POWERFUL POLITICIAN WAS, INSTANTLY, THE BIGGEST NEW YORK SCANDAL-- AND MYSTERY--IN YEARS. MANES' CRONIES PUT OUT A COVER STORY.

NEW YORK POST
MANES SLASHED IN HOOKER TRYST

IN FACT, AS HE SOON ADMITTED, MANES SLASHED HIMSELF. BUT WHY?

LIFE JUST ISN'T WORTH LIVING ANYMORE.

DONALD MANES WAS NOTHING BUT A STRONG-ARM MAN.

DON'T WORRY PAL. THE CITY'LL BE HAPPY TO RENEW IT'S CONTRACT WITH YOUR COMPANY. WE'RE ALL FRIENDS HERE.

SOMEONE KNEW MANES' SECRET: RUDOLPH GIULIANI, THE INCORRUPTIBLE FEDERAL PROSECUTOR WHOSE ONLY WEAKNESS WAS A LOVE OF PUBLICITY.

THERE'S NOBODY WORSE THAN A PUBLIC OFFICIAL WHO SELLS HIS OFFICE AND CORRUPTS OTHERS--EXCEPT MAYBE A MURDERER.

GIULIANI TAPED MANES' BAGMAN, GEOFF LINDENAUER, TAKING CASH FROM A SECRET INFORMER, BUSINESSMAN BERNIE SANDOW.

HERE'S YOUR FIVE GRAND, GEOFF!

THANKS, BERNIE! SEE YA IN TWO WEEKS!

WHEN MANES GOT WIND OF THE INVESTIGATION IN LATE 1985, HE STARTED ACTING STRANGELY.

THERE'S ONLY ONE WAY OUT OF THIS, GEOFF.

WHEN GIULIANI'S INVESTIGATION WENT PUBLIC--AFTER MANES' SURREAL SUICIDE ATTEMPT, ED KOCH QUICKLY ABANDONED HIS LONG-TIME BACKER.

DONALD MANES IS A *CROOK!*

ON MARCH 13, 1986, MANES--NOW PUBLICLY DISGRACED--WAS HOME TALKING ON THE PHONE WITH HIS PSYCHIATRIST WHEN...

KA-SHRUNK

THE DAY AFTER MANES' DEATH, KOCH WAS HIS OLD, BUOYANT SELF.

HOW'M I DOIN'?!

IT WAS A CASE OF PREMATURE ELATION. THE SCANDAL WAS FAR FROM FINISHED.

OTHER KOCH COHORTS FELL ON VARIOUS CORRUPTION CHARGES: BRONX BOSS STANLEY FRIEDMAN, BROOKLYN KINGMAKER MEADE ESPOSITO AND SEVERAL OTHER MEMBERS OF THE MACHINE THAT PROPPED KOCH INTO POWER.

US MARSHALL SERVICE EDNY

53

BUT THE UNKINDEST CUT FROM THE LEAST LIKELY QUARTER: BESS MYERSON, THE FIRST JEWISH MISS AMERICA. SHE'D GONE ON TO A CAREER IN CITY GOVERNMENT.

LIFELONG BACHELOR KOCH STAGED A BOGUS "ROMANCE" WITH MYERSON IN HIS 1978 CAMPAIGN.

THE SHAM HELPED KOCH WIN, BUT LEFT HIM FOREVER LINKED TO MYERSON IN THE PUBLIC MIND.

IN 1987, MYERSON'S *REAL* LOVER WAS GETTING DIVORCED. MYERSON GAVE A CUSHY CITY JOB TO THE JUDGE'S DAUGHTER.

BESS HAS, UH, FALLEN FROM, UH, GRACE.

THEN KOCH'S OFFICE *SUPPRESSED* A REPORT THAT NAILED MYERSON.

THAT WAS KOCH'S DEATH BLOW. HE RAN FOR RE-ELECTION AND LOST TO DAVID DINKINS, NEW YORK'S FIRST BLACK MAYOR.

FOUR YEARS LATER, DINKINS WAS DEPOSED BY ANOTHER NEW MAYOR--RUDOLPH GIULIANI.

CHAPTER FOUR

DIRTY BUSINESS

If there's one thing this amusingly imperfect society worships more than fame, power or status, it's money. And we worship the people who know how to make lots of money. We think of businessmen as successful, competent, efficient, respectable, with limitless reservoirs of common sense.

We now present a series of stories dedicated to the proposition that, guess what—it just isn't so! The business world is no more immune to idiocy, incompetence and outright malfeasance than any other segment of society. Feast your eyes, then, on exploding automobiles, poisoned playgrounds, international bribery, extortion and even murder. None of it an accident—all of these business scandals sprang straight from some businessman's arrogance or amorality in the pursuit of cold, hard cash. Money talks, but in these cases, it talks dirty.

ROBERT VESCO WAS A HIGH-SCHOOL DROPOUT FROM DETROIT WITH A BRILLIANT MIND FOR BUSINESS. IT MADE HIM A MILLIONAIRE BEFORE HE WAS 30. BUT IT ALSO MADE HIM...

LONG BEFORE IVAN BOESKY, VESCO WAS THE ORIGINAL HARD-DRIVING WALL STREET MAVERICK.

THAT CLOCK SAYS 7:02!! YOU'RE SUPPOSED TO BE AT WORK BY 7:00!! YOU'RE FIRED!!!

BY 1968 HIS COMPANY OWNED AN AIRLINE AND SEVERAL MANUFACTURING FIRMS. AT AGE 33, VESCO HELD SHARES WORTH *FIFTY MILLION!*

GIMME MONEY! THAT'S WHAT I WANT!

HIS COMPANY'S NAME REFLECTED VESCO'S ASPIRATIONS: INTERNATIONAL CONTROLS.

VESCO STYLED HIMSELF A HARDWORKING FAMILY MAN, DEVOTED TO HIS WIFE AND FOUR KIDS.

IN REALITY, HIS REAL LOVES-- BESIDES BUSINESS-- WERE BOOZE, GAMBLING AND PHILANDERING. HIS REPUTATION WAS ALWAYS A LITTLE SHADY.

THE STREETWISE VESCO'S FATE INTERTWINED WITH BERNIE CORNFELD, SUPER-RICH GLOBAL SOPHISTICATE AND BUDDY OF HUGH HEFNER.

CORNFELD HAD MADE A FORTUNE RUNNING A GENEVA MUTUAL FUND CALLED INVESTORS OVERSEAS SERVICES.

IN 1970, IOS WAS CRUMBLING. VESCO TURNED ON HIS ROUGH-HEWN CHARM AND OFFERED HIMSELF AS THE COMPANY'S SAVIOR.

GENTLEMEN, ONLY *I* CAN SAVE YOUR $%#@*! COMPANY!

IOS INTERESTED HIM BECAUSE, BEING OVERSEAS, IT WAS UNREGULATED.

THERE WAS ONE PROBLEM: BERNIE CORNFELD. THE JET-SETTER LIVED IN A DIFFERENT UNIVERSE THAN THE HARD-HAT MILLIONAIRE VESCO.

NICE SUIT.

GET IT AT K-MART?

HE VOWED...

THAT *THUG* VESCO NEVER GETS CONTROL OF THIS COMPANY!!

VESCO STARTED A **VERY** HOSTILE TAKE-OVER. HE EVEN BOUGHT SHARES HELD IN A SWISS BANK'S SAFE-DEPOSIT BOX -- ON A SUNDAY.

THEY'RE MINE -- AND I WANT THEM **NOW!!**

VESCO'S MACHINATIONS EARNED HIM A HUMILIATING NIGHT IN A SWISS JAIL. IT WAS ONE NIGHT TOO MANY FOR HIM.

IF THEY TREAT ME LIKE A CROOK, THEN DAMMIT, I'LL ACT LIKE A CROOK! I'LL STEAL EVERY DIME I CAN!

DURING THIS PERIOD, 1971, VESCO COLLECTED A COUPLE OF KEY ASSETS. ONE WAS "DON-DON" NIXON, THE PRESIDENT'S CALLOW NEPHEW, WHO CAME TO WORSHIP VESCO.

I'LL DO **ANYTHING** FOR YOU, BOBBY!

DAMN RIGHT YOU WILL, YA PUNK!

THE OTHER -- A 707 JET, PURCHASED AND RENOVATED AT INTERNATIONAL CONTROLS' EXPENSE. VESCO TURNED IT INTO HIS OWN FLYING PLEASURE PALACE, COMPLETE WITH DISCO, BEDROOM AND, FREQUENTLY, HIGH-PRICED EUROPEAN CALL GIRLS.

WITH A PERSONAL JET -- AND A PERSONAL NIXON -- AT HIS DISPOSAL, VESCO HAD EASY ACCESS TO INFLUENTIAL PEOPLE.

VESCO FINALLY BOUGHT OUT CORNFELD BY DISGUISING HIS PURCHASE BEHIND A NETWORK OF DUMMY CORPORATIONS.

THE BEST PART IS VESCO GETS NOTHING!

HEH HEH!

WITH CORNFELD OUT OF THE WAY, VESCO WAS FREE TO SUCK IOS DRY.

WHEN HE WAS DONE, VESCO HAD LOOTED IT OF ABOUT A QUARTER-BILLION DOLLARS.

FOR THAT TYPE OF OPERATION, HE NEEDED AN INSURANCE POLICY. HE CALLED HARRY SEARS, A RESPECTED REPUBLICAN POLITICIAN.

I WANT YOU TO DELIVER $200,000 TO NIXON'S REELECTION CAMPAIGN.

NIXON'S MEN, CHARACTERISTICALLY, WERE ENGAGED IN SUBTERFUGE OF THEIR OWN. CAMPAIGN TREASURER MAURICE STANS TOLD SEARS...

WE'D LIKE THE DONATION IN, UH, **CURRENCY.**

YOU MEAN...?

ON APRIL 10, 1972 -- THREE DAYS AFTER A NEW LAW PROHIBITING SECRET DONATIONS TOOK EFFECT...

MR. STANS, HERE IS YOUR "CURRENCY."

WHAT VESCO MAY OR MAY NOT HAVE KNOWN IS THAT HIS MONEY FINANCED NIXON'S COVERT SQUAD OF FIXERS, "THE PLUMBERS," THE SAME CADRE THAT PULLED OFF THE WATERGATE BREAK-IN.

VESCO WAS MORE CONCERNED WITH THE SECURITIES AND EXCHANGE COMMISSION, WHICH WAS PURSUING HIM RELENTLESSLY.

WE'LL NAIL YOU, VESCO!

GET LOST! I GOT FRIENDS!

BUT VESCO HAD MISCALCULATED. IN THE WAKE OF WATERGATE, STANS AND NIXON'S ATTORNEY GENERAL JOHN MITCHELL WERE INDICTED IN CONNECTION WITH VESCO'S ILLEGAL DONATION.

VESCO WAS INVESTIGATED TOO. AT THE SAME TIME, THE S.E.C. FILED A FRAUD COMPLAINT AGAINST HIM. HIS LEGAL PROBLEMS PILED UP. SO ROBERT VESCO FLED THE COUNTRY.

ADIOS, AMERICA! ICH BEN EIN COSTA RICAN!

IN COSTA RICA, VESCO WAS SHELTERED BY PRESIDENT JOSE "DON PEPE" FIGUERES. IT HELPED THAT VESCO POURED $2.1 MILLION INTO FIGUERES' COMPANY. FIGUERES PASSED THE "VESCO LAW," WHICH GUARANTEED:

WE WILL NEVER EXTRADITE ROBERT VESCO!

FOR THE MILLIONAIRE FUGITIVE, HOWEVER, KIDNAPPING AND ASSASSINATION WERE A MUCH GREATER CONCERN THAN EXTRADITION.

HE SURROUNDED HIMSELF WITH ARMED GUARDS.

AT ONE POINT HE TRIED TO PURCHASE 2,000 MACHINE GUNS WITH, SUSPICIOUSLY, SILENCERS.

IT'S A COMPANY OPERATION. I WORK FOR THE CIA!

HE WAS PROBABLY LYING, BUT VESCO WAS DEFINITELY UP TO SOMETHING.

IN 1978, FIGUERES LOST POWER AND THE VESCO LAW WAS REPEALED. VESCO HIGHTAILED TO NASSAU, THEN TO ANTIGUA.

GOSH, THIS LIFE AS A FUGITIVE IS REALLY ROUGH!

HE WASN'T WELCOME THERE LONG, HOWEVER. PURSUED BY U.S. AGENTS, HE SLIPPED AWAY, AT ONE POINT SWIMMING FROM A SMALL BOAT TO SHORE.

HE TRIED TO GO BACK TO COSTA RICA, BUT WASN'T ALLOWED OUT OF THE AIRPORT.

WELCOME TO COSTA RICA

SORRY, SENOR VESCO. ORDERS OF EL PRESIDENTE!

THE LEGEND OF OUTLAW VESCO FLOURISHED. SOME SAID THAT HE WAS THE FORCE BEHIND COLOMBIAN DRUG LORD CARLOS LEHDER, AMONG OTHER HIGH-FLYING ACTIVITIES.

JUST LISTEN TO ME, KID, AND YOU'LL BE ALL RIGHT.

IN REALITY, BY THE MID-80s, VESCO HAD RENOUNCED HIS CITIZENSHIP AND SETTLED IN CUBA.

WE DON'T CARE WHAT VESCO DID IN THE U.S.! HE IS WELCOME HERE!

FOR 13 YEARS, VESCO LIVED MODESTLY IN A HAVANA SUBURB. HE WAS STILL WHEELING AND DEALING, THOUGH.

BUT EVENTUALLY, THE CUBAN GOVERNMENT TIRED OF HIM.

ON MAY 31, 1995, CUBAN POLICE SHOWED UP AT VESCO'S HOME.

SENOR VESCO, YOU ARE UNDER ARREST FOR FRAUD!

THE U.S. MADE LITTLE ATTEMPT TO EXTRADITE HIM. IT'S UNLIKELY THAT THE POWERS-THAT-BE, ESPECIALLY REPUBLICANS, WANTED TO REVISIT THE DARK DAYS OF TWO DECADES EARLIER.

YEAH, WE REALLY WANT TO GO THROUGH THAT AGAIN!

HIS LONG RUN WAS OVER. IN 1996, CUBA SENTENCED THE 61-YEAR-OLD VESCO TO 13 YEARS BEHIND BARS.

THE FUGITIVE HAD BECOME THE PRISONER.

OCTOBER 19, 1982: JOHN Z. DELOREAN, GLAMOROUS MULTIMILLIONAIRE AUTOMOBILE ENTREPRENEUR, SCRAWLS A DESPERATE LETTER TO HIS ATTORNEY.

By the time you open this, I will be dead. Tomorrow, I sell my company to organized crime.

BUT BY THE TIME THE DAY CAME TO A CLOSE, DELOREAN WAS NOT DEAD. IN A WAY, HIS FATE WAS WORSE.

HE HAD BEEN ARRESTED BY THE FBI FOR CONSPIRACY TO DISTRIBUTE COCAINE.

HARD-DRIVING DELOREAN'S DOWNFALL SHOCKED THE NATION. BUT IN RETROSPECT, IT WAS INEVITABLE. FOR YEARS THE SPORTS CAR MAGNATE HAD BEEN RIDING ON A FAST TRACK THAT WAS DESTINED TO BECOME A...

COLLISION COURSE

WITH DISASTER!

SON OF A DETROIT AUTOWORKER, DELOREAN WAS THE CHIEF ENGINEER OF PONTIAC, A GM COMPANY MAN. BUT IN THE EARLY 60s HE HAD AN IDEA.

WE NEED A CAR THE "KIDS" CAN "DIG." A "FAB" SET OF "WHEELS."

HE CREATED THE GTO, AN INSTANT SMASH FOR GM. THE CAR WAS SO POPULAR AMONG DRAG-RACE-CRAZED YOUTH THAT IT WAS IMMORTALIZED IN RONNIE AND THE DAYTONAS' MILLION-SELLING SINGLE, "GTO".

♪LITTLE GTO, YOU'RE REALLY LOOKIN' FINE, THREE DEUCES AND A FOUR-SPEED AND A 389!♪

FLUSH WITH SUCCESS, DELOREAN BECAME A JET-SETTER. HE SHED 60 POUNDS, DYED HIS GRAYING HAIR, DIVORCED HIS WIFE AND MARRIED A 20-YEAR-OLD MODEL -- EVEN GOT A FACE LIFT.

HEY, I DIDN'T GET A FACE LIFT!

WELL, OKAY. I DID.

BY 1973 HE HAD, IN HIS OWN MIND ANYWAY, GROWN BIGGER THAN HIS MIGHTY CORPORATE EMPLOYER.

I'M NOT QUITTING MY JOB, I'M FIRING GENERAL MOTORS!

HE ALSO GOT DIVORCED AGAIN AND MARRIED ANOTHER MODEL, CRISTINA FERRARE.

DELOREAN CULTIVATED HIS HOLLYWOOD HIGH-LIVING IMAGE. BUT SOME OF HIS BUSINESS PARTNERS ALLEGED THAT HE FINANCED HIS LIFESTYLE WITH A SERIES OF SHADY BUSINESS DEALS. HE FOUGHT OFF SEVERAL LAWSUITS.

HE'S LIVIN' IT UP -- AND BLEEDIN' *US* DRY!

ALL THE WHILE, HE PLOTTED TO CREATE HIS ULTIMATE MONUMENT TO HIMSELF, THE DELOREAN MOTOR COMPANY.

WE WILL BUILD AN "ETHICAL SPORTS *CAR*," USING SAFE MATERIALS AND PROVIDING JOBS FOR THE NEEDY.

HE ROUNDED UP $3.5 MILLION IN CAPITAL, SOME FROM HIGH-PROFILE INVESTORS LIKE JOHNNY CARSON AND OTHERS...

HEY—O!

...BUT MOST OF THE MONEY CAME FROM THE BRITISH GOVERNMENT, OVER $100 MILLION IN LOANS.

IN EXCHANGE, DELOREAN BUILT HIS PLANT IN VIOLENCE-TORN BELFAST, NORTHERN IRELAND.

HE MAINTAINED HIS CHAMPAGNE LIFESTYLE-- AT THE EXPENSE OF A COMPANY THAT HAD YET TO PRODUCE A CAR.

MY ATTORNEY SAYS WE'LL DO FINE -- IF WE CAN KEEP FROM EVER BUILDING A CAR! HA HA HA!

IN 1980 THE FIRST STAINLESS STEEL DELOREANS ROLLED ON TO SHOWROOM FLOORS. THEY WERE FILLED WITH DEFECTS AND RECALLED. THEY WERE ALSO OVERPRICED AND, EVEN WITH THE KINKS IRONED OUT, FAILED TO SPARK PUBLIC IMAGINATION.

AND THEY DIDN'T EVEN BOTHER TO PAINT 'EM.

JMC

WITH SALES SLUGGISH, DELOREAN GREW DESPERATE. FOR THE FIRST TIME IN HIS LIFE, HE WAS FAILING. THE HE GOT A CALL OUT OF THE BLUE FROM AN OLD NEIGHBOR.

JOHN, I HAVE SOME FRIENDS WHO'D LIKE TO HELP YOUR COMPANY.

I'LL MEET YOU IN NEWPORT BEACH!

DELOREAN DIDN'T KNOW THAT HIS FRIEND JOHN HOFFMAN, A ONETIME DRUG DEALER, WAS NOW AN FBI INFORMANT.

THE FUNDS WILL COME FROM OFFSHORE THROUGH EUREKA SAVINGS AND LOAN. I KNOW THE BANK PRESIDENT.

I NEED TO MEET HIM.

HE ALSO DIDN'T KNOW THAT BANK PRESIDENT "JAMES BENEDICT" WAS REALLY AN UNDERCOVER FBI AGENT.

DON'T WORRY, MR. DELOREAN. WE'VE GOT MONEY TO BURN. - HEH-HEH -

---

OBLIVIOUS TO THE FBI PRESENCE, HE THOUGHT HE WAS DEALING WITH MOBSTERS. HE TRIED TO BACK OUT BUT WAS TOLD...

YOU KNOW TOO MUCH, DELOREAN. PULL OUT NOW AND YOUR KIDS ARE DEAD! IT'LL BE A BLOODY MESS!

HIS NEW "ASSOCIATES" BEGAN MENTIONING DRUGS FREQUENTLY.

FROM THAT COCAINE PURCHASE YOU'LL SEE $10 MILLION IN 48 HOURS.

I DON'T BELIEVE THEY'RE SERIOUS ABOUT THE DRUGS. THEY JUST WANT MY COMPANY.

IT ALL LED TO THE OCT. 19, 1982 MEETING WHERE THE UNDERCOVER MEN SHOWED DELOREAN A SUITCASE FULL OF COCAINE...

THIS STUFF IS BETTER THAN GOLD.

...THEN ARRESTED HIM.

THE SCANDAL STUNNED THE NATION, WHICH UNTIL THEN NEVER QUESTIONED THE DELOREAN MYTH.

BUSTED

BUT JOHN Z. DELOREAN WAS MERELY DOWN, NOT OUT.

I'M AN ABSOLUTELY INNOCENT MAN. THIS IS A PURE FRAME-UP, AN FBI CHEAP SHOT.

NONETHELESS, HIS DREAM WAS DEAD FOREVER. THE BRITISH GOVERNMENT SEIZED HIS COMPANY ON THE SAME DAY HE WAS ARRESTED.

BECAUSE HE'D THOUGHT THE "MOBSTERS" WERE GOING TO KILL HIM, DELOREAN FELT GOD HAD PREPARED HIM FOR DEATH. HE WANTED TO MAKE SURE HIS FAMILY WAS TAKEN CARE OF.

CRISTINA, MY LOVE, I'M GOING TO KILL MYSELF SO YOU AND THE KIDS GET THE INSURANCE MONEY.

DON'T BOTHER, JOHN, LIFE INSURANCE DOESN'T COVER SUICIDE.

OH. WELL, FORGET IT THEN.

SHORTLY BEFORE THE DELOREAN TRIAL WAS SCHEDULED TO START, A SURREAL EVENT OCCURRED.

HELLO, 60 MINUTES? THIS IS LARRY FLYNT, PUBLISHER OF HUSTLER MAGAZINE. YEAH, THAT HUSTLER MAGAZINE. WANNA SEE SOME VIDEOTAPE OF JOHN DELOREAN? NO, NOT THAT KIND OF VIDEOTAPE.

FLYNT HAD OBTAINED THE FBI SURVEILLANCE TAPES. CBS AIRED THEM.

THE TRIAL WAS DELAYED AS POTENTIAL JURORS WERE SCREENED FOR BIAS.

IN COURT, THE GOVERNMENT SPARED NOTHING IN ITS ATTACK ON DELOREAN.

THIS MAN DELOREAN IS THE FACE OF GREED! THE FACE OF EVIL!

BUT AFTER JUST ONE BALLOT, THE JURY DECIDED THAT THE GOVERNMENT STING OPERATION WAS THE REAL EVIL. THE VERDICT: NOT GUILTY ON ALL COUNTS.

THIS SENDS A MESSAGE TO THE GOVERNMENT THAT THIS TYPE OF CONDUCT WILL NOT BE TOLERATED.

PRAISE THE LORD!

IF IT WAS A SET-UP, WHO WAS BEHIND IT?

COULD BE GENERAL MOTORS. OR THE BRITISH, OR THE IRA. I JUST DON'T KNOW.

CRISTINA LEFT HIM AND HE STILL FACED FRAUD AND EMBEZZLEMENT CHARGES UNRELATED TO THE COKE BUST.

IN 1986, HE WAS ACQUITTED OF THOSE, TOO, AND RETIRED INTO OBSCURITY.

THE DELOREAN SPORTS CAR, WITH A BELATED CULT FOLLOWING, WAS FEATURED IN BACK TO THE FUTURE. THE DELOREAN OWNERS ASSOCIATION MAINTAINS 3,000 MEMBERS. REPORTEDLY, JOHN DELOREAN MAILS IN HIS $30 ANNUAL DUES FAITHFULLY.

THE MID-1980s. AMERICA'S ERA OF BIG MONEY. FAST MONEY. *BORROWED* MONEY. EVERY YEAR, THE MEGA-MONEY MEN THREW THEMSELVES A PARTY. THEY CALLED IT "THE PREDATOR'S BALL" AND ITS 1,500 GUESTS WERE--

The PIRATES of FINANCE

THE BALL WAS STAGED BY INVESTMENT FIRM DREXEL BURNHAM LAMBERT. ITS STAR TRADER, THE MYSTERIOUS MICHAEL MILKEN -- FEARLESS INNOVATOR OF THE FINANCIAL TOOL THAT DROVE THE '80s: THE JUNK BOND.

WE'RE GOING TO TEE UP GM, FORD, AND IBM -- AND MAKE THEM *CRINGE!*

AT BERKELEY IN THE '60s, MILKEN IGNORED DRUGS, FREE LOVE, AND PROTEST, BURYING HIMSELF IN FINANCIAL TEXTS. THERE HE "DISCOVERED" JUNK BONDS BY READING A BOOK.

LOW-RATED AND DEFAULTED BONDS, HANDLED CORRECTLY, PAY OFF *BIG-TIME!*

YOUNG MILKEN GOT A JOB WITH DREXEL IN THE EARLY '70s. HE WAS SO DRIVEN, HE WORE A MINER'S HAT TO WORK SO HE COULD PERUSE CORPORATE REPORTS ON DARK COMMUTER TRAINS.

BY THE MID-'70s HE'D RE-MADE THE MODEST FIRM INTO A WALL STREET GIANT WITH HIS JUNK-BOND DEALS.

HE'S THE SMARTEST MAN I'VE EVER MET!

THEN HE MOVED HIS WHOLE OPERATION TO HIS NATIVE L.A.

HIS UNDERLINGS WERE GETTING SO RICH THEY DIDN'T BALK AT THE MOVE -- OR AT MILKEN'S FANATICAL WORKING CONDITIONS. THE DAY BEGAN AT 4:30 A.M.

USUALLY MILKEN WAS ALREADY AT WORK, LEAVING NOTES ON THEIR DESKS.

MILKEN'S TRADERS COULD NOT LEAVE THE OFFICE UNTIL ABOUT 8 P.M. EVEN FOR LUNCH OR DINNER, WHICH WERE CATERED.

I'M REALLY TIRED. I'M GOING TO READ CORPORATE REPORTS AT HOME.

READ THEM HERE! YOU CAN NAP LATER!

MILKEN BROUGHT IN A QUARTER OF DREXEL'S PROFITS. HIS PERSONAL FORTUNE MAY HAVE HIT $5 BILLION!

DREXEL ANNUAL REPORT

?

BUT ALWAYS SECRETIVE, HE WOULDN'T PUT HIS PICTURE IN THE COMPANY'S ANNUAL REPORT.

"JUNK BONDS" PAID HIGH INTEREST AND CARRIED HIGH RISK. MILKEN CONVINCED INVESTORS THAT THEY WERE ACTUALLY A *BETTER* INVESTMENT THAN STANDARD BONDS. BACKED BY BILLIONS IN MILKEN JUNK, CORPORATE RAIDERS TOOK OVER DOZENS OF COMPANIES.

SAFEWAY

DON'T CALL THEM "JUNK". THEY'RE "HIGH YIELD BONDS."

THE DEALS OFTEN PUT HUNDREDS OUT OF WORK AND BURDENED THE U.S. ECONOMY WITH CRIPPLING DEBT. BUT THEY MADE MILKEN AND HIS COHORTS FABULOUSLY RICH.

BUT MILKEN'S REAL STRENGTH CAME FROM THE S&Ls, INSUR-ANCE FIRMS, AND PENSION FUNDS IN HIS EMPIRE.

BROTHER CAN YOU SPARE A HUNDRED BILLION?

CLOS

MILKEN'S BILLIONS WERE BACKED BY AVERAGE AMERICANS' *HONESTLY-EARNED* MONEY.

ON OCT. 1, 1986 MILKEN RECEIVED A CALL FROM A CLIENT, IVAN BOESKY, WALL STREET'S TOP ARBITRAGE MAN.

I WANT TO ARRANGE A MEETING, MICHAEL, TO DISCUSS -- *CERTAIN TOPICS.*

I UNDER-STAND.

WHAT MILKEN DIDN'T KNOW...

...WAS THAT BOESKY WAS NOW A GOVERNMENT INFORMANT.

THE SON OF A RUSSIAN JEWISH IMMIGRANT, BOESKY HUSTLED HIS WAY ONTO WALL STREET WITHOUT A COLLEGE DEGREE. HIS SPECIALTY: HIGH-RISK ARBITRAGE, BUYING STOCK IN COMPANIES TARGETED FOR TAKEOVER, THEN SELLING AT A MASSIVE PROFIT-- IF THE TAKEOVER WENT THROUGH.

A DANGEROUS GAME, BUT BOESKY ALWAYS SEEMED TO WIN.

A PRETERNATURALLY DRIVEN MAN, BOESKY ONCE TOLD A COLLEAGUE...

I SEE MYSELF AS A LATTER-DAY ROTHSCHILD.

HE DROVE HIS EMPLOYEES EVEN HARDER.

TELL ME WHO'S BUYING *NOW*, YOU LOUSY $@#%#!!

AS HARD AS THEY WORKED FOR HIM, STRANGELY, HE OFTEN SEEMED TO IGNORE THEIR ADVICE.

SORRY, KID, I'VE GOT BETTER INFORMATION.

ON DEC. 20, IVAN BOESKY, WALL STREET'S WORST CRIMINAL, SHOWED UP TO BE SENTENCED.

I'M SO ASHAMED. ALL I WANT NOW IS TO REDEEM MYSELF.

BOESKY WENT OFF TO A MINIMUM-SECURITY PRISON AND ENJOYED PLENTY OF PERKS, SERVING TWO YEARS OF HIS THREE-YEAR SENTENCE.

NOW THIS IS WHAT I CALL REDEMPTION!

THOUGH HIS WORLD WAS ABOUT TO CAVE IN, 1987 WASN'T A BAD YEAR FOR MILKEN. HE TOOK HOME A TIDY $550 MILLION.

NEVER COUNT YOUR MONEY, JUST DRIVE YOUR-SELF TO MAKE MORE.

1989 AND '90 WEREN'T AS KIND. INDICTED ON 98 COUNTS OF RACKE-TEERING, FRAUD, AND INSIDER TRADING, MILKEN PLED GUILTY TO SIX FELONIES.

BUCKING FOR A LIGHT SENTENCE, MILKEN'S DESPERATE PR CAMPAIGN CONTINUED.

HE EVEN HUNG OUT WITH MICHAEL JACKSON.

I'M BAD! UH-HUH! YA KNOW IT!

IT DIDN'T WORK. WHEN HE HEARD HIS SENTENCE, A WHOPPING 10 YEARS, HE COLLAPSED.

OXYGEN!

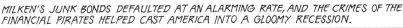

MILKEN'S JUNK BONDS DEFAULTED AT AN ALARMING RATE, AND THE CRIMES OF THE FINANCIAL PIRATES HELPED CAST AMERICA INTO A GLOOMY RECESSION.

STILL, SOME WONDERED IF MILKEN, BOESKY, AND OTHERS WEREN'T SCAPEGOATS. THEY WERE OUTSIDERS, MOSTLY JEWISH, WHO ROCKED THE WASP-ISH WALL STREET OLD-BOY NETWORK WHICH REMAINED UNTOUCHED BY THE '80S DEBACLE.

MILKEN SURE THOUGHT SO. HE SERVED TWO YEARS, SURVIVED PROSTATE CANCER, AND TAUGHT MATH TO HIGH SCHOOL KIDS WHILE MAKING MILLIONS AS A "CONSULTANT" AND STRIVING TO REBUILD HIS REPUTATION.

I GOT OFF EASY. MOST REVOLUTIONARIES ARE KILLED.

MIKE'S MATH CLUB

NINE MONTHS AFTER HIS NEW YORK TRIUMPH, MAXWELL RELAXED ON HIS BELOVED YACHT OFF THE CANARY ISLANDS. ONE NIGHT HE LEFT HIS CABIN AND EMERGED ALONE ONTO THE DECK.

AND THEN...

SPLASH

MAXWELL'S SONS KEVIN AND IAN, WHO WERE ALSO HIS TWO TOP EXECUTIVES, WERE THE FIRST TO GET THE NEWS.

DAD SEEMS TO HAVE FALLEN OFF THE BOAT. HE'S FALLEN INTO THE SEA!

PFUUU

THE FOLLOWING DAY CONFIRMED THE WORST.

IT'S HIM, ALL RIGHT. IT'S MAXWELL.

FUNNY HOW HE'S FLOATING FACE UP! THAT'S NOT NORMAL.

HIS WIFE BETTY FLEW TO SPAIN AND IDENTIFIED THE BODY.

HE'S A COLOSSUS LYING HERE--AS HE HAD BEEN IN LIFE.

NO MOLESTAR LOS MUERTES

LIKE THE ORIGINAL COLOSSUS, HIS FALL WAS ONLY A MATTER OF TIME. AFTER HIS DEATH, HIS SONS WERE HELD ACCOUNTABLE FOR HIS SHADY DEALINGS.

YOU'RE NICKED FOR FRAUD AND CONSPIRACY, MATIES!

THEY WERE CLEARED, BUT ONLY AFTER A LONG TRIAL.

WITH "CAP'N BOB" GONE, THE GLOBAL MAXWELL CONGLOMERATE STOOD EXPOSED AS A SHAM. EVEN HIS MIRACULOUS DAILY NEWS RESCUE TURNED OUT TO BE A MONEY-LAUNDERING SCHEME.

HE MOVED $238 MILLION OUT OF HERE IN NINE MONTHS! THIS PAPER'S FLAT BROKE!

MAX!!!

DAILY NEWS
PARKER SAVES LIEB

FORD TO CITY: DROP DEAD

INTERM SETS N

THE NEWS FILED BANKRUPTCY 10 MONTHS AFTER MAXWELL "SAVED" IT. FROM HIS GLOBAL OPERATION HE PLUNDERED $2 BILLION THROUGH FRAUDULENT LOANS AND PILFERED PENSION FUNDS.

THE BUSINESS COULDN'T RUN WITHOUT HIM BECAUSE HE RAN IT SINGLEHANDEDLY, IGNORING NORMAL CORPORATE FORMALITIES.

B-B-BUT WE CAN'T INVEST THESE PENSION FUNDS WITHOUT CONSULTING THE BOARD OF DIRECTORS!!

DAMN YOU! I AM THE BOARD OF DIRECTORS!!

BOORISH AND CRASS, HE RULED THROUGH TANTRUMS AND INTIMIDATION.

NEVER FORGET-- I OWN THE STADIUM!! YOU'RE MERELY THE MANAGERS!!

BAM BAM BAM

HE BULLIED HIS OWN KIDS, WHOM HE DEMANDED ACT LIKE PROPER ENGLISH GENTLEMEN--THE OPPOSITE OF HIMSELF.

THIS OUGHT TO TEACH YOU SOME MANNERS!

BONK

MAXWELL YEARNED FOR POWER. HE WON A SEAT IN PARLIAMENT, CONFIDENT HE'D SOON RISE TO PRIME MINISTER. INSTEAD, HE FOUND HE WAS OUT OF HIS LEAGUE.

THIS JUST ISN'T MY SCENE!

MAXWELL, WHO'D LONG TERRORIZED THE BRITISH PRESS WITH SCATTERSHOT LIBEL SUITS, KNEW WHERE REAL POWER LAY. IN 1984 HE BOUGHT THE STRUGGLING, BUT PROFITABLE MIRROR GROUP, ONE OF BRITAIN'S LEADING NEWSPAPER CHAINS.

Daily Mirror

MAXWELL SAVES MIRROR

A GOD ON ROBERT

RRIPP

AND WHAT'S BEST IS THAT I PLEDGE NEVER TO INTERFERE IN THE JOURNALISTIC PROCESS!

HE PROCEEDED TO USE THE PAPER FOR HIS OWN FLAGRANT SELF-AGGRANDIZEMENT. HE HOBNOBBED WITH ROYALTY.

MIRROR

HE EVEN TURNED UP IN FAMINE-TORN ETHIOPIA.

I'LL SAVE YOUR STARVING PEOPLE JUST LIKE I SAVED THE MIRROR!

HIS PAPERS DUTIFULLY REPORTED HIS EVERY MOVE.

WHILE BASKING IN LUXURY, HE TIGHTENED THE CLAMPS ON THE MIRROR'S UNIONS.

TELL THEM THE GRAVY TRAIN IS ABOUT TO HIT THE BUFFERS!

MAXWELL STORMED INTO AMERICA, BUYING MACMILLAN PUBLISHING AND THE *THE NEWS*, PUTTING HIMSELF ON PAR WITH HIS ARCHRIVAL, AUSTRALIAN MEDIA BARON RUPERT MURDOCH.

I THINK BOB MAY BE IN OVER HIS HEAD ON THIS ONE.

HE WAS. BACK HOME, THE PRESS WAS CATCHING ON TO THE SORRY STATE OF MAXWELL'S "EMPIRE." HE RESPONDED THE WAY HE ALWAYS HAD.

MAXWELL LOSING MILLIONS

MAXWELL FINANCES RICKETY

I'LL SUE EACH AND EVERY ONE OF YOU *BASTARDS!*

BEFORE THE SCANDAL ENGULFED HIM, HE DIED. HE WAS BURIED IN ISRAEL, WHERE HE HAD MADE HUGE AND SUCCESSFUL INVESTMENTS...

...USING MONEY SHUTTLED OUT OF BRITISH PENSION FUNDS.

HIS DEATH WAS A MYSTERY. ONE PATHOLOGIST THOUGHT HIS FALL MAY HAVE RESULTED FROM WHAT DOCTORS CALL "MICTURITION SYNCOPE."

AAHH! WHAT A RELIEF! SAY, I FEEL FU--FU--F... UH-OH!

IN PLAIN ENGLISH: HE FAINTED WHILE TAKING A LEAK.

ROY GREENSLADE, MAXWELL'S MIRROR EDITOR WHO BATTLED MIGHTILY WITH HIS BOSS, HAD A GRIMMER SUSPICION.

THE 20TH CENTURY'S GREATEST CON MAN *COMMITTED SUICIDE* BECAUSE HE KNEW HE WAS ABOUT TO BE FOUND OUT AT LAST.

STILL OTHERS THOUGHT HIS DEATH WAS CONNECTED TO A CHARGE LEVELED BY U.S. JOURNALIST SEYMOUR HERSH.

ROBERT MAXWELL WAS AN AGENT OF THE *MOSSAD!*

THE ALLEGATION WAS NEVER SUBSTANTIATED.

WHAT *IS* KNOWN IS THAT HIS MASSIVE DEBTS ENABLED HIM TO FULFILL A CRUEL PROMISE HE'D ONCE MADE TO HIS FAMILY.

WHEN I DIE, I PLAN TO LEAVE YOU-- *NOTHING!!*

IN FACT, IT WAS WORSE THAN THAT.

GENTLEMEN, I'M AFRAID YOUR FATHER DIED A PAUPER-- AND LIVED A THIEF!

HE DIED A POOR MAN IN A MUCH MORE MEANINGFUL SENSE. THIS ACQUAINTANCE OF PRINCES AND PRESIDENTS WAS A LONELY MAN.

I CANNOT HAVE ANY FRIENDS BECAUSE I CANNOT GIVE ANY TIME TO FRIENDSHIP. I ONLY KNOW THIS WAY.

FACTOID BOOKS

The LOCKHEED SCANDAL

BANZAI! BANZAI!!!

MARCH 25, 1976. CHOFU PREFECTURAL AIRPORT, JAPAN.

MITSUYASU MAENO, 29, ULTRA-NATIONALIST AND, ODDLY-ENOUGH, PORN-FILM ACTOR, COMMANDEERS A SMALL PLANE. DESTINATION: TOKYO.

LONG LIVE THE EMPEROR!

MAENO ZEROES IN ON THE HOME OF YOSHIO KODAMA, JAPAN'S BEHIND-THE-SCENES POLITICAL--AND CRIMINAL--KINGMAKER. THEN, KAMIKAZE-STYLE...

KER-BLAM

WHAT WOULD COMPEL A YOUNG MAN TO DO SUCH A THING?

THE ANSWER LAY DEEP AMONG THE SECRETS OF ONE OF THE WORLD'S LARGEST MILITARY CONTRACTORS, A COMPANY THAT SOLD BILLIONS OF DOLLARS IN WEAPONS EVERY YEAR...

...WHILE COVERTLY FUNCTIONING AS ONE OF THE WORLD'S LARGEST ORGANIZED CRIME SYNDICATES. THE STORY GOES BACK AT LEAST TO THE LATE 1950s WHEN LOCKHEED CAME OUT WITH ITS NEW MILITARY PLANE, THE STARFIGHTER.

A NEXT-GENERATION AIRCRAFT, THE ROCKET-LIKE STARFIGHTER FLEW TWO TIMES THE SPEED OF SOUND...

..BUT THERE WAS ONE SMALL PROBLEM...

...THE PLANE CRASHED CONSTANTLY, EARNING ITS NICKNAME, "THE WIDOWMAKER."

KABWOW

OF ABOUT 1,100 STAR-FIGHTERS SOLD TO GERMANY AND JAPAN, TWENTY PERCENT CRASHED.

THERE GOES ANOTHER ONE!

HOW DID LOCKHEED SELL THIS FLYING COFFIN TO AIR FORCES THROUGH-OUT EUROPE AND ASIA? THE OLD-FASHIONED WAY:

BRIBERY!

THE SCANDAL BROKE IN THE MID-70s, THANKS TO U.S. SENATOR FRANK CHURCH AND HIS INVESTIGATIVE COMMITTEE.

THIS IS A SORDID TALE OF BRIBERY AND SHADOWY FIGURES BEHIND THE SCENES, RIGHT OUT OF A SPY NOVEL!

IT STARTED WITH AN ADMISSION BY TOM JONES, CHAIRMAN OF LOCKHEED'S SMALLER RIVAL, NORTHROP CORPORATION.

SURE, WE BRIBED PEOPLE. WE WERE JUST FOLLOWING **LOCKHEED'S** BUSINESS MODEL.

LOCKHEED'S COMBATIVE CHAIRMAN DAN HAUGHTON STONEWALLED AS BEST HE COULD.

WE PREFER TO CALL THEM "KICKBACKS," AND I'M NOT NAMING NAMES!

WORSE, LOCKHEED RECENTLY NEEDED A BAILOUT FROM UNCLE SAM, COLLECTING $191 MILLION IN TAXPAYER CASH.

BUT NAMES DID EMERGE. AMONG THEM, THE NETHERLANDS' PRINCE BERNHARD, WHO WAS RICH ENOUGH AS IT WAS.

BUT HE COULD USE ANOTHER MILLION FOR HIS MISTRESS...

...AND ILLEGITIMATE DAUGHTER.

LOCKHEED WAS SO ENAMORED OF BERNHARD THAT IT PAID HIM $100,000 IN 1968, EVEN THOUGH HE'D THEN **REFUSED** TO HELP THEM, TURNING DOWN A $500,000 PAYOFF.

YOUR HIGHNESS, HOW CAN WE SHOW OUR GRATITUDE...

...FOR YOUR HONESTY?

IN INDONESIA, LOCKHEED'S GREASE MONEY WENT INTO AN ACCOUNT CALLED "THE WIDOWS AND ORPHAN'S FUND."

JUST CONSIDER IT **HUMANITARIAN AID**. HEH HEH.

LOCKHEED'S AGENT IN THE MIDDLE EAST WAS SYRIAN ARMS MERCHANT ADNAN KHASHOGGI. HE PLAYED UP MIDDLE-EASTERN STEREOTYPES TO PUSH WESTERNER'S BUTTONS...

IT'S NOT MY FAULT-- BRIBERY IS THE **CUSTOM** AMONG MY PEOPLE.

KHASHOGGI ACCRUED $106 MILLION IN LOCKHEED "COMMISSIONS," USING THE CASH TO LEVERAGE HIS POSITION IN THE U.S.A.

THESE BRIBES COME BACK, RECYCLED AS FOREIGN OWNERSHIP OF AMERICAN ASSETS!

AMONG HIS PRIME AMERICAN ASSETS, A CERTAIN POLITICIAN.

HE ALLEGEDLY SLIPPED A COOL MILLION TO NIXON'S CAMPAIGN.

ADNAN, THIS LOOKS LIKE THE BEGINNING OF A BEAUTIFUL FRIENDSHIP.

LOCKHEED'S "LOCUST" (ITS CODE WORD FOR "AGENT") IN JAPAN WAS YOSHIO KODAMA.

KODAMA WAS A WAR CRIMINAL, RIGHT-WING NATIONALIST, AND GANGSTER WHO GOT OFF-- COURTESY OF THE C.I.A.

ON SEPTEMBER 1, 1972, NIXON MET IN PRIVATE WITH JAPAN'S PRIME MINISTER KAKUEI TANAKA.

THREE DAYS LATER, JAPAN DECIDED TO BUY A BILLION DOLLARS WORTH OF ANTI-SUBMARINE PLANES FROM LOCKHEED.

AND KODAMA BEGAN RECEIVING CRATES FULL OF YEN.

JUST LEAVE IT OVER THERE, PLEASE.

SHORTLY AFTER ALL-NIPPON AIRWAYS ORDERED $400 MILLION WORTH OF LOCKHEED TRISTAR PASSENGER JETS, BOTH NIXON AND TANAKA DIED IN 1994, NEVER REVEALING WHAT THEY DISCUSSED THAT DAY.

CURIOUSLY, LOCKHEED WAS THE ONLY MAJOR CORPORATION **NOT** TO DONATE HUGE SUMS TO NIXON'S RE-ELECTION COMMITTEE. NOT ON THE RECORD, ANYWAY.

C.R.E.E.P. CONTRIBUTIONS—

GENERAL MOTORS
GENERAL ELECTRIC
STANDARD OIL
LOCKHEED

THE SCANDAL TOOK ITS TOLL. LOCKHEED TREASURER ROBERT WATERS KILLED HIMSELF AFTER THE CHURCH COMMITTEE ANNOUNCED HE'D BE SUBPOENAED.

IN JAPAN, KODAMA SUFFERED A STROKE.

HE WAS BEDRIDDEN WHEN KAMIKAZE MAENO, OUTRAGED THAT HIS FORMER HERO HAD SHAMED THE NATION, CRASHED INTO HIS HOUSE. KODAMA ESCAPED UNHURT BUT DISGRACED.

MAENO'S ACTING OEUVRE BECAME A METAPHOR FOR THE LOCKHEED OBSCENITY IN JAPAN.

BUT IN THE U.S., LOCKHEED REHABILITATED ITS IMAGE. IN THE 80s, IT WON THE CONTRACT FOR AMERICA'S MOST SECRET-- AND EXPENSIVE-- PLANE, THE STEALTH FIGHTER.

FACTOID BOOKS

WHEN YOU THINK OF BANKERS, YOU THINK OF MEN IN GRAY SUITS. CAUTIOUS. CONSERVATIVE. PILLARS OF THE COMMUNITY. BUT SADLY, THAT'S NOT ALWAYS THE CASE...

WHEN BANKERS GO BAD

YOU T'INK A SQUIRT LIKE *YOU* IS GONNA GET A LOAN FROM *ME?*

Poit!

T'INK *AGAIN!*

IN 1973, AUSTRALIAN BANKER FRANK NUGAN TEAMED UP WITH AMERICAN EX-GREEN BERET MICHAEL HAND.

WE'LL OFFER HIGH INTEREST, TAX SHELTERS, AND SECRET CASH TRANSFERS!

MY CIA CONTACTS WILL HELP WITH THAT!

THE AUSTRALIAN NUGAN HAND BANK OPENED A BRANCH IN CHIANG MAI, THAILAND-- HEART OF THE "GOLDEN TRIANGLE," EPICENTER OF WORLDWIDE HEROIN TRAFFIC.

THE BANK'S THAILAND BRANCH MANAGER NEIL EVANS ALLEGED--

IN SEVEN MONTHS I COLLECTED $6 MILLION IN DEPOSITS FROM MAJOR DRUG KINGPINS.

NUGAN HAND BANK COLLECTED MORE THAN $10 MILLION IN DEPOSITS FROM AMERICANS STATIONED IN SAUDI ARABIA.

THANKS A LOT, BOYS!

WE CAN'T WAIT TO SEE THOSE HIGH RETURNS!

MOST OF THEM NEVER SAW THEIR MONEY AGAIN...

...BECAUSE ON JAN. 27, 1980 FRANK NUGAN WAS FOUND SHOT TO DEATH IN HIS CAR, OUT ON A LONELY AUSTRALIAN HIGHWAY.

IT WAS RULED A SUICIDE.

MICHAEL HAND ORDERED THE BANK'S RECORDS RANSACKED. AND HE WASN'T KIDDING WHEN HE TOLD THE BANK'S DIRECTORS:

DO WHAT WE SAY-- OR YOUR WIVES WILL BE CUT UP AND RETURNED TO YOU IN BITS AND PIECES!

IT TURNED OUT THAT THE TWO BANKERS HAD BEEN DRAINING NUGAN HAND. DEBTS OUTWEIGHED ASSETS BY $50 MILLION. ALL OF THE DEPOSITORS' MONEY WAS GONE.

I WONDER WHERE IT ALL WENT.

THE BANK'S OFFICERS SEEMED UNFAZED. SEVERAL WERE MILITARY MEN, ONE OF WHOM SAID--

I DON'T FEEL *GUILTY* BECAUSE SOME GUY GOT *SWINDLED!*

MICHAEL HAND, HOWEVER, VANISHED WITHOUT A TRACE

A DECADE LATER, ANOTHER INTERNATIONAL BANK COLLAPSED, THIS ONE ALSO FAVORED BY TERRORISTS, DRUG DEALERS, AND CIA AGENTS. PANAMANIAN DICTATOR MANUEL NORIEGA DEPOSITED OVER $30 MILLION DOLLARS THERE.

THE INNOCUOUS NAME "BANK OF CREDIT AND COMMERCE INTERNATIONAL" MASKED THE FACT THAT IT WAS A GLOBAL CRIME SYNDICATE.

FOUNDED IN 1972 BY AGHA ABEDI, A PAKISTANI FINANCIER WITH STRANGE BELIEFS, BCCI RECEIVED ACCOLADES FOR INVESTING HEAVILY IN THE THIRD WORLD.

FEEL THE FORCE INSIDE YOU!

IT LATER TURNED OUT THAT BCCI WAS COMMITTING MASSIVE FRAUD, FAILING TO RECORD HUNDREDS OF MILLIONS OF DOLLARS IN DEPOSITS.

UM, COULD I GET A RECEIPT FOR THAT?

WHY? DON'T YOU *TRUST* ME?

BCCI AVOIDED SCRUTINY BY COURTING POWERFUL CONTACTS. IN THE U.S. IT HIRED ESTEEMED ATTORNEY CLARK CLIFFORD -- ADVISOR TO SEVERAL PRESIDENTS--

--AND HIS LAW PARTNER ROBERT ALTMAN.

IN THE U.S. ONLY MANHATTAN D.A. ROBERT MORGENTHAU TRIED TO INVESTIGATE BCCI. HE FOUND HIMSELF OBSTRUCTED BY FEDERAL OFFICIALS.

HERE'S A HOT TIP, BOB. BCCI'S *CLEAN!* GET IT?

IN 1991 BCCI, WHICH HAD ILLEGALLY HIDDEN UP TO *$15 BILLION* IN LOSSES, WAS SEIZED BY REGULATORS. THE SHUTDOWN CRIPPLED MANY THIRD WORLD GOVERNMENTS.

CAMEROON, FOR EXAMPLE, HAD ONE-THIRD OF ITS FOREIGN EXCHANGE RESERVES IN BCCI.

CLIFFORD AND ALTMAN WERE INDICTED. BUT THE CASE AGAINST CLIFFORD WAS DROPPED BECAUSE OF HIS FAILING HEALTH, WHILE ALTMAN WAS ACQUITTED.

I WAS *DUPED!*

I'M *EXONERATED!*

THEIR BILLING FOR THEIR LEGAL SERVICES, HOWEVER, MADE THEM BOTH MILLIONS.

BCCI FOUNDER ABEDI STAYED SAFELY IN PAKISTAN WHERE HE DIED IN 1995.

MAY THE FORCE BE WITH YOU!

THE FATE OF BCCI'S LOST BILLIONS REMAINS A MYSTERY.

IF BCCI'S FALL PROVED THE MOST EXPENSIVE BANK SCANDAL EVER, THEN ITALY'S BANCO AMBROSIANO COLLAPSE WAS SURELY THE MOST SINISTER. THE $1.3 BILLION DISASTER WAS TIED INTIMATELY TO THE SECRET MASONIC-FASCIST CULT "P-2," LED BY FORMER BLACKSHIRT LICIO GELLI -- AND TO THE VATICAN!

WE ARE PREPARED TO FACE DEATH SO THAT WE MAY DESTROY THIS GOVERNMENT!

P-2 HAD POWERFUL MEMBERS THROUGHOUT ITALIAN SOCIETY. ONE WAS BANCO AMBROSIANO PRESIDENT ROBERTO CALVI--OFTEN CALLED "GOD'S BANKER."

P-2 DREW FUNDS FROM PANAMANIAN DUMMY COMPANIES CREATED BY CALVI--WHOSE INVESTMENTS WERE GUARANTEED BY VATICAN BANK PRESIDENT ARCHBISHOP PAUL MARCINKUS.

I DIDN'T KNOW THAT THOSE COMPANIES WERE REALLY OWNED BY BANCO AMBROSIANO! REALLY!

WHEN THE BANK FELL, DRAINED BY P-2'S PANAMANIAN COMPANIES, CALVI WAS TRIED AND CONVICTED. HE FLED--THEN TURNED UP IN 1982, HANGING FROM LONDON'S BLACKFRIAR'S BRIDGE.

IN HIS POCKETS: $20,000 AND 12 POUNDS OF BRICKS.

MARCINKUS HOLED UP INSIDE VATICAN CITY WHERE ITALIAN POLICE HAD NO AUTHORITY.

BUT I DID NOTHING WRONG!

ITALIAN AUTHORITIES SAID THEY WOULDN'T PROSECUTE. HE RETURNED TO HIS NATIVE ILLINOIS.

P-2 BANKER MICHELE SINDONA, WHO OWNED THE PANAMA COMPANIES WITH GELLI, CALVI, AND THE VATICAN, WAS CONVICTED IN AMERICA ON NUMEROUS FRAUD COUNTS.

HE TRIED TO POISON HIMSELF, BUT SURVIVED.

LICIO GELLI WAS ARRESTED WHILE TRYING TO WITHDRAW $100 MILLION FROM P-2'S SWISS ACCOUNT.

I SHOULD'A' USED AN ATM!

P-2 WAS SMASHED, BUT THE SCANDAL SHAMED THE VATICAN AND SHOOK WORLD FINANCIAL MARKETS TO THEIR CORE.

FACTOID BOOKS 100% TRUE

Thalidomide Nightmare

1954. THE GERMAN PHARMACEUTICAL FIRM CHEMIE GRUNENTHAL IS ON A MISSION TO BOOST PROFITS. AND THAT MEANS...

DRUGS! DRUGS! WE MUST HAVE NEW DRUGS!

THE PROJECT PAID OFF.

WE'VE CREATED A-- A-- A WONDER DRUG!! I'LL CALL IT-- *THALIDOMIDE!*

THIS WILL MAKE US ALL RICH!

THALIDOMIDE WAS DESIGNED TO BE A SLEEPING PILL.

AND BEST OF ALL, IT HAS NO *HARMFUL* SIDE EFFECTS!

BUT GRUNENTHAL STAFF DOCTORS REPORTED ALL KINDS OF *DIFFERENT* AND FABULOUS USES FOR THE WONDER DRUG.

DOCTOR! DOCTOR! THE PILL HAS DIMINISHED OUR MORALLY TROUBLING DESIRE TO MASTURBATE!

IT IS TRULY A MIRACLE OF SCIENCE!

OTHER DOCTORS FOUND MORE DISTURBING EFFECTS.

...DIZZINESS, NAUSEA, BUZZING IN THE EARS, CONSTIPATION, NUMBNESS OF THE EXTREMITIES...

GRUNENTHAL NEVER BOTHERED WITH THE CRUCIAL "PLACENTAL BARRIER" TEST, WHICH DETERMINES IF A DRUG TAKEN BY A PREGNANT WOMAN REACHES THE FETUS.

IT'S NOT REQUIRED, SO WHY WASTE THE TIME?

OMINOUSLY, TESTS ON RATS SHOWED THEY WEREN'T AFFECTED BY THE SEDATIVE THE SAME WAY HUMANS WERE.

THEY DON'T SEEM TO BE GETTING VERY SLEEPY.

IN OTHER WORDS, EVEN THOUGH THE DRUG SEEMED SAFE FOR RATS, PEOPLE MIGHT BE AT RISK ANYWAY. BUT GRUNENTHAL DIDN'T THINK OF THAT.

THE COMPANY QUICKLY LAUNCHED THE DRUG ALL ACROSS EUROPE WITH A VIGOROUS PUBLICITY CAMPAIGN. THE PRODUCT WAS A HUGE SUCCESS.

OH, DEAR--IT SAYS HERE THAT THALIDOMIDE IS THE FIRST SLEEPING PILL THAT'S *COMPLETELY SAFE!*

THEN IT MUST BE TRUE, SO COULD YOU PICK ME UP SOME THALIDOMIDE TOMORROW?

THALIDOMIDE MIRACLE! NEW DRUG

DAMNING EVIDENCE ROLLED IN. GRUNENTHAL FINALLY PERFORMED THAT PLACENTAL BARRIER TEST.

WELL--HEH HEH--IT SEEMS THAT, UM, THE DRUG *DOES* REACH THE -; KOFF! KOFF! - FETUS AFTER ALL.

AACCH!

A RESEARCHER FOR BRITAIN'S THALIDOMIDE MAKER RAN A TEST ON RABBITS RATHER THAN RATS.

UH-OH.

GRUNENTHAL TRIED TO SUPPRESS THE FINDINGS, BUT THE BRITISH RESEARCHER PUBLISHED THEM ANYWAY.

...induced deformities in rabbits remarkably similar to those in humans...

IN THE U.S., RICHARDSON-MERREL AT LAST WITHDREW ITS APPLICATION -- WHICH DR. KELSEY HAD NIXED SIX TIMES.

SHE EMERGED AS A TRUE HEROINE AND WAS DECORATED BY THE PRESIDENT. HER RESOLVE SPARED MISERY FOR THOUSANDS OF FAMILIES.

THE MILLIONS OF TABLETS DISTRIBUTED BY DOCTORS AS PART OF MERREL'S MARKETING--DRIVEN "CLINICAL TRIAL" POSED A PROBLEM. EVEN PRESIDENT KENNEDY JOINED THE FIGHT.

EVERY WOMAN IN THIS COUNTRY SHOULD CHECK THEIR MEDICINE CABINET AND TURN THIS DRUG IN.

SHERRI FINKBINE, A PREGNANT ARIZONA WOMAN WHO'D TAKEN THE DRUG, SPARKED A NATIONAL MINI-SCANDAL WHEN SHE ANNOUNCED...

I'M GOING TO SWEDEN TO GET A *LEGAL ABORTION.*

DESPITE WIDESPREAD CONDEM-NATION, SHE GOT HER ABORTION. THE FETUS WAS INDEED DEFORMED.

IN THE U.S., THE THALIDOMIDE SCANDAL LED TO TIGHTER FEDERAL CONTROL OF THE DRUG INDUSTRY. AMONG THE MANY NEW RULES:

ALL RESEARCHERS MUST BE FULLY QUALIFIED AND A DRUG'S EFFECT ON THE FETUS MUST BE DETERMINED.

BUT THE BEST NEWS IS THAT MANY OF THE SURVIVING THALIDOMIDE CHILDREN HAVE GROWN UP TO LEAD DIGNIFIED, PRODUCTIVE LIVES. THEY ARE ARTISTS, TV PRODUCERS, ENTREPRENEURS, AND JUST PLAIN HAPPY PARENTS.

POSTSCRIPT: 35 YEARS AFTER THE SCANDAL, THALIDOMIDE IS MAKING A COMEBACK AS A THERAPEUTIC DRUG FOR AIDS AND LEPROSY PATIENTS.

FACTOID BOOKS

WHOSE VIRUS *IS* IT, ANYWAY?

IN THE EARLY 1980s A NEW AND TERRIFYING DISEASE RAVAGED THE U.S. IT DESTROYED THE HUMAN IMMUNE SYSTEM -- OUR DEFENSE AGAINST DISEASE. APPARENTLY YOU COULD CATCH THE DISEASE THROUGH SEX.

"ACQUIRED IMMUNE DEFICIENCY SYNDROME"--AIDS-- WAS A MYSTERY. WHY DID IT STRIKE SO MANY GAY MEN? WHERE DID IT COME FROM? MOST IMPORTANT, WHAT CAUSED IT?

IN APRIL, 1984 ROBERT GALLO, ONE OF THE GOVERNMENT'S TOP BIOMEDICAL RESEARCHERS, MADE A DRAMATIC ANNOUNCEMENT.

I, ROBERT GALLO, HAVE DISCOVERED THE PROBABLE *CAUSE OF AIDS!*

IT WAS, HE SAID, A VIRUS. HE NAMED IT "HIV."

IT MADE HIM THE WORLD'S MOST FAMOUS BIOLOGIST OVERNIGHT. SIGNIFICANTLY, GALLO HAD DEVELOPED A *TEST* FOR THE AIDS VIRUS.

GOOD NEWS! YOU'RE HIV-NEGATIVE!

-PHEW!-

LAB

THE PATENT ON THE TEST WAS, OBVIOUSLY, A GOLDMINE.

NOT EVERYONE WAS THRILLED WITH GALLO -- LEAST OF ALL FRENCH BIOLOGIST LUC MONTAIGNE.

SACRE BLEU! GALLO'S VIRUS IS IDENTICAL TO THE ONE WE *FRENCH* DISCOVERED LAST YEAR!

FRENCH

TEST E GALLO

INDEED, MONTAIGNE *HAD* SENT GALLO SAMPLES OF HIS VIRUS FOR RESEARCH PURPOSES, AND THEN, SUDDENLY, GALLO "DISCOVERED" HIV. COULD THE SAMPLES HAVE SOMEHOW BEEN MIXED UP?

ABSOLUTELY IMPOSSIBLE!

GALLO CHANGED THAT TUNE IN 1992 WHEN MONTAIGNE'S TESTS PROVED THAT HIS SAMPLE *WAS* IN FACT THE SOURCE OF GALLO'S "DISCOVERY."

UH, LET'S JUST CALL ME THE "CO-DISCOVERER" OF HIV. OKAY?

THE GOVERNMENT PROBED GALLO FOR FRAUD, BUT LET HIM GO BECAUSE IT COULDN'T PROVE HE'D *CONSCIOUSLY* PLANNED TO FABRICATE RESULTS. GALLO CLAIMED...

I'M *FULLY EXONERATED!*

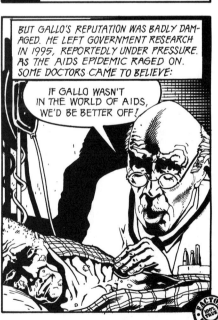

BUT GALLO'S REPUTATION WAS BADLY DAMAGED. HE LEFT GOVERNMENT RESEARCH IN 1995, REPORTEDLY UNDER PRESSURE. AS THE AIDS EPIDEMIC RAGED ON, SOME DOCTORS CAME TO BELIEVE:

IF GALLO WASN'T IN THE WORLD OF AIDS, WE'D BE BETTER OFF!

FACTOID BOOKS

THROUGHOUT THE **50**s AND **60**s HUNDREDS OF FAMILIES MOVED TO THIS PICTURE-PERFECT LITTLE SUBURB IN UPSTATE NEW YORK. IT SEEMED THE IDEAL PLACE TO RAISE CHILDREN AND CATCH A LITTLE PIECE OF THE AMERICAN DREAM. THEY NEVER DREAMED THAT, INSTEAD, THEY WOULD FIND...

DEATH AT LOVE CANAL

IT WAS AN ERA BEFORE EARTH DAY, WHEN "GREEN" MEANT JUST ONE THING: MONEY.

THE BUSINESS OF AMERICA WAS *BUSINESS* -- AND BUSINESS WAS BOOMING. OF COURSE, EVEN BUSINESS HAD TO DUMP ITS WASTE *SOMEWHERE*.

FROM 1947 TO 1953, THE *HOOKER CHEMICAL AND PLASTICS CORPORATION* BURIED AT LEAST 21,000 TONS OF INDUSTRIAL WASTE INTO AN UN-FINISHED CANAL, NAMED FOR THE MAN WHO'D TRIED TO BUILD IT IN 1892, *WILLIAM T. LOVE*.

IN 1953, HOOKER SOLD THE LAND TO THE LOCAL SCHOOL BOARD FOR $1.

AND BY THE WAY, HOOKER CORP. IS *NOT* LIABLE FOR *PHYSICAL HARM* OR *DEATH* RESULTING FROM CHEMICALS THERE.

IT'S A DEAL!

THE TOWN BUILT A SCHOOL AND A CHILDREN'S PLAY-GROUND ON THE LAND, OBLIVIOUS TO THE TOXIC THREAT JUST BELOW THE GROUND.

AS EARLY AS 1958, CHILDREN WERE BURNED BY SUBSTANCES SEEPING UP FROM THE CANAL.

HOOKER INVESTIGATED AND FOUND HIGHLY TOXIC *BENZENE HEXACHLORIDE* ON THE GROUND.

BUT THE COMPANY CHOSE NOT TO WARN THE TOWN'S RESIDENTS OF ANY HAZARD.

WE COULD INCUR *SUBSTANTIAL LIABILITIES*.

THE CHEMICALS STAYED NEAR THE CANAL -- UNTIL THE MID-70s WHEN HEAVY RAINS RAISED THE GROUNDWATER LEVEL...

...BRINGING THE POISONOUS WASTE RIGHT INTO PEOPLE'S HOMES.

SOMETHING'S JUST NOT RIGHT HERE, HONEY.

IN 1978, ALMOST **30%** OF PREGNANT WOMEN IN LOVE CANAL MISCARRIED.

DON'T WORRY, DARLING. WE CAN TRY AGAIN.

OVER **20%** OF BABIES THAT SURVIVED THEIR GESTATION HAD BIRTH DEFECTS.

YOUNG HOUSEWIFE **LOIS GIBBS** WAS ALARMED WHEN HER SON BEGAN HAVING SEIZURES AFTER STARTING SCHOOL. SHE CONFRONTED THE SCHOOL SUPERINTENDENT.

MRS. GIBBS, THERE IS **NO CONTAMINATION** AT THIS SCHOOL!

GIBBS BEGAN KNOCKING ON NEIGHBORS' DOORS AROUND THE CANAL -- AND SHE FOUND SOME DISTURBING FACTS.

MY...MY BABY. SHE JUST **DIED** IN HER CRIB!

THAT'S THE **FIFTH** ONE IN JUST A FEW BLOCKS!

OUR DAUGHTER'S IN THE HOSPITAL. HER **KIDNEYS** ARE FAILING.

I'VE BEEN IN THE HOSPITAL FOUR TIMES THIS YEAR MYSELF -- IT'S THESE DAMNED **MIGRAINES!**

NOT EVERYONE WAS WILLING TO HELP.

DON'T ROCK THE BOAT, LOIS! THE PROBLEM'S BEING TAKEN CARE OF.

GIBBS MANAGED TO ORGANIZE MANY RESIDENTS ANYWAY. FINALLY, THE STATE AGREED TO HOLD A HEARING -- IN ALBANY, A SIX-HOUR DRIVE AWAY. LOIS AND A FEW OF HER NEIGHBORS MANAGED TO ATTEND, WHERE THEY HEARD...

WE RECOMMEND THAT ALL PREGNANT WOMEN AND CHILDREN UNDER AGE **TWO** MOVE OUT OF THE AREA.

WHAT?!? WHAT ABOUT THE **REST** OF US? THIS IS **MURDER!**

HOOKER CHEMICAL WAS OWNED BY *OCCIDENTAL PETROLEUM*, CHAIRED BY *ARMAND HAMMER*, ONE OF THE WORLD'S RICHEST MEN.

THE PROBLEM OF LOVE CANAL HAS BEEN BLOWN UP OUT OF CONTEXT!

A SPOKESPERSON FOR THE CHEMICAL INDUSTRY DISPLAYED EQUAL COMPASSION.

THE RESIDENTS OF LOVE CANAL MAY BE EXAGGERATING THEIR ILLNESSES, THE WAY HYPOCHON-DRIACS DO.

THERE WAS NO COVERING UP THIS TRAGEDY, HOWEVER. CONGRESS HEARD TESTIMONY FROM *DR. BEVERLY PAIGEN*, WHO'D INVESTIGATED LOVE CANAL AND FOUND...

...CANCER, EPILEPSY, BRONCHITIS, UTERINE BLEEDING, BIRTH DEFECTS, PNEUMONIA...

IN 1980, RESIDENTS -- INCLUDING A NUN -- TRAV-ELED TO CALIFORNIA FOR OCCIDENTAL'S SHAREHOLDER'S MEETING. THEY MET WITH A WARM RECEPTION FROM CHAIRMAN HAMMER.

GO BACK TO BUFFALO, SISTER!

PRESIDENT CARTER DECLARED LOVE CANAL A DISASTER AREA. THE GOVERNMENT PAID *$250 MILLION* TO EVACUATE THE FAMILIES.

FOR SALE

LOVE CANAL BECAME A GHOST TOWN.

IN 1990, THE GOVERNMENT DECLARED LOVE CANAL "CLEAN" AND LET HOMES SELL -- AT *VERY* LOW PRICES. GIBBS NOW A PROMINENT TOXIC WASTE ACTIVIST, SAID...

IT'S *UNETHICAL!* NOW *POOR PEOPLE* WILL BE THE VICTIMS!

IN 1995, OCCIDENTAL FINALLY AGREED TO PAY THE GOVERNMENT *$129 MILLION* TO COMPENSATE FOR THE LOVE CANAL CLEANUP.

THIS SETTLEMENT IS GOOD FOR THE GOVERNMENT AND GOOD FOR US.

OCCIDENTAL PETROLEUM

BUT THERE WERE NO REAL HAPPY ENDINGS TO THE LOVE CANAL SCANDAL.

SINCE 1978, AT LEAST 22 RESIDENTS TOOK THEIR OWN LIVES.

EXPLODING PINTOS

BUCKLE UP, KIDS!

FORD. THE ALL-AMERICAN CAR. IN THE 1950s FORDS WERE THE BEST-- AND THE SAFEST.

A DECADE LATER, MARKETS WERE CHANGING. THE COMPANY'S FAST-RISING VICE-PRESIDENT, LEE IACCOCA, HAD A BRAINSTORM.

BUILD ME A CAR THAT WEIGHS *UNDER* 2,000 POUNDS AND COSTS *LESS THAN* $2,000!

FORD EXECUTIVES WERE CHANGING, TOO--AS EVIDENCED BY IACCOCA'S STATED PHILOSOPHY.

SAFETY DOESN'T SELL!

IACCOCA WAS FAR FROM ALONE IN THAT VIEW. HIS BOSS, HENRY FORD II, SCION OF THE FORD FAMILY DYNASTY, FELT THE SAME WAY, SAYING...

WE COULD BUILD THE SAFEST CAR IN THE WORLD, BUT NOBODY WOULD BUY IT! THE AMERICAN PEOPLE WANT *GOOD-LOOKING* CARS, *FAST* CARS, CARS WITH *POWER* AND *STYLING*. THAT'S THE KIND OF CARS WE BUILD!

A NEW CAR USUALLY TOOK 43 MONTHS TO DEVELOP. BUT IN JUST OVER A FRANTIC 35, IACCOCA'S BABY WAS BORN.

LADIES AND GENTLEMEN-- THE FORD PINTO!

THE PINTO WAS AN INSTANT HIT, QUICKLY BECOMING THE MOST POPULAR CAR ON THE AMERICAN ROAD.

NICE CAR, BOB!

SPORTY WHEELS, DON!

BUT THE PINTO HAD A SECRET. IN ALL BUT THREE OF 40 CRASH TESTS, THE CAR'S FUEL TANK RUPTURED.

HMMM. INTERESTING RESULT.

YES. INTRIGUING.

NO ONE DARED BRING THE PROBLEM TO IACCOCA'S ATTENTION. SAFTY, THEY SAID, WAS A "TABOO" TOPIC WITH HIM.

UH, MR. IACCOCA, SIR--? IT SEEMS THERE'S A SMALL PROBLEM WITH, ER...

WHAT??

NOTHING.

IACCOCA

IT WAS A SECRET THAT WOULDN'T LAST. A FEW MONTHS AFTER THE PINTO'S RELEASE, LILY GRAY WAS PULLING OUT ONTO A CALIFORNIA FREEWAY WHEN...

STALLED, GOSH DARN IT!

SPUTTER SPUTTER

LOOK OUT!

SSKREEEEE!

KEERASH!

FA-SHOOM!

THE MASSIVE FIREBALL KILLED LILY GRAY. HER PASSENGER, 13-YEAR-OLD RICHARD GRIMSHAW, SURVIVED, BUT WITH BURNS OVER 90 PERCENT OF HIS BODY, HE WAS HORRIBLY MUTILATED. THE TRAGEDY WOULD BE THE FIRST OF MANY.

BY ONE ESTIMATE, AS MANY AS 900 PEOPLE DIED IN CRASHES THAT WOULD NOT HAVE CAUSED SERIOUS INJURIES IF THEIR PINTOS HADN'T EXPLODED LIKE INCENDIARY BOMBS.

BANG! BLAM! POOF BOOM

IN 1977, THE INVESTIGATIVE MAGAZINE MOTHER JONES, GAINING ACCESS TO INTERNAL FORD DOCUMENTS, RAN A LENGTHY AND SHOCKING EXPOSE.

FORD EXECUTIVES KNEW ABOUT THE PINTO'S FLAWS IN ADVANCE, BUT REFUSED TO CORRECT THEM!

PERHAPS THE MOST APPALLING OF MJ'S REVELATIONS: FORD'S COLD NUMERICAL ANALYSIS.

BASED ON THESE NUMBERS, IT'S MORE COST-EFFECTIVE TO ALLOW 360 DEATHS OR INJURIES THAN TO MAKE THE CAR SAFE.

FORD'S CALCULATIONS WERE BASED ON A FIGURE ARRIVED AT BY EQUALLY "OBJECTIVE" GOVERNMENT BUREAUCRATS.

BASED ON 12 QUANTIFIABLE SOCIETAL FACTORS, WE CALCULATE THE VALUE OF AN INDIVIDUAL HUMAN LIFE AT *$200,725.*

BUREAUCRAT

MEANWHILE, RICHARD GRIMSHAW -- WHO'D UNDERGONE NEARLY 70 SURGERIES SINCE THE ACCIDENT-- SUED FORD.

THIS MEMO PROVES FORD COULD HAVE FIXED THE PROBLEM FOR JUST *$10 PER CAR,* BUT *DIDN'T*--KNOWING PEOPLE WOULD *DIE!*

OUTRAGED, THE JURY AWARDED GRIMSHAW A RECORD *$125 MILLION!*

WE CAME UP WITH THIS HIGH AMOUNT SO THAT FORD WOULDN'T DESIGN CARS THIS WAY AGAIN. THE PINTO IS A *LOUSY* AND *UNSAFE* PRODUCT!

EXIT

EVEN THE GOVERNMENT JOINED THE UNIVERSAL CONDEMNATION OF FORD AND ITS PINTO, WRITING A LETTER TO IACCOCA THAT SAID...

...BASED ON OUR INVESTIGATION, A DEFECT EXISTS IN THESE PINTOS THAT COULD RESULT IN FIRE.

AGAINST THE TIDAL *WAVE* OF BAD PUBLICITY, FORD TOOK ACTION ON JUNE 9, 1978 -- STILL REFUSING TO ADMIT THAT ANYTHING WAS WRONG.

TO *END PUBLIC CONCERN,* WE WILL RECALL THE AFFECTED PINTOS.

BUT IT TOOK FORD MONTHS TO SEND OUT RECALL NOTICES. IN THE MEANTIME, THREE TEENAGE GIRLS IN INDIANA WERE INCINERATED.

SCHOOL

MATH

DISTRICT ATTORNEY MICHAEL COSENTINO, A HARD-NOSED REPUBLICAN, WAS OUTRAGED.

THAT DOES IT, I'M CHARGING FORD MOTOR COMPANY WITH *HOMICIDE!!*

GAZZETTE

3 TEENS DIE IN PINTO

FORD POURED $2 MILLION INTO ITS DEFENSE, HIRING FORMER WATERGATE PROSECUTOR JAMES NEAL.

WHAT I'M DOING IS RIGHT. COMPANIES JUST CAN'T KEEP UP WITH FEDERAL REGULATIONS.

THANKS TO NEAL, FORD WON ACQUITTAL.

IACCOCA TOOK RESPONSIBILITY FOR THE DEBACLE. SORT OF.

HEY, I DIDN'T MAKE AN UNSAFE CAR ON *PURPOSE!*

THE SCANDAL DIDN'T TAINT HIM. AS HEAD OF CHRYSLER, HE SAVED THE COMPANY (WITH $2 BILLION FROM UNCLE SAM) AND BECAME A BUSINESS ICON.

FACTOID BOOKS

CYBER PORN SCARE

IN THE MID-1990s THE *INTERNET*--A GLOBAL NETWORK LINKING MILLIONS OF COMPUTERS--REVOLUTIONIZED COMMUNICATION. SUDDENLY THE WORLD BECAME A LOT SMALLER, AND ANYTHING THE HUMAN MIND COULD THINK OF APPEARED "ON LINE."

AND WE *ALL KNOW* WHAT THE HUMAN MIND LIKES TO THINK OF.

FROM THE BEGINNING, *SEX* (A DIGITAL, IMPERSONAL VERSION OF IT, ANYWAY) WAS AMONG THE INTERNET'S MOST POPULAR APPLICATIONS.

I'M--TAKING--OFF--MY--PANTS--

Clickety *Clickety Clickety*

IT'S ONLY NATURAL.

AND JUST AS IT HAD WITH TV AND MOVIES, THIS LED TO CRIES OF...

SAVE OUR CHILDREN...

...OUR CHILDREN...

...FROM THIS *SMUT!*

ON JULY 3, 1995 *TIME MAGAZINE,* SENSING A "HOT BUTTON" CONTROVERSY, RAN A SENSATIONAL "CYBERPORN" COVER STORY.

THE STORY WAS BASED ON A COLLEGE PAPER BY 30-YEAR-OLD UNDERGRAD MARTIN RIMM WHO SIGNED AN EXCLUSIVE DEAL WITH *TIME* AND WOULDN'T EVEN ANSWER QUESTIONS ABOUT HIMSELF.

IT WOULD *DETRACT* FROM THE *IMPORTANCE* OF MY *FINDINGS!*

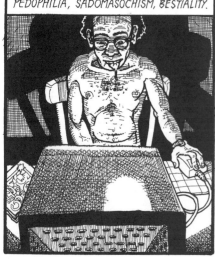

THOSE INFLAMMATORY "FINDINGS" PORTRAYED THE INTERNET AS A PERILOUS WILDERNESS OF DEVIANT PORN: PEDOPHILIA, SADOMASOCHISM, BESTIALITY.

SCHOLARS DISCREDITED RIMM'S "STUDY" AS SLIPSHOD AND MISLEADING, OVERBLOWING THE "THREAT."

RIMM HIMSELF, IT TURNED OUT, WAS THE SECRET AUTHOR OF A BOOK TITLED THE PORNOGRAPHER'S HANDBOOK.

IT WAS *SATIRE!* YEAH! THAT'S IT!

THOUGH *TIME* LATER RAN AN ARTICLE CRITICIZING ITS OWN COVER STORY, POLITICIANS WEREN'T CONFUSED BY THE FACTS. CONGRESS PASSED THE 1996 "COMMUNICATIONS DECENCY ACT" REGULATING ONLINE "INDECENCY."

AND I KNOW IT'S BAD BECAUSE I'VE SEEN *PLENTY* OF IT!

FACTOID BOOKS

WRITER

JONATHAN VANKIN

Award-winning journalist Jonathan Vankin wrote two previous books: the critically acclaimed 1991 *Conspiracies, Cover-Ups and Crimes* and (with John Whalen) its 1995 companion volume, *60 Greatest Conspiracies of All Time*. Neither contained pictures, so he is pleased that this, his third, is a comic book. His fascination with scandal stems from a lengthy newspaper career in which he witnessed many important people do some pretty stupid things. His own conduct is of course, at all times, utterly beyond reproach. So back off!

ARTISTS

CHARLES ADLARD

"Don't listen to those men in the long coats—I didn't draw The X-Files...ever...no, no really...I didn't. But I do draw *Shadowman!* Oh yes! Oh yes!" (Page 106)

SERGIO ARAGONÉS

Sergio is the creator of the award-winning comic *Groo*. His comics and illustrations have appeared in *MAD*, and most recently in *Sergio Aragonés' Louder Than Words* from Dark Horse Comics. (Page 118)

GLENN BARR

Glenn's projects have included the graphic novels and comics *Cliff's Wild Life, Technocracy Blues, Mars on Earth*, as well as *Brooklyn Dreams* for Paradox Press. His animation work includes *The Ren & Stimpy Show* and *Baby Huey*. (Page 179)

HILARY BARTA

Eats food, breathes air, and draws comics. (Page 8)

GREGORY BENTON

Gregory's cartooning wonderment has appeared in *Details, High Times*, and in his own comic book *Hummingbird*. He's that cat who won't cop out, when there's danger all about — can you dig it? (Page 50)

BRIAN BUNIAK

In addition to his hectic schedule as a double agent for the British Secret Service, Brian draws *Bunitoons*, which is available on the Internet. (Page 26)

DON CAMERON

Although voted Most Lovable Artist by the Editors For a Better America, Don manages to remain as humble as ever. Don's next eagerly-awaited project is a four-volume miniseries on the life and times of Morey Amsterdam drawn entirely with his penis. (Page 113)

ANTHONY CASTRILLO

Anthony's latest work includes DC's *Supergirl* and *Impulse* Annuals. (Page 52)

JOHN CEBOLLERO

John is currently studying for his urine test. He could not be contacted for a bio. (Page 88)

STEPHEN DESTEFANO

Stephen has been a professional cartoonist for over 15 years. He was born in Queens, New York. (Page 5 and 183)

D'ISRAELI D'EMON DRAUGHTSMAN

D'Israeli still lives in Sheffield with his mummy, but his nice kitty has fled. Perhaps that business with the bulldog clips was too much for him. (Page 46)

COLLEEN DORAN

Colleen is the writer, artist, and creator of the series *A Distant Soil*. She worked on *Sandman* and is drawing a *Wonder Woman* graphic novel which is due out in '98. (Page 32)

RANDY DUBURKE

Randy's work for DC Comics includes covers of *Animal Man, Darkstars, Ms. Tree*, and *The Shadow*. He drew the story "Tunnel Rats" for the DC/Vertigo anthology *Weird War Tales*, as well as *Hunter's Heart,* a graphic novel in the Paradox Mystery line. (Page 68)

HUNT EMERSON

Hunt Emerson lurks 100 feet in the air, in sight of the New Hindu Temple on Soho Road. At night, the dome is lit from below in blue light. (Page 82)

BOB FINGERMAN

When Bob isn't drawing weird stuff for Paradox, he's illustrating his comic *Minimum Wage* from Fantagraphics. It's like Vitamin C and sex—it's good for you. So just go buy it. (Page 176)

RICK GEARY

Rick's illustrations appear occasionally in *MAD*. He continues to write and illustrate a series of children's books featuring "The Mask" for Dark Horse Comics. His new graphic novel is *The Borden Tragedy* for NBM. (Page 40)

DICK GIORDANO

Dick was born July 20, 1932. The rest, as they say, is ancient history. (Page 154)

PAUL GULACY

Gulacy is well known for getting Helfer's butt out of the sling in crunch-time situations. (Page 16)

BOB HALL

Bob has been a theater director, playwright, actor, and cartoonist. He currently writes and draws the comic *Armed and Dangerous* for Acclaim. (Page 150)

CRAIG HAMILTON

No stranger to scandals, Craig was informed once, by a gypsy fortune teller, that he actually *was* Rudy Valentino in a past life. His Big Book work includes *Urban Legends, Weirdos*, and *Death*. (Page 11)

CULLY HAMNER

Cully learned to tap at an early age, and danced on Broadway along such idols as Sammy Davis, Jr. However, tragedy struck at age forty when he developed heel cancer. Crestfallen, he turned to comics. (Page 104)

DANNY HELLMAN

...With a clumsy yank the blindfold was gone. I could see the girl again. She had made a costume change—she was now wearing crisp surgical scrubs. "Don't look so worried, sweetie," she said, twirling a scalpel in her hand,"what do you need a brain stem for, anyway?" (Page 100)

SHEPHERD HENDRIX

Shep has spent five years dancing with the big boys (DC, Dark Horse, Milestone, and Kitchen Sink). Now he is a co-creator and co-owner of *Glyph*, a group-owned magazine. (Page 135)

DAN LAWLIS

Dan is best known for his work at Dark Horse on *Barb Wire* and *Agents of Law*. The last big job he did was for Marvel—a fully painted sci-fi story called *Starlord*. (Page 114)

STEVEN LIEBER
Steven pronounces his surname LEE-burr, not LYE-burr. He's worked on *Hawkman*, *Lady Justice*, *Detective Comics*, *Dark Horse Presents*, *Roadways*, and a three-part *Grendel Tales* story arc due out in '97. (Page 162)

DAVID LLOYD
Other work by David can be seen in the classic graphic novel *V for Vendetta*, in *The Horrorist*, and in *Weird War Tales*, published by DC/Vertigo. Be good to yourself and buy all of them. (Page 17)

LENNIE MACE
"Don't call me a cartoonist. Don't call me an illustrator or an artist, either. But whatever you do, don't, repeat, *don't* call me 'that ballpoint pen guy.'" (Page 172)

GRAHAM MANLEY
Graham is believed to be in hiding from the police somewhere in Scotland. He is wanted for crimes against the comic-strip form. (Page 94)

STEVE MANNION
Steve says he has no idea *what's* going on. But we know better. (Page 146)

ANTHONY MODANO
Anthony can be found running around the streets of Boston, playing with his band Kicked in the Head, and pursuing his art career. Please give his sorry ass a job. (Page 77)

JOE ORLANDO
Joe edited all those great DC Comics in the '60s and '70s that didn't have superpeople in them, like *Angel and the Ape*, and the original *House of Secrets*. He recently retired after being a big VP and Creative Director for DC and *MAD*. And you thought his only asset was his good looks. (Page 78)

TAYYAR OZKAN
Tayyar's collection *Caveman: Evolution Heck* was published by NBM. He inked a story arc for *The Dreaming* for DC/Vertigo as well as drawing *Bushwacked*, *Pet*, and *Cave Bang* for Eros. (Page 126)

JEAN-CLAUDE PADILLA
Jean-Claude is a third-year cartooning major at the School of Visual Arts who plans to take over the world with his captivating ideas, stories and art. Thanks, Andy and Jim! Thanks, Mom! (Page 67)

ARNOLD PANDER
Arnold's most recent work includes "Jack Zero," and (with his brother Jacob) *Triple•X*, both for Dark Horse Comics. (Page 28)

RICK PARKER
Rick drew *MTV's Beavis and Butt-head* for Marvel, and many Big Book stories for Paradox. His most recent scandal involved his attempt to white out the "C" on each of the signs at the Canal Street subway stop. He is still at large. (Page 72)

JAMES PASCOE
James enjoys drawing pictures. He also enjoys drinking beer and watching movies, but no one will pay him for that. (Page 175)

MIKE PERKINS
Mike has worked for Fleetway in the U.K., Nowa Fantastyka in Poland, and Caliber in the States. You can find his current work—*Doctor Faustus*, *Black Mist*, and *Necroscope*—at a comic shop near you! (Page 22)

STEVE PUGH
Steve lives in Worcester, U.K. with the lady wrestler "Tartan Apokalips." (Page 37)

JOE SACCO
Joe is the author of *Palestine*, which won the American Bookseller's Association Award and is published by Fantagraphics. Currently, he is working on a series of stories about his experiences in Bosnia. (Page 123)

MARIE SEVERIN
Started as a colorist at EC Comics and as an artist for the Federal Reserve Bank of New York. She then found a home at Marvel for 30 years—and will stay there doing her thing till she gets it right! (Page 24)

ERIC SHANOWER
Eric's current comics work can be seen in *Weird War Tales*, *Harlan Ellison's Dream Corridor*, and *Oz-Story*. He is working on a major comics project involving the most beautiful woman in the world. (Page 62)

GALEN SHOWMAN
Galen likes to draw. He has done album covers for The Wipers, illustrated for various magazines and co-created and illustrated *The Lost* and *Renfield* for Caliber Comics. (Page 132)

WALTER SIMONSON
Here's the book on Walter from a local high school student: "Mr. Simonson's so *old*, and he's been doing comics for so *long*, and he's *still* totally twisted!" (Page 166)

ROBIN SMITH
Robin was the art director for *2000 AD*, and an artist on *Judge Dredd*. He is the illustrator of the recently released *Green Candles* and forthcoming book *The Bogie Man*, two graphic novels in the Paradox Graphic Mystery line. (Page 158)

ROBERT SNYDER
Robert was an editorial cartoonist at *The Baltimore Sun*. He routinely drew corrupt police officers with pig snouts and stupid politicians with their pants around their ankles. He got canned. (Page 71)

JOE STATON
Joe has worked for Marvel on *The Incredible Hulk*, and for DC illustrating *Superman*, *Batman*, *Plastic Man*, *Green Lantern*, and many others. Joe illustrated *Family Man*, a graphic novel in the Paradox Mystery line written by Jerome Charyn. (Page 140)

WARD SUTTON
Ward is: a syndicated cartoonist (*Ward's Cleaver*, *Schlock 'N Roll*), a comic-book author (*Ink Blot*), a rock poster artist (for Pearl Jam and Beck) and a freelance illustrator (*Rolling Stone*, *Entertainment Weekly*, and others). (Page 122)

S.M. TAGGART
Girded against the coming apocalypse, Mr. Taggart asks that you all knock before entering his bunker as this would allow him time to load his rifle. (Page 169)

ALWYN TALBOT
Alwyn just finished a B.A. in illustration. His work has appeared in *Vorgarth*, *Negative Burn*, and *Kimota*. He says thanks to Andy for the chance. (Page 182)

BRYAN TALBOT
Bryan's award-winning work has ranged from *Nemesis*, *Judge Dredd*, *Luther Arkwright*, *Batman*, *Sandman*, and his recent *The Tale of One Bad Rat*. He is currently working on a new Luther Arkwright book for Dark Horse Comics. (Page 80)

TY TEMPLETON
Ty was born in downtown Canada and was raised by show-business gypsies. His comics work includes *Batman & Robin Adventures*, *Secret Origins*, and *Mad Dog*. (Page 55)

ALEX WALD
Alex is currently riding high in the charts with covers for *Supersnazz*, *The Galaxy Trio*, and *Southern Culture on the Skids*. He has frolicked nude on Mt. Fuji, but was demurely clothed for his July, 1968 *Playboy* pictorial. (Page 58)

ALAN WEISS
Alan has worked for DC, Marvel, Defiant, and Broadway Comics and has split his time between comics and advertising. (Page 12)

ANDREW WENDEL
Andrew was a portrait artist for *The New Yorker* and is fueled by passions for music, cycling, and the bizarre. His work has also appeared in five Paradox Big Books. (Page 110)

BIBLIOGRAPHY

CHAPTER 1 TAWDRY TINSELTOWN

"FATTY" ARBUCKLE: NO TEARS FOR THE FAT MAN
Anger, Kenneth. *Hollywood Babylon*. New York: Dell, 1975.
Edmonds, Andy. *Frame-Up! The Untold Story of Roscoe "Fatty" Arbuckle*. New York: William Morrow, 1991.
Oderman, Stuart. *Roscoe "Fatty" Arbuckle: A Biography of the Silent Film Comedian 1887-1933*. Jefferson, NC: McFarland and Company, Inc., 1994.
Yallop, David A. *The Day The Laughter Stopped: The True Story of Fatty Arbuckle*. New York: St. Martin's Press, 1976.
Young, Robert, Jr. *Roscoe "Fatty" Arbuckle: A Bio-Bibliography*. Westport, CT: Greenwood Press, 1994.

THE GREAT LOVER
Anger, Kenneth. *Hollywood Babylon*. New York: Dell, 1975.
Kohn, George C. *Encyclopedia of American Scandal*. New York: Facts on File, 1989.
Scagnetti, Jack. *The Intimate Life of Rudolph Valentino*. Middle Village, NY: Jonathan David Publishers, 1975.

DEATH OF A MYSTERY MAN
Anger, Kenneth. *Hollywood Babylon*. New York: Dell, 1975.
Giroux, Robert. *A Deed of Death: The Story Behind the Unsolved Murder of Hollywood Director William Desmond Taylor*. New York: Knopf, 1990.
Hynd, Alan. "Murder in Hollywood," *American Mercury* #69 (Nov. 1949), pp. 594-601.
King, Ed C. "I Know Who Killed Desmond Taylor," *Taylorology* #50 (Feb. 1997).
Kirkpatrick, Sidney. *A Cast of Killers*. New York: Dutton, 1986.
Long, Bruce. "The Case Against Edward Sands," *Taylorology* #19 (July, 1994).
Sherman, William. "In Defense of Mabel Normand," *Taylorology* #15 (March, 1994).

ALL-AMERICAN JUNKIE
Anger, Kenneth. *Hollywood Babylon*. New York: Dell, 1975.
Bodeen, DeWitt. *From Hollywood*. New York: A.S. Barnes and Co., 1976.
Kohn, George C. *Encyclopedia of American Scandal*. New York: Facts on File, 1989.

CHARLIE CHAPLIN
Anger, Kenneth. *Hollywood Babylon*. New York: Dell, 1975.
Chaplin, Charles. *My Autobiography*. New York: Plume Books, 1992.
McCabe, John. *Charlie Chaplin*. Garden City, NY: Doubleday and Co., 1978.
Milton, Joyce. *Tramp: The Life of Charlie Chaplin*. New York: HarperCollins, 1996.
Robinson, David. *Chaplin: His Life and Art*. New York: McGraw-Hill Publishing Co., 1985.

THE ICE-CREAM BLONDE
Anger, Kenneth. *Hollywood Babylon*. New York: Dell, 1975.
Edmonds, Andy. *Hot Toddy: The True Story of Hollywood's Most Sensational Murder*. New York: William Morrow & Co., 1989
Kohn, George C. *Encyclopedia of American Scandal*. New York: Facts on File, 1989.

Munn, Michael. *The Hollywood Murder Casebook*. New York: St. Martin's Press, 1987.

MARY ASTOR'S LITTLE BLUE BOOK
Anger, Kenneth. *Hollywood Babylon*. New York: Dell, 1975.
Astor, Mary. *A Life on Film*. New York: Delacorte Press, 1971.
Kohn, George C. *Encyclopedia of American Scandal*. New York: Facts on File, 1989.

IN LIKE FLYNN
Anger, Kenneth. *Hollywood Babylon*. New York: Dell, 1975.
Flynn, Errol. *My Wicked, Wicked Ways*. New York: G.P. Putnam, 1959.
Godfrey, Lionel. *The Life and Crimes of Errol Flynn*. New York: St. Martin's Press, 1977.
Kohn, George C. *Encyclopedia of American Scandal*. New York: Facts on File, 1989.
Munn, Michael. *Hollywood Rogues*. New York: St. Martin's Press, 1991.
Thomas, Tony. *Errol Flynn: The Spy Who Never Was*. New York: Citadel Press, 1990.

THE SWEATER GIRL AND THE GANGSTER
Anger, Kenneth. *Hollywood Babylon*. New York: Dell, 1975.
Kohn, George C. *Encyclopedia of American Scandal*. New York: Facts on File, 1989.
Morella, Joe and Edward Z. Epstein. *Lana: The Public and Private Lives of Miss Turner*. New York: Citadel Press, 1971.
Turner, Lana. *Lana: The Lady, the Legend, the Truth*. New York: E.P. Dutton, 1982.
Updike, John. "Legendary Lana." *The New Yorker*, Feb. 12, 1996.
Valentino, Lou. *The Films of Lana Turner*. Secaucus, NJ; Citadel Press, 1976.

THE LOVES OF INGRID BERGMAN
Bergman, Ingrid and Alan Burgess. *Ingrid Bergman: My Story*. New York: Delacorte Press, 1972.
Brown, Curtis F. *Ingrid Bergman*. New York: Pyramid Books, 1973.
Leamer, Laurence. *As Time Goes By: The Life of Ingrid Bergman*. New York: Harper and Row, 1987.

E!
Baumgold, Julie. "Midnight in the Garden of Good and Elvis." *Esquire*, March, 1995.
Geller, Larry and Joel Spector. *If I Can Dream: Elvis' Own Story*. New York: Simon and Schuster, 1989.
Hammontree, Patsy Guy. *Elvis Presley: A Bio-Bibliography*. Westport, CT: Greenwood Press, 1985.
Latham, Caroline and Jeanne Sakol. *"E" is for Elvis*. New York: NAL Books, 1990.
Marsh, Dave. *Elvis*. New York: Thunder's Mouth Press, 1992.
Nash, Alanna. *Elvis Aaron Presley: Revelations From the Memphis Mafia*. New York: HarperCollins, 1995.

THE SCANDAL THAT SANK A STUDIO
Alpert, Hollis. *Burton*. New York: Putnam, 1986.
Brown, Peter Harry and Patte B. Barham. *Marilyn: The Last Take*. New York: Signet, 1993.

Heymann, C. David. *Liz: An Intimate Biography of Elizabeth Taylor*. New York: Birch Lane Press, 1995.

Kelley, Kitty. *Elizabeth Taylor: The Last Star*. New York: Simon and Schuster, 1981.

Sheppard, Dick. *Elizabeth*. Garden City, NY: Doubleday, 1974.

Spoto, Donald. *A Passion For Life: The Biography of Elizabeth Taylor*. New York: HarperCollins, 1995.

MURDER, MAYHEM, COTTON CLUB

Cowie, Peter. *Coppola*. New York: Charles Scribner's Sons, 1990

Daly, Michael. "The Making of the Cotton Club." *New York*, May 7, 1984.

Evans, Robert. *The Kid Stays in the Picture*. Beverly Hills: Dove Books, 1995.

Lewis, Jon. *Whom God Wishes to Destroy : Francis Coppola and the New Hollywood*. Durham, NC: Duke University Press, 1995.

Newton, Michael. *Raising Hell: An Encyclopedia of Devil Worship and Satanic Crime*. New York: Avon Books, 1993.

Terry, Maury. *The Ultimate Evil*. Garden City, NY: Dolphin Books, 1987.

Wick, Steve. *Bad Company: Drugs, Hollywood and the Cotton Club Murder*. New York: Harcourt Brace Jovanovich, 1990.

DON SIMPSON: FAST TRACK

Biskind, Peter. "Good Night, Dark Prince." *Premiere*, April, 1996.

Masters, Kim. "Days of Thunder, Nights of Despair." *Vanity Fair*, April, 1996.

Philips, Chuck and Carla Hall. "Narcotics Unit Probes Don Simpson's Death." *The Los Angeles Times*, Feb. 6, 1996.

——. "Fatal Attraction." *The Los Angeles Times*, Oct. 23, 1995.

Philips, Chuck. "Suit Claims Conspiracy in Fatal Overdose." *The Los Angeles Times*, August 15, 1996.

HEIDI FLEISS, HOLLYWOOD MADAM

Heidi Fleiss: Hollywood Madam. A film by Nick Broomfield. Distributed by IN Pictures.

Hirschberg, Lynn. "Heidi Does Hollywood." *Vanity Fair*, Feb. 1994.

Hubler, Shawn and James Bates. "Heidi's Arrest is the Talk of Tinseltown." *The Los Angeles Times*, August 1, 1993.

Hubler, Shawn. "Actor Says He Got Call Girls From Fleiss..." *The Los Angeles Times*, July 21, 1995.

——. "Fleiss Sentenced to 37 Months for Tax Evasion." *The Los Angeles Times*, Jan. 8, 1997.

Murphy, Dean and Terry Pristin. "The Heidi Chronicles." *The Los Angeles Times*, August 8, 1993.

Rensin, David. "Heidi Fleiss Interview." *Playboy*, August, 1996.

Shah, Diane. "The Hardest Working Girl in Show Business." *Esquire*, Nov. 1993.

Singer, Mark. "Heidi's Outtakes." *The New Yorker*, Aug. 23, 1993.

WOODY AND MIA

Corliss, Richard. "Scenes From a Breakup." *Time*, August 31, 1992.

Goldman, John J. "Woody Allen Says Battle is Like a 'Cosmic Explosion.'" *The Los Angeles Times*, August 25, 1992.

Groteke, Kristi. *Mia and Woody: Love and Betrayal*. New York: Carroll and Graf, 1994.

Hoban, Phoebe. "Everything You Always Wanted to Know About Woody and Mia (But Were Afraid to Ask)." *New York*, Sept. 21, 1992.

Lax, Eric. *Woody Allen: A Biography*. New York: Alfred A. Knopf, 1991.

Orth, Maureen. "Mia's Story." *Vanity Fair*, November, 1992.

White, Diane. "If You Ask Mia, Woody's Bananas." *Boston Globe*, February 19, 1997.

HOLLYWOOD BAD BOYS

Anger, Kenneth. *Hollywood Babylon*. New York: Dell, 1975.

Eells, George. *Robert Mitchum*. New York: Franklin Wats, 1984.

Munn, Michael. *Hollywood Rogues*. New York: St. Martin's Press, 1991.

CHAPTER 2 SOCIETY SLEAZE

MURDER OF THE CENTURY

Baker, Paul R. *Stanny: The Gilded Life of Stanford White*. New York: Free Press, 1989.

Baldwin, Charles C. *Stanford White*. New York: Dodd, Mead & Co., 1931.

Knappman, Edward W., ed. *Great American Trials*. Detroit: Visible Ink Press, 1994.

Lessard, Suzannah. *Architect of Desire: Beauty and Danger in the Stanford White Family*. New York: Dial Press, 1996.

Mooney, Michael M. *Evelyn Nesbit and Stanford White: Love and Death in the Gilded Age*. New York: William Morrow, 1976

THE PRINCESS AND THE ICE QUEEN

Balzar, John. "Harding Pleads Guilty to Obstructing Justice." *The Los Angeles Times*, March 17, 1994.

Coffey, Frank and Joe Layden. *Thin Ice: The Complete Uncensored Story of Tonya Harding*. New York: Pinnacle Books, 1994

Haight, Abby and J.E. Vader. *Fire on Ice*. New York: Times Books, 1994.

McGrory, Brian and Jane Meredith Adams. "Harding Traveled Harsh Path to Stardom." *Boston Globe*, January 30, 1994.

Smolowe, Jill. "The Slippery Saga of Tonya Harding." *Time*, February 15, 1994.

DEATH AND THE DIET DOCTOR

Alexander, Shana. *Very Much a Lady*. New York: Little, Brown and Co., 1983.

Knappman, Edward W., ed. *Great American Trials*. Detroit: Visible Ink Press, 1994.

Kohn, George C. *Encyclopedia of American Scandal*. New York: Facts on File, 1989.

Trilling, Diana. *Mrs. Harris: The Death of the Scarsdale Diet Doctor*. New York: Harcourt Brace Jovanovich, 1981.

JIMMY SWAGGART IN HELL

Associated Press. "Church Leader Tells How Swaggart Was Caught." Feb. 24, 1988.

Hackett, George. "A Sex Scandal Breaks Over Jimmy Swaggart." *Newsweek*, Feb. 29, 1988.

Kohn, George. *Encyclopedia of American Scandal*. New York: Facts on File, 1989.

Ostling, Richard. "Now It's Jimmy's Turn." *Time*, March 7, 1988.

Wright, Lawrence. "False Messiah." *Rolling Stone*, July 14, 1988.

THE BALLAD OF JIM & TAMMY

Associated Press. "No Longer Lavish." October 5, 1996.

Brower, Montgomery. "Unholy Roller Coaster." *People Weekly*, Sept. 18, 1989.

Gaillard, Frye. "The Rise and Fall of Jim Bakker." *Charlotte Observer*, March 29, 1987.

Golson, Barry. "The Jessica Hahn Story." *Playboy*, November, 1987.

Levin, Eric. "It's Jim and Tammy Time Again!" *People Weekly*, July 4, 1988.

Shepard, Charles E. *Forgiven: The Rise and Fall of Jim Bakker and the PTL Ministry*. New York: Atlantic Monthly Press, 1989.

Storch, Charles. "A Story of Struggle." *Charlotte Observer* (from *Chicago Tribune*), August 30, 1987.

SEX, DRUGS AND ROX

Knappman, Edward W., ed. *Great American Trials*. Detroit: Visible Ink Press, 1994

Kohn, George C. *Encyclopedia of American Scandal*. New York: Facts on File, 1989.

Marx, Linda. "Pulitzer Reprise." *People Weekly*, Nov. 9, 1992.

Pallesen, Tim. "Psychic Recalls Mrs. Pulitzer's Affairs." *Miami Herald*, Sept 29, 1982.

——. "Pulitzers Are Pulling No Punches at Trial." *Miami Herald*, Sept. 22, 1982.

Pulitzer, Roxanne and Kathleen Maxa. *The Prize Pulitzer*. New York: Random House, 1989.

CYRIL BURT: INTELLIGENCE MAN

"The Burt Scandal." *Living Marxism*, Dec. 1992.

Fletcher, Ronald. *Science, Ideology and the Media: The Cyril Burt Scandal*. New Brunswick, NJ: Transaction Publishers, 1991.

Hearnshaw, L.S. *Cyril Burt, Psychologist*. Ithaca, NY: Cornell University Press, 1979.

Jensen, Arthur. "IQ and Science: The Mysterious Burt Affair." *Public Interest*, Sept. 1, 1991.

Samelson, Franz. "Rescuing the Reputation of Sir Cyril Burt." *Journal of the History of the Behavioral Sciences*, July, 1992.

Panati, Charles. "An Epitaph for Sir Cyril?" *Newsweek*, Dec. 20, 1976.

THE KING AND MRS. SIMPSON

Allen, Peter. *The Windsor Secret*. New York: Stein and Day, 1984.

Bloch, Michael. *The Secret File of the Duke of Windsor*. New York: Harper and Row Publishers, 1988.

Bryan, J. III and Charles J.V. Murphy. *The Windsor Story*. New York: William Morrow and Co., 1979.

Ziegler, Philip. *King Edward VIII: A Biography*. New York: Alfred A. Knopf, 1991.

CHARLES AND DIANA

Benson, Ross. *Charles: The Untold Story*. New York: St. Martin's Press, 1993.

Buskin, Richard. *Princess Diana: The Real Story*. New York: Signet, 1992.

Davies, Nicholas. *Diana: A Princess and Her Troubled Marriage*. New York: Bantam Books, 1993.

Henican, Ellis. "Now, Divorce of Century." *Newsday*, August 29, 1996.

Moore, Sally. *The Definitive Diana*. Chicago: Contemporary Books, 1991.

Morton, Andrew. *Diana: Her New Life*. New York: Simon and Schuster, 1994.

Whitaker, James. *Diana vs. Charles: Royal Blood Feud*. New York: Dutton, 1993.

Wong, Betty. "Diana Shocks With Adultery Confession." *Reuters News Service*, Nov. 21, 1995.

O.J.'S FINAL RUN & CIRQUE DU O.J.

Bugliosi, Vincent. *Outrage: The Five Reasons Why O.J. Simpson Got Away With Murder*. New York: W.W. Norton & Co., 1996.

Darden, Christopher. *In Contempt*. New York: Regan Books, 1996.

Fuhrman, Mark. *Murder in Brentwood*. Washington, DC: Regnery Publishing, 1997.

Goldberg, Hank. *The Prosecution Responds*. Secaucus, NJ: Birch Lane Press, 1996.

Lange, Tom and Phillip Vannatter. *Evidence Dismissed: The Inside Story of the Police Investigation of O.J. Simpson*. New York: Pocket Books, 1997.

Schiller, Lawrence. *American Tragedy: The Uncensored Story of the Simpson Defense*. New York: Random House, 1996.

Shapiro, Robert L. *The Search for Justice: A Defense Attorney's Brief on the O.J. Simpson Case*. New York: Warner Books, 1996.

Rantala, M.L. *O.J. Unmasked: The Trial, the Truth and the Media*. Chicago: Catfeet Press, 1996.

Toobin, Jeffrey. *The Run of His Life: The People v. O.J. Simpson*. New York: Random House, 1996.

WACKO JACKO

Cerone, Daniel. "Michael's Video Takes a Beating." *The Los Angeles Times*, Nov. 16, 1991.

Corliss, Richard. "Who's Bad?" *Time*, Sept. 6, 1993.

Fink, Mitchell. "Spielberg: Earth to Michael." *People Weekly*, July 10, 1995.

"Michael Jackson and Wife Lisa Marie Presley Reveal Intimate Side..." *Jet*, July 3, 1995.

Newton, Jim. "Jackson Not Charged but Not Absolved." *The Los Angeles Times*, Sept. 22, 1994.

"Photo Pop." *People Weekly*, April 21, 1997.

Willman, Chris. "Michael Jackson's Falling Down." *Entertainment Weekly*, July 28, 1995.

CHAPTER 3 POLITICS AS USUAL

THE WAYS AND MEANS OF LUST

"A Bit of the Bubbly." *Time*, Oct. 28, 1974.

Frady, Marshall. "Wilbur's Blue Angel." *New Times*, Dec. 27, 1974.

Green, Stephen and Margot Hornblower. "Mills Admits Being Present During Tidal Basin Scuffle." *Washington Post*, Oct. 11, 1974.

The Los Angeles Times. "Wilbur Mills, Former Powerful Lawmaker, Dies." May 3, 1992.

Shapiro, Walter. "Wilbur Mills: The Ways and Means of Conning the Press." *Washington Monthly*, ..Dec. 1974.

"Wilbur's Argentine Firecracker." *Time*, Oct, 21, 1974.

THE PROFUMO AFFAIR

Irving, Clive et al. *Anatomy of a Scandal: A Study of the Profumo Affair*. New York: William Morrow and Co., 1963.

Knightley, Philip and Caroline Kennedy. *An Affair of State: The Profumo Case and the Framing of Stephen Ward*. New York: Athaneum, 1987.

X-RATED CONGRESS

Adler, Jerry. "Congress: An X-Rated Tale." *Newsweek*, March 16, 1981.

Christy, Marian. "Rita Jenrette: Her Motives." *The Boston Globe*, March 5, 1981.

Garment, Suzanne. *Scandal: The Culture of Mistrust in American Politics*. New York: Times Books, 1991.

Jenrette, Rita and Kathleen Maxa. "Diary of a Mad Congresswife." *The Washington Post Magazine*, Dec. 7, 1980.

——. "The Liberation of a Congressional Wife." *Playboy*, April, 1981.

Kohn, George C. *Encyclopedia of American Scandal*. New York: Facts on File, 1989.

ROCKY

Colby, Gerard with Charlotte Dennett. *Thy Will Be Done*. New York: HarperCollins, 1995.

Jackovich, Karen and Gary Clifford. "Megan Marshack: The Ambitious Aide Whose Silence Deepens the Mystery of Rockefeller's Death." *People Weekly*, Feb. 26, 1979.

Persicco, Joseph E. *Imperial Rockefeller: A Biography of Nelson Rockefeller*. New York: Simon and Schuster, 1982.

"Rocky's Final Hour." *Newsweek*, Feb. 19, 1979.

FROM CAMELOT TO CHAPPAQUIDDICK

Burke, Richard E. *The Senator: My Ten Years With Ted Kennedy*. New York: St. Martin's Press, 1992.

Damore, Leo. *Senatorial Privilege: The Chappaquiddick Cover-Up*. Washington, DC: Regnery Gateway, 1988.

David, Lester. *Good Ted, Bad Ted: The Two Faces of Edward M. Kennedy*. New York: Birch Lane Press, 1993.

Hersh, Burton. *The Education of Edward Kennedy*. New York: William Morrow and Co., 1972.

Olsen, Jack. *The Bridge at Chappaquiddick*. Boston: Little, Brown and Co., 1970.

Ulasewicz, Tony. *The President's Private Eye*. Westport, CT; MASCAM Publishing Co., 1990.

HE SAID, SHE SAID

Borger, Gloria et al. "The Untold Story." *U.S. News and World Report*. Oct. 12, 1992.

Brock, David. *The Real Anita Hill*. New York: The Free Press, 1993.

Mayer, Jane and Jill Abramson. *Strange Justice: The Selling of Clarence Thomas*. Boston: Houghton Mifflin Company, 1994.

Simon, Senator Paul. *Advice and Consent*. Washington, DC: National Press Books, 1992.

PANTS-FREE PRESIDENTS

Hagood, Wesley O. *Presidential Sex: From the Founding Fathers to Bill Clinton*. New York: Citadel Press, 1996.

Hunt, Irma. *Dearest Madame: The Presidents' Mistress*. New York: McGraw-Hill, 1978.

Ross, Shelley. *Fall From Grace: Sex, Scandal and Corruption in American Politics from 1702 to the Present*. New York: Ballantine Books, 1978.

WATERGATE

Colodny, Len and Robert Gettlin. *Silent Coup: The Removal of a President*. New York: St. Martin's Press, 1991.

Haldeman, H.R. *The Ends of Power*. New York: Times Books, 1978.

Hougan, Jim. *Secret Agenda: Watergate, Deep Throat and the CIA*. New York: Random House, 1984.

Kutler, Stanley I. *The Wars of Watergate*. New York: Knopf, 1990.

Lukas, J. Anthony. *Nightmare: The Underside of the Nixon Years*. New York: Penguin Books, 1988.

Woodward, Bob and Carl Bernstein. *All the President's Men*. New York: Simon and Schuster, 1974.

IRAN-CONTRA

Draper, Theodore. *A Very Thin Line: The Iran-Contra Affairs*. New York: Hill and Wang, 1991.

Garment, Suzanne. *Scandal: The Culture of Mistrust in American Politics*. New York: Times Books, 1991.

Ledeen, Michael A. *Perilous Statecraft: An Insider's Account of the Iran-Contra Affair*. New York: Charles Scribner's Sons, 1988.

Moyers, Bill. *The Secret Government: The Constitution in Crisis*. Washington, DC: Cabin Locks Press, 1988.

National Security Archive. *The Chronology: The Documented Day-by-Day Account of the Secret Military Assistance to Iran and the Contras*. New York: Warner Books, 1987.

President's Special Review Board. *The Tower Commission Report*. New York: Bantam Books, 1987.

Sick, Gary. *October Surprise*. New York: Times Books, 1991.

Walsh, Lawrence E. *Iran-Contra: The Final Report*. New York: Times Books, 1994.

THE WRONG ARM OF THE LAW

Domanick, Joe. *To Protect and to Serve: The LAPD's Century of War in the City of Dreams*. New York: Pocket Books, 1994.

Ownes, Tom. *Lying Eyes: The Truth Behind the Corruption and Brutality of the LAPD and the Beating of Rodney King*. New York: Thunder's Mouth Press, 1994.

Whitman, David. "The Untold Story of the L.A. Riot." *U.S. News and World Report*, May 31, 1994.

THE GREAT S & L ROBBERY

Adams, James Ring. *The Big Fix: Inside the S&L Scandal*. New York: John Wiley and Sons, 1990.

Day, Kathleen. *S&L Hell: The People and the Politics Behind the $1 Trillion Savings and Loan Scandal*. New York: W.W. Norton & Co., 1993.

Fritz, Sara. "Mr. Ed's Revenge." *The Los Angeles Times*, March 25, 1990.

Lowy, Martin E. *High Rollers: Inside the Savings and Loan Debacle*. New York: Praeger Publishers, 1991.

Mayer, Martin. *The Greatest-Ever Bank Robbery: The Collapse of the Savings and Loan Industry*. New York: Charles Scribner's Sons, 1990.

Pizzo, Stephen, Mary Fricker and Paul Muolo. *Inside Job: The Looting of America's Savings and Loans*. New York: McGraw Hill, 1989.

THE WILSON-TERPIL AFFAIR

Associated Press. "CIA Dealt with Fugitive, Judge Told." Sept. 30, 1982.

Corn, David. *Blond Ghost: Ted Shackley and the CIA's Crusades*. New York: Simon and Schuster, 1994.

Hersh, Seymour M. "The Qaddafi Connection." *The New York Times Magazine*, June 14, 1981.

———. "Exposing the Libyan Connection." *The New York Times Magazine*, June 21, 1981.

Maas, Peter. *Manhunt*. New York: Random House, 1986.

Magnuson, Ed. "Trafficking in Terror For Libya." *Time*, June 29, 1981.

THE FRIENDS OF EDDIE KOCH

Moscow, Warren. *The Last of the Big-Time Bosses: The Life and Times of Carmine DeSapio*. New York: Stein and Day, 1971.

Moses, Paul. "Year Later: Political Core Unshaken." *Newsday*, Jan. 11, 1987.

Newfield, Jack and Wayne Barrett. *City For Sale: Ed Koch and the Betrayal of New York*. New York, Harper and Row, 1988.

CHAPTER 4 DIRTY BUSINESS

THE FUGITIVE

Bardach, Ann Louise. "Vesco's Last Gamble." *Vanity Fair*, March, 1996.

"Cuba Sentences Fugitive Businessman to 13 Years for Fraud." *The New York Times*, Aug. 27, 1996.

Herzog, Arthur. *Vesco: His Rise, Fall and Flight*. New York: Doubleday, 1987.

Hougan, Jim. *Spooks: The Haunting of America & The Private Use of Secret Agents*. New York: Bantam Books, 1979.

Hutchison, Robert A. *Vesco*. New York: Praeger Publishers, 1974.

COLLISION COURSE

Andersen, Kurt. "A Life in the Fast Lane." *Time*, Nov. 1, 1982.

Daly, Michael. "The Real DeLorean Story." *New York*, Nov. 8, 1982.

DeLorean, John Z. *DeLorean*. Zondervan Books: Grand Rapids, MI, 1985.

Kohn, George C. *Encyclopedia of American Scandal*. New York: Facts on File, 1989.

Latham, Aaron. "Anatomy of a Sting." *Rolling Stone*, March 17, 1983.

Serrill, Michael S. "The Case of the Purloined Tapes." *Time*, Nov. 7, 1983.

Starr, Mark. "DeLorean: Not Guilty." *Time*, Aug. 27, 1984.

PIRATES OF FINANCE

Fischel, Daniel. *Payback: The Conspiracy to Destroy Michael Milken and his Financial Revolution*. New York: HarperBusiness, 1995.

Frantz, Douglas. "The Unraveling of Dennis Levine." *Esquire*, Sept. 1987.

Kinkead, Gwen. "Crook of the Year." *Fortune*, Jan. 5, 1987.

Kornbluth, Jesse. *Highly Confident: The Crime and Punishment of Michael Milken*. New York: William Morrow and Co., 1992.

Serwer, Andrew Evan. "Mystery Man of Mergers." *Fortune*, Jan. 5, 1987.

Stavro, Barry and Patrice Apodaca. "Milken Redux." *The Los Angeles Times*, Feb. 18, 1996.

Stein, Benjamin J. *A License to Steal: The Untold Story of Michael Milken and the Conspiracy to Bilk the Nation*. New York: Simon and Schuster, 1992.

Stewart, James B. *Den of Thieves*. New York: Touchstone, 1992.

FAREWELL TO CAP'N BOB

Bower, Tom. *Maxwell: The Outsider*. New York: Viking, 1992.

Garneau, George. "Maxwell's Money Laundry." *Editor and Publisher*, March 19, 1994.

Greenslade, Roy. *Maxwell: The Rise and Fall of Robert Maxwell and his Empire*. New York: Birch Lane Press, 1992.

"The Father: Bullying Buccaneer Casts a Shadow Over Sons' Trial." *Daily Telegraph*, January 22, 1996.

THE LOCKHEED SCANDAL

Boulton, David. *The Grease Machine: The Inside Story of Lockheed's Dollar Diplomacy*. New York: Harper and Row, 1978.

Hougan, Jim. *Spooks: The Haunting of America & The Private Use of Secret Agents*. New York: Bantam Books, 1979.

Sampson, Anthony. *The Arms Bazaar: From Lebanon to Lockheed*. New York: Viking Press, 1977.

WHEN BANKERS GO BAD

Bates, James. "BCCI: Behind the Bank Scandal." *The Los Angeles Times*, July 30, 1991.

Cornwell, Rupert. *"God's Banker."* New York: Dodd, Mead & Company, 1983.

DiFonzo, Luigi. *St. Peter's Banker: Michele Sindona*. New York: Franklin Watts, 1983.

Frantz, Douglas. "BCCI: Odd Bank With the Air of Cult." *The Los Angeles Times*, Sept. 3, 1991.

Fritz, Sara and James Bates. "BCCI May be History's Biggest Bank Fraud Scandal." *The Los Angeles Times*, July 11, 1991.

Kwitny, Jonathan. *The Crimes of Patriots*. New York: Touchstone Books, 1987.

Lernoux, Penny. *In Banks We Trust*. Garden City, NY: Anchor Press/Doubleday, 1984.

Polk, Peggy. "Marcinkus Ends Vatican Career, Will Return to Chicago." *Chicago Tribune*, Oct. 31, 1990.

Truell, Peter and Larry Gurwin. *False Profits: The Inside Story of BCCI, the World's Most Corrupt Financial Empire*. Boston: Houghton Mifflin, 1992.

THALIDOMIDE NIGHTMARE

"The Drug That Left a Trail of Heartbreak." *Life*, August 10, 1962.

"Inside Story of a Medical Tragedy." *U.S News and World Report*, August 13, 1962.

Fine, Ralph Adam. *The Great Drug Deception: The Shocking Story of MER/29 and the Folks Who Gave You Thalidomide*. New York: Stein and Day, 1972.

Freiman, Fran Lochner and Neil Schlager. *Failed Technology: True Stories of Technological Disasters*. New York: U.X.L., 1995.

Insight Team of the Sunday Times of London. *Suffer the Children: The Story of Thalidomide*. New York: Viking Press, 1979.

Jerome, Richard and Simon Perry. "Undefeated" *People Weekly*, March 3, 1997.

WHOSE VIRUS IS IT ANYWAY?

Ansley, David. "AIDS Discovery Wasn't His Own, Scientist Admits." *San Jose Mercury News*, May 31, 1991.

Crewdson, John. "Burden of Proof." *Chicago Tribune*, Dec. 6, 1992.

Duesberg, Peter. *Inventing the AIDS Virus*. Washington, DC: Regnery Publishing, 1996.

Gallo, Robert. *Virus Hunting: AIDS, Cancer and the Human Retrovirus*. New York: Basic Books, 1991.

DEATH AT LOVE CANAL

Freiman, Fran and Neil Schlager. *Failed Technology: True Stories of Technological Disasters*. New York: U.X.L., 1995.

Gibbs, Lois Marie. *Love Canal: My Story*. Albany, NY: State University of New York Press, 1982.

Hoffman, Andrew J. "Love Canal Lives." *E Magazine*, Nov. 1, 1994.

Machacek, John. "17 years later: Chemical Company Agrees to Pay $129M to Clean Up Love Canal." *Gannett News Service*, Dec. 21, 1995.

Mokhiber, Russell. *Corporate Crime and Violence: Big Business and the Abuse of Public Trust*. San Francisco: Sierra Club Books, 1988.

Setterberg, Fred and Lonny Shavelson. *Toxic Nation*. New York: John Wiley and Sons, 1993.

Zipko, Stephen J. *Toxic Threat*. New York: Julian Messner, 1986.

EXPLODING PINTOS

Cullen, Francis T. et al. *Corporate Crime Under Attack: The Ford Pinto Case and Beyond*. Cincinnati: Anderson Publishing, 1987.

Lacey, Robert. *Ford: The Men and the Machine*. Boston: Little Brown and Co., 1986.

Freiman, Fran and Neil Schlager. *Failed Technology: True Stories of Technological Disasters*. New York: U.X.L., 1995.

Mokhiber, Russell. *Corporate Crime and Violence: Big Business and the Abuse of Public Trust*. San Francisco: Sierra Club Books, 1988.

CYBER PORN SCARE

Chapman, Gary. "Not So Naughty." *The New Republic*, July 31, 1995.

Elmer-Dewitt, Philip. "Cyberporn." *Time Magazine*, July 3, 1995.

——. "Fire Storm on the Computer Nets." *Time Magazine*, July 24, 1995.

Meeks, Brock. "How Time Failed." *Hotwired*, October, 1995.

COPYRIGHT INFORMATION

INTRODUCTION copyright © 1997 Jonathan Vankin and Stephen DeStefano

"FATTY" ARBUCKLE: NO TEARS FOR THE FAT MAN copyright © 1997 Jonathan Vankin and Hilary Barta

THE GREAT LOVER copyright © 1997 Jonathan Vankin and Craig Hamilton

DEATH OF A MYSTERY MAN copyright © 1997 Jonathan Vankin and Alan Weiss

ALL-AMERICAN JUNKIE copyright © 1997 Jonathan Vankin and Paul Gulacy

CHARLIE CHAPLIN copyright © 1997 Jonathan Vankin and David Lloyd

THE ICE CREAM BLONDE copyright © 1997 Jonathan Vankin and Mike Perkins

MARY ASTOR'S LITTLE BLUE BOOK copyright © 1997 Jonathan Vankin and Marie Severin

IN LIKE FLYNN copyright © 1997 Jonathan Vankin and Brian Buniak

THE SWEATER GIRL AND THE GANGSTER copyright © 1997 Jonathan Vankin and Arnold Pander

THE LOVES OF INGRID BERGMAN copyright © 1997 Jonathan Vankin and Colleen Doran

E! copyright © 1997 Jonathan Vankin and Steve Pugh

THE SCANDAL THAT SANK A STUDIO copyright © 1997 Jonathan Vankin and Rick Geary

MURDER, MAYHEM, AND THE COTTON CLUB copyright © 1997 Jonathan Vankin and D'Israeli D'Emon Draughtsman

DON SIMPSON: FAST TRACK copyright © 1997 Jonathan Vankin and Gregory Benton

HEIDI FLEISS, HOLLYWOOD MADAM copyright © 1997 Jonathan Vankin and Anthony Castrillo

WOODY AND MIA copyright © 1997 Jonathan Vankin and Ty Templeton

HOLLYWOOD BAD BOYS copyright © 1997 Jonathan Vankin and Alex Wald

MURDER OF THE CENTURY copyright © 1997 Jonathan Vankin and Eric Shanower

THE PRINCESS AND THE ICE QUEEN copyright © 1997 Jonathan Vankin and Jean-Claude Padilla

DEATH AND THE DIET DOCTOR copyright © 1997 Jonathan Vankin and Randy DuBurke

JIMMY SWAGGART IN HELL copyright © 1997 Jonathan Vankin and Robert Snyder

THE BALLAD OF JIM & TAMMY copyright © 1997 Jonathan Vankin and Rick Parker

SEX, DRUGS AND ROX copyright © 1997 Jonathan Vankin and Anthony Modano

CYRIL BURT: THE INTELLIGENCE MAN copyright © 1997 Jonathan Vankin and Joe Orlando

THE KING AND MRS. SIMPSON copyright © 1997 Jonathan Vankin and Bryan Talbot

CHARLES AND DIANA copyright © 1997 Jonathan Vankin and Hunt Emerson

O.J.'S FINAL RUN copyright © 1997 Jonathan Vankin and John Cebollero

CIRQUE DU O.J. copyright © 1997 Jonathan Vankin and Graham Manley

WACKO JACKO copyright © 1997 Jonathan Vankin and Danny Hellman

THE WAYS AND MEANS OF LUST copyright © 1997 Jonathan Vankin and Cully Hamner

THE PROFUMO AFFAIR copyright © 1997 Jonathan Vankin and Charles Adlard

X-RATED CONGRESS copyright © 1997 Jonathan Vankin and Andrew Wendel

ROCKY copyright © 1997 Jonathan Vankin and Don Cameron

FROM CAMELOT TO CHAPPAQUIDDICK copyright © 1997 Jonathan Vankin and Dan Lawlis

HE SAID, SHE SAID copyright © 1997 Jonathan Vankin and Sergio Aragonés

PANTS-FREE PRESIDENTS copyright © 1997 Jonathan Vankin and Ward Sutton

WATERGATE copyright © 1997 Jonathan Vankin and Joe Sacco

THE IRAN-CONTRA SCANDAL copyright © 1997 Jonathan Vankin and Tayyar Ozkan

THE WRONG ARM OF THE LAW copyright © 1997 Jonathan Vankin and Galen Showman

THE GREAT S & L ROBBERY copyright © 1997 Jonathan Vankin and Shepherd Hendrix

THE WILSON-TERPIL AFFAIR copyright © 1997 Jonathan Vankin and Joe Staton

THE FRIENDS OF EDDIE KOCH copyright © 1997 Jonathan Vankin and Steve Mannion

THE FUGITIVE copyright © 1997 Jonathan Vankin and Bob Hall

COLLISION COURSE copyright © 1997 Jonathan Vankin and Dick Giordano

PIRATES OF FINANCE copyright © 1997 Jonathan Vankin and Robin Smith

FAREWELL TO CAP'N BOB copyright © 1997 Jonathan Vankin and Steven Lieber

THE LOCKHEED SCANDAL copyright © 1997 Jonathan Vankin and Walter Simonson

WHEN BANKERS GO BAD copyright © 1997 Jonathan Vankin and S. M. Taggart

THALIDOMIDE NIGHTMARE copyright © 1997 Jonathan Vankin and Lennie Mace

WHOSE VIRUS IS IT ANYWAY? copyright © 1997 Jonathan Vankin and James Pascoe

DEATH AT LOVE CANAL copyright © 1997 Jonathan Vankin and Bob Fingerman

EXPLODING PINTOS copyright © 1997 Jonathan Vankin and Glenn Barr

CYBER PORN SCARE copyright © 1997 Jonathan Vankin and Alwyn Talbot

AFTERWORD copyright © 1997 Jonathan Vankin and Stephen DeStefano

THINK YOU KNOW EVERYTHING?

THINK AGAIN.

63 TRUE TALES OF THE WORLD'S MOST INCOMPETENT JAILBIRDS!

THE BIG BOOK OF LITTLE CRIMINALS

LITTLE MEN. BIG SCHEMES. TOUGH LUCK.

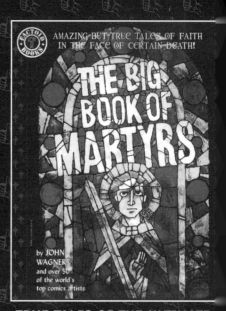

AMAZING-BUT-TRUE TALES OF FAITH IN THE FACE OF CERTAIN DEATH!

THE BIG BOOK OF MARTYRS

by JOHN WAGNER and over 50 of the world's top comics artists

TRUE TALES OF THE ULTIMATE SACRIFICE!

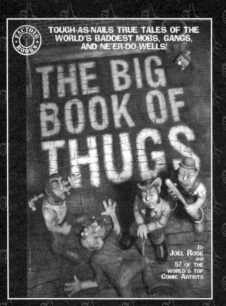

TOUGH-AS-NAILS TRUE TALES OF THE WORLD'S BADDEST MOBS, GANGS, AND NE'ER-DO-WELLS!

THE BIG BOOK OF THUGS

By JOEL ROSE AND 57 OF THE WORLD'S TOP COMIC ARTISTS

YOU WANT TOUGH? WE GOT TOUGH!

ALLEGEDLY TRUE TALES OF PARANORMAL PHENOMENA!

THE BIG BOOK OF THE UNEXPLAINED

BY DOUG MOENCH and over 40 of the world's top comics artists!

STRANGE PHENOMENA REVEALED!

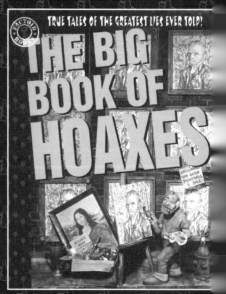

TRUE TALES OF THE GREATEST LIES EVER TOLD!

THE BIG BOOK OF HOAXES

BIG LIES THE WHOLE WORLD BELIEVED!